A CIVI UNI

("KISS ME GOODNIGHT SERGEANT MAJOR")

Being the true experiences of a
National Serviceman

Only the Name has been changed
to protect the guilty!

RAY SKINNER

Published by M-Y Books
187 Ware Road
Hertford
SG13 7EQ

m-y Books
m-ybooks.co.uk

CHAPTER 1

IN WHICH I TRAVEL TO MY
TWO YEARS NATIONAL SERVICE

It had happened to me at last! It was 17th June 1954 and I was on the 10:50hrs train out of Waterloo heading for Blandford Forum, in a compartment full of young men who looked as apprehensive as I felt.

As I looked out of the window on that beautiful summer's morning and watched the scenery flashing by, I tried to recollect my thoughts and establish the events that had led me to being on this particular train destined for a place that until recent days I'd never even heard of.

The culprit was obviously the National Service Act, there was no doubt about that. This was the law whereby all young men on attaining the age of eighteen were required to serve two years in one of her Majesty's armed forces. If, however, you were following a course of training, then you could apply for deferment which in my experience was rarely refused. As I was studying building construction at the Tottenham Technical College (albeit only three nights a week) I had applied for and been granted deferment until I took my Higher National examination. That is how I came to find myself, at the age of twenty two, in a compartment full of eighteen-year-olds.

Gaining deferment at the age of eighteen seemed fine at the time. Now however that I had taken my exam, and had been called up, and at the present time was on my way to No. 1 Training Battalion R.E.M.E., I wished that I had gone in the forces at eighteen. My military service would have been over with and a thing of the past. However I hadn't and it wasn't. The hubbub in the compartment gained in intensity as all the young men spoke at the same time. I half listened.

The conversation subject varied from football to fornication, the usual schoolboy stuff. I reverted to looking out of the window and back to my own personal thoughts.

Getting married on last New Year's Eve hadn't really helped the situation either, but then Doreen and I had wanted to get married before I got called up to serve my two years' National Service. When the possibility of a bed-sit cropped up Doreen and I jumped at the opportunity. Unfortunately the female landlord had proved to be mentally unstable which made living in the house totally unbearable for the pair of us. Consequently, only the previous week we had been forced to move into a spare room at my parents' house where Doreen was now living and would probably have to live for the duration of my National Service. All in all therefore, I felt that I had far more problems than all the young men around me, who whilst unsettled over taking a trip into the unknown were, to a certain extent, excited as if setting out on an adventure. I, on the other hand, didn't feel that way, at all. Instead I was bothered over the circumstances in which I was leaving a wife behind me.

My mind drifted back to the day when I arrived home to find a letter directing me to attend a medical the following week prior to my two years' service.

On the appointed day, the 13th of April, (I've been suspicious about the figure thirteen ever since) I travelled to a hospital in Central London where I had x-rays taken and then continued on to East London for the rest of my medical. I duly arrived at Wanstead Flats, where a collection of timber sheds awaited me, all looking forlorn standing as they did on that relatively barren part of London.

I climbed the ramshackle wooden steps to what appeared to be the entrance to this collection of timber sheds, opened the paint-peeled door and entered the building. I was immediately confronted by a throng of young men sitting on hard wooden benches along the sides of a corridor, none of whom looked particularly happy with themselves.

I was just about to enquire if anybody was interested in the fact that I had arrived, when without ceremony one of these young men fell heavily to the floor groaning and moaning as he went, and seemingly foaming from the mouth. I was astounded I had never ever seen anything quite like this before. A second young man who had been sitting next to him, immediately threw himself to his knees and started loosening his collar and tie at the same time looking up and calling for assistance.

At first glance the prone figure on the floor looked very ill indeed, but before any of the other men sitting on the wooden benches had time to help, the door at the end of the corridor burst open and two white smocked figures came hurrying along the corridor towards the commotion. As they bent over the two figures on the floor, I realised that they had khaki uniforms under their white smocks. They were presumably Army medical men. I was confronted with the Army sooner than I had expected! The two white-smocked figures whirled into action with what appeared to be a well-rehearsed plan, the young helper on his knees was lifted bodily to his feet and placed none too gently back on the wooden bench whence he came. The recumbent figure on the floor was then dragged roughly and rapidly by his arms through an open door off the corridor by the two white-smocked figures, the door slamming loudly as the poor unfortunate's feet had passed through it.

I took a quick glance around the railway carriage to confirm that none of the occupants were either of the two young men I had seen that day at Wanstead. It would have been a fantastic coincidence if any had been but such coincidences did occur, but no they weren't.

I looked out of the window again just in time to see us fly through a station, too fast to read the name. I hadn't realised it at the time but the scene that I had witnessed at Wanstead was a scene which was apparently a regular occurrence there, where numerous young men "swung the lead" in the hope of dodging National Service. With hindsight how they hoped to achieve this with their pseudo theatricals I couldn't begin to understand. I was nevertheless to witness a number of similar incidents such as this before these before my two years National Service was completed, but I was to bear no malice whatsoever against anyone who managed to obtain their release for whatever reason. For as far as I was concerned it was to be two years of my life utterly wasted. Not that I knew this fact at the time of my journey to join the Army.

The chattering in the carriage reached a crescendo once again just as it did in the corridor. Those in the carriage were talking about their childish exploits and those in the corridor about the spectacle we had all had just witnessed and pandemonium reigned supreme in both instances for a few seconds.

The young man who had gone to the aid of an apparent violently sick person now sat on his hard wooden bench trying to look totally unconcerned about the whole incident. As the noise increased to a crescendo, the door through which the three had just disappeared opened as if by magic, there was no one to be seen by it, and a voice yelled out

"Silence!"

The corridor subsided into the commanded silence and all eyes were focused upon a white clad figure who had suddenly appeared framed within the doorway. I'm sure that the fellow was just about to say. "I'll put you all on a charge unless you all shut up," a phrase I was to get used to in the next two years, when sadly the figure realised he couldn't do that as we weren't in the Army yet. He turned on his heel and retreated through the doorway whence he came, the door slammed to. A few moments later a second white-clad figure came through the doorway with a clipboard in his hand. I noticed that this personage had three stripes sewn onto knicker elastic dangling from his right arm. Seeing this phenomenon for the very first time I was mildly amused but I soon learnt that in the Army that you didn't laugh at Sergeants, knicker elastic or not.

"What's your name laddie", he questioned looking at me with his piercing eyes.

"Skinner", I replied, adding "Sir" as an afterthought, and regretting it immediately. Even at that stage I realised that you didn't call a Sergeant 'Sir.' Although I was to find out that sergeants at basic training camps were not averse to insisting that recruits called them "sar," a subtle difference, or was it?

"Raymond Francis?" he queried.

"Er, yes Sergeant." I got it right that time.

A titter ran round the corridor from the assembled young men. The name Francis always raised a retort especially on occasions like this in all male company, though heaven knows why, it could have been far worse. Francis, known as Frank, had been my father's name and I was quite proud of the fact that I carried it also.

"Right, sit there and wait until you're called," he instructed.

I found a space on one of the wooden benches and did as I was told. Time went by very slowly as people at the head of the queue disappeared through the various doors leading off the corridor and conversely more men came in through the entrance door and gave their names to the Sergeant and joined the end of the queue.

As I sat there that day and indeed that day on the train it began to dawn on me how much older I appeared to be compared with the majority of the people around me. The age difference of four years when you are twenty two years old and the others are only eighteen years old is quite significant in my opinion. Unfortunately it didn't seem to make any difference to the Sergeant and his compatriots with regard to their attitude towards me on that day!

Time dragged very heavily, there was nothing to read, and very few people wanted to enter into conversation. After what seemed an eternity, though in truth was probably only half an hour later, the ubiquitous Sergeant yelled out my name and bade me follow him into a room leading off the corridor.

My recollections of what happened next have dimmed over the years, but I recall that on passing through the doorway I entered a large open plan area reminiscent of a room at a hospital. Numerous desks were positioned around the room at which sat white-coated gentlemen, presumably doctors.

I was instructed to strip to my underwear. I was then passed from desk to desk, doctor to doctor and asked searching questions, some predictable, some not.

"Yes, I had had Chicken Pox and Measles, and Whooping Cough".

"No, I really hadn't ever had that disease!" I replied indignantly.

A blood sample here, a water sample there.

"Fill that bottle over there with a sample of your water,"

"What from over here doctor?" Not a smile, no sense of humour, and they weren't even Army personnel either as far as I was aware.

The one amusing incident that stands out in my mind even to this day over that medical is the elderly doctor, well I assume he was a doctor, who must have been eighty years old if he was a day, dressed in Norfolk Jacket and Plus Fours whose only task in life in that particular medical room seemed to consist in asking you to drop your trousers and bend over. Watch it! I thought! He then proceeded to look at my backside. He did this from all of four feet Six inches away. Or for those readers who are not conversant with pre-metric measurement, eighteen hundred and fifty millimetres. What he hoped to discover I never did find out, but he appeared to be happy carrying out his task and he was being paid by the Government to do it so who was I to ask, "If his journey was really necessary?, (An old wartime saying that younger readers may not be conversant with, but certainly all budding National Servicemen of the time would have been.)

On reflection perhaps he was an optician and this was his own particular method on checking the colour of my eyes!

I was only approximately halfway round the circuit of doctors when one of the doctors, who was obviously charged with checking the condition of my heart, appeared to become a little anxious, or at any rate excited. On asking him if there was anything wrong, he informed me that my heart appeared to be a trifle enlarged.

My heart missed a beat, metaphorically speaking that is. Could this be the ailment that would unexpectedly keep me out of the forces? Perhaps I was still thinking about the two young men I had seen in the corridor earlier on.

The doctor was speaking to me again. Did I do any sports he enquired? I had only recently given up cycle racing, after some six years in the sport and told the doctor so.

"Ah that would account for the condition", he replied. "That's all right, that's fine".

Fine! Bedamned! I thought, and my heart sunk back to its normal level again, Unfortunately, National Service still seemed to be on programme.

After some half an hour of further examinations, I arrived at the final desk in the room. The doctor sitting at it bade me take a seat as he took a cursory glance at the notes he had before him.

He signed them in the appropriate space, looked up at me smiled, and said, "You will be pleased to know that you have been passed A.1."

I wasn't at all sure that I was pleased, but there was nothing

I could do about it. It's the only time in my life that I wished that there was something wrong with me. Nothing too severe, of course, just enough to keep me out of the forces.

However, judging by some of the pitiful wrecks I was to meet in the Army whilst carrying out my National Service, I now realise that the only way to have failed that medical was to have a leg missing, or something similar, and I'm not so sure about that anymore!

My medical was at an end and I was bade to wait out in the corridor once more, until my name was called. Banished to the corridor I met the knicker elastic sergeant once again.

"Youze wait there until the h'officer calls your name. When he does, youze go through the door over there," he said indicating a door opposite me. With that "Youze" disappeared down the corridor.

I sat on the, by now familiar, wooden benches and took stock of my surroundings, as I was now taking stock of my surroundings today sitting in the coach. We were passing a large expanse of tidal water glittering and shimmering in the sunlight.

"That's Poole harbour", called out someone within the compartment, "Not long to go now."

Oh that the journey would go on forever. I just didn't want to arrive at the Army. I just knew that I wasn't going to like it. My interview with the Captain at Wanstead had planted that opinion in my mind.

When my name was yelled out I recoiled then I crossed the corridor knocked on the half open door, heard a "Come in", and entered what I found to be a cubicle-like office. Confronting me across a desk was, even with my limited knowledge of military matters I knew to be an Army Captain, in uniform.

"Sit down," he ordered, "I see that you have expressed a preference to serve your National Service in the Army" he said looking at the papers before him. "Very wise, well done," he informed me in a very brusque manner. "The idea of this interview", he continued "is to give you some background information about the Army and what you can expect when you are called to the colours."

'Called to the colours' I thought? this sounds like something out of 'Beau Geste' or 'Gunga Din' - what on earth is he going on about?

"No, just a moment, Sir," I protested, "I haven't expressed a preference to join the Army for my National Service , what in fact I have said is that I wish to serve in the Royal Engineers, in view of the fact that I know something about civil engineering. If service in the Royal Engineers isn't possible, then I would wish to serve my National Service in the Royal Air Force."

"Ah well yes, as far as we are concerned that means that you have expressed a wish to serve in the Army," the Captain explained.

"I'm sorry I don't see it that way at all," I retorted

Hell I thought they might treat eighteen year olds in this manner but not me, after all I'm twenty two!

"Whether you do, or whether you don't is besides the point," he replied, "It has been decided that you're going in the Army and that's that." he informed me.

So much for my choice in the matter and indeed for being twenty-two I thought.

"Now then about the Army," he then went on to give me a dissertation about the various Regiments and Corps and the opportunities for learning a trade, furthering, my education, and even gaining promotion whilst in the Army carrying out my National Service, none of which I was particularly interested in.

I was still smarting over the injustice of the situation as I saw it. Over the fact that it was said that you had a choice over which branch of the forces you wished to serve out your National Service in. I had certainly expressed a clear desire to carry out my National Service in the Royal Engineers or, failing that, the R.A.F. And yet here was I now being told that I would have to carry it out in an old branch of the Army. Perhaps even in the Army Catering Corps! Now if it had been the W.R.A.Cs!

The voice in front of me was still droning on about the Army, and all the time I was becoming more and more incensed over the injustice of it all, leastways as it appeared to me. We had now got to the point where I was being offered the possibility of signing on as a regular, only of course if I was found to be suitable, suitable for what I thought?

"Excuse me", I interjected, breaking the officer's train of

thought.

"Yes", He said "What is it?"

"If as you say it's been decided that I'm going in the Army anyway, what are my chances of going in the Royal Engineers as my preferred regiment?"

"Corps." He said

"Corps?" I queried.

"Yes, Corps, The Royal Engineers is a corps not a regiment," he explained with a trace of irritation in his voice.

"Oh well what are my chances of going in the Royal Engineers anyway?" I queried.

"I'll tell you what your chances are Skinner." I was impressed he got my name right! "When we have a new intake into the Army, we have all your names put in one pile, and in another pile we put all the branches of the Army where we are requiring men. Royal Engineers, Royal Artillery, Catering Corps, etc., etc., etc. If when we turn up your name we turn up sapper, then you'll go into the Royal Engineers as a sapper,"

"Oh good".

"If on the other hand when we turn up your name we turn up cook, Army Catering Corps, then you go into the Catering Corps as a cook."

"Oh not so good," said I.

"Hm"? He murmured looking up momentarily

"I said that doesn't seem to me to be a very scientific method of selection. Why don't you put people in a trade or profession they already know something about? They wouldn't need training if you were to do that".

The Captain on the other side of the desk, I realised wasn't taking a blind bit of notice of what I was saying. He was treating me as if I were a child straight out of school and that he was some kind of headmaster. He was totally ignoring the fact that I was a married man of twenty two who had been at work for six years and was fairly well qualified at my job. I was to find out that with very few exceptions this was the Army's standard attitude towards the National Serviceman, and one that I was going to experience for the next two years. The fact was that the Army was unable to or didn't wish to differentiate between eighteen year olds straight from school and relatively mature young men of twenty two or more, who were often married and sometimes with a family

I realised that the Army's representative had suddenly stopped droning on and was staring at me.

Was it a corps or a regiment he belonged to I wondered not too seriously.

"Well?" he enquired

Well what? I thought."

"Well," he repeated, and as an afterthought, "Any questions?"

"No I suppose not," I said dejectedly, "But are you absolutely certain that I've got to go into the Army and there's no way I can change it to the R.A.F. now?

"Absolutely."

"I see."

Then one bright ray of hope.

"What are the chances of getting a commission in the Army?" I queried

"You can apply for one once you're in the Army. Now I can't answer any more questions as I have already overrun my allotted time with you, I've still got dozens of lads like you to see this afternoon," he informed me.

I had a feeling he was exaggerating somewhere along the line. He probably wanted to get away early to see West Ham play. But then did officers watch football? I wasn't sure.

"When will I know which regiment or corps I'm going in?" I queried. Not that I knew the difference, in fact after serving two years National Service I still didn't know the exact difference.

"When you get your call-up papers," he retorted looking at me in a manner that indicated that the interview was definitely at an end. I decided to make a strategic withdrawal, as the bishop said to the actress (I was an avid reader of the Saint books at the time).

I made my exit with rather a dazed feeling, with the twit behind the desk making some remark about hoping that I'd enjoy my two years with the colours. There was that word again. Perhaps he was Gunga Din's son? Beau Geste's maybe?

Outside in the corridor I met the Sergeant who had ushered me in to see the officer.

"Where do I go next, Sergeant?" I enquired.

"No that's you finished for the day, you won't hear from us now until your receive your call-up papers."

"I see."

I made my exit along the corridor by which I had made my entry. Was it really only three hours previously? There were still a number of young men sitting on the hard wooden benches either staring at the ceiling, or at their shoes, or else talking amongst themselves in hushed voices.

I was cross with myself. I had made up my mind that I was going to stand my ground today, one way or the other, and on reflection I hadn't so much as said "boo to a goose," I was disappointed with myself. As I made my way to the door at the end of the corridor I passed through it into what was to be my world, at least for a few more weeks. It was strange however because I remember that although it was a bright sunny spring day with clear blue skies when I arrived, the world to me now seemed suddenly dull. It had gradually dawned on me how unpleasant my next two years were likely to be.

I was jerked out of my day dreaming by the train pulling into Blandford Station. Everyone in the compartment grabbed their possessions and prepared to alight from the train. Looking through the window I could see that the platform was swarming with khaki clad figures who were yelling out orders to all those poor unfortunates who were bound for No.1. Training Battalion to board the lorries that were parked in the road outside the station.

The few civilian passengers that alighted with us had a slightly amused look on their faces. Clearly they had all seen this performance many times before and were quietly making their way towards the ticket collector. I started to make my exit with them pretending that I wasn't with all these young men. This was the young man who wasn't going to be herded along with all the others, he was going to be independent and have a stroll around town before reporting for duty or so he kidded himself.

Standing alongside the ticket collector was an Army Sergeant who when I handed over my travel warrant, barked out. "Over there lad, up into the lorry waiting outside. How did he know that I was bound for the Army? Was it the dazed looking expression on my face? Or was it the fact that they assumed that all young men arriving on that train were destined for the Army? Then the penny dropped. The Sergeant was standing next to the ticket collector for the purpose of looking for travel warrants being offered up to the official instead of tickets.

Anyhow I was so intimidated by all the yelling and shouting that was going on around me, all of which appeared to be directed at me personally, that all thoughts of a gentle stroll around the town totally deserted me and I climbed aboard the lorry along with a lot of other lost looking souls.

CHAPTER 2

IN WHICH I ARRIVE AT
NO.1 TRAINING BATTALION R.E.M.E.

As soon as the lorry filled up it was driven off through the town towards the camp, that was situated on a hill some mile or so outside Blandford. I remember thinking at the time at least we had a beautiful day for the journey. The sun was shining and a breeze was blowing quite nicely through the lorry where the canvass tilt had been raised at the sides. The only thing that spoilt the generally pleasant atmosphere was the sight of two Army Corporals sitting at the back of the lorry. They looked ominously like guards intent on stopping any desertions. Come to think of it though we weren't in the Army yet, so we could hardly be accused of deserting, could we? I took another look at the two Corporals. I reckoned that they were in the mood to accuse us of anything!

We soon got to the top of the hill and reached the camp. At first glance it appeared to consist of a collection of single storey brick built buildings at its centre, surrounded by a far larger number of old timber hutments. The brick buildings at the centre turned out to be the administration buildings and the collection of timber hutments were, you've guessed it, our living quarters. A closer inspection of the timber hutments proved them to be built on the "Spider" principle, that is with the ablution block in the middle with the living accommodation radiating from it in the form of a spider's web. I had already experienced the doubtful pleasure of staying in such accommodation years ago when I slept in my Father's room in wartime, at a gun site at Lipitts Hill in Epping Forest when my Mother and I visited him one Christmas. I recalled that on Christmas Day the guard at the entrance gate was smoking a large cigar and calling out Hi-De-Hi to all those entering and leaving the camp, including officers, and not letting in anyone who didn't give the password of Ho-De-Ho. Everybody appeared to be very happy on that occasion.

Old memories came floating back to me as I looked upon these buildings recalling fond memories. Perhaps the Army might not be so bad after all!

"When you're bloody ready lad we'd be pleased to have the pleasure of your bloody company. Get out of that bloody lorry, bloody quick. Or have you decided that you don't like the look of us and want to go back home to Mummy?"

I was rudely awoken from my day dreams by the Sergeant roaring at me. I looked around and realised that the lorry was now empty except for me, and that the previous occupants were all lined up at the side of the road grinning at my discomfort, alongside the Sergeant who had yelled the words at me. I jumped off the lorry and joined them.

"Right," said the Sergeant, "Now listen carefully. You're going into this building to be documented, later you'll draw your kit and be allocated to a platoon and a barrack room.

"Any questions?" There were none. "Right," said the Sergeant again. "Bloody move."

We piled into the building indicated. Little did I realise it was the last time I would pile in, anywhere for a long time to come. Henceforth it would be "marching, in a smart and orderly fashion - anywhere and everywhere including, would you believe it, to the bog (toilet)!

On entering the building I was a trifle surprised to find that the first bit of "documentation" we were to undergo was a haircut. Even those amongst us who had obviously undergone some fearsome looking haircuts prior to joining the Army were subjected to a further scalping. The barbers were clearly being paid on the number of heads attended to. No one escaped the demon barbers, or were they instead sheep shearers? For I had never seen barbers like these before.

After the haircut we were then progressed through to the next room where the formality of joining the Army and the general documentation process took place. I was surprised to find out later that all this documentation was carried out by National Servicemen of only a few weeks standing. We were then allocated to a platoon and introduced to our Platoon Sergeant, Sergeant Pearce. A middle aged, fairly short, and jolly looking man. He explained to us that we were now in No.8 Platoon of 'B' Company, the best Company in the Battalion. We soon learnt that first impressions can be very deceptive

I was then very pleasantly surprised to find that after each of us had been issued with a knife, fork, and spoon, not forgetting the pint-sized mug, it was my introduction to Army cooking. It was disgusting and in my opinion totally un-eatable. I recall leaving the cookhouse, and still feeling hungry queuing up at an ice cream van parked outside the cookhouse for a cone to stem the pangs of hunger.

One of the unusual aspects of the Blandford camp was the fact that a public highway ran through the centre of the camp, and that various entrepreneurs, such as the ice cream vendor used to ply their trade from it. This and the fact that you could see buses and cars running through the camp lessened the feeling of isolation that otherwise appeared to surround us all

After tea we were marched down to the stores, where we were issued with the rest of our kit, very little attention seemingly being given to whether or not the articles fitted you so long as you had the right number of everything. We were then marched back to the barrack room, a polite name for a decrepit old timber hut, where we proceeded to try on our new wardrobe of clothes.

One point that sticks out in my memory even now over the issue of clothing, is the fact that out of the two pairs of boots issued to me, one of them was a repaired second hand pair to be used as my second best boots. I was disgusted over this fact, as I had never used second-hand shoes before in my life! It was no good my saying that I wasn't going to start now as I had no choice in the matter.

Once clothed in our new regalia we were then directed to package up our civilian clothes ready to be posted home courtesy of the Army. It was then that we learnt that we would not be allowed to wear our civilian clothes again until we had been in the Army six months and had obtained our permanent passes, whatever they were.

That evening we worked long and hard in an effort to settle in and get ourselves in to some form of order for the following morning. Although "Lights out" was meant to be ten thirty, or to be more correct now, 22:30hrs we kept working until about 00:30hrs or so. On more than one occasion the patrolling two man guard called in to tell us we must turn our lights out, but they informed us that if we wanted to turn them on again once they were out of sight, it was okay by them, they considered that they would have done their duty. After this procedure had happened two or three times we felt that we knew the guard well enough to enter into conversation with them. They then told us that they'd only been in the Army five weeks themselves. Only five weeks! To us that had only arrived that day it seemed that their National Service was almost completed. We eventually put our lights out at about 01:30hrs and went to bed, but such was our enthusiasm that first morning that, come 5:15am or so or as we were beginning to say 05:15hrs, everyone was up and roaring to go, the only thing was we didn't know where to go, so to speak. This factor was soon put right however just after 06:00hrs, when a person, who it transpired was to be our platoon Lance-Corporal emerged from his room at the end of the hut. In only his underpants, he looked an unassuming and mediocre person. Rubbing the sleet from his eyes he demanded to know, what all the fucking noise was about? And ordered us to be bleeding quiet as he'd got a bleeding hangover from the night before. We complied with his order immediately.

He supposed quite correctly that we all wanted to go to breakfast now. He then proceeded to enquire if there were any amongst us who had been in the Army cadets. When one of our number volunteered the fact that he had been in the Cadet Force for four years the Corporal instructed him to line us up on the road outside as soon as we were ready. Then to march us down to the cookhouse for breakfast and woe betide him if anything went wrong. If it did he'd find himself on a fucking charge, fucking quick. So much for volunteering I thought! Having done his duty the Corporal promptly went back to bed.

The Army Cadet duly lined us up on the road outside as instructed, and then marched us down to the cookhouse in what I thought was a very efficient manner. The breakfast I received was the most revolting meal I have ever had served up to me in the whole of my life. No wonder our Corporal hadn't bothered to partake of it.

This was my introduction to leathery eggs floating in a sea of grease, and strange plum-like tomatoes drowned in a red liquid, Cold fried bread stuck together with congealed fat, all served from a counter swarming with bugs of various species. I just couldn't believe my eyes, and walked out having eaten nothing, heaving gently. Once outside I marched back to the hut in a smart and orderly fashion, feeling disappointed that there was no one around to see me performing this pristine operation.

Unfortunately it appeared to be too early for the ice cream vendor!

Back at the billet we were informed by our estimable Lance-Corporal, who had now risen from his bed, henceforth to be known as a "pit", and by the more obscene of the N.C.O.s as a "wanking pit," that we were all going on muster parade that morning, for 08:00hrs. "So bleeding get ready," he ordered us.

The thought of going on parade struck terror into my heart if no one else's, I wasn't at all sure that I could march correctly let alone perform such intricate manoeuvres such as turning and halting with any degree of accuracy. The Lance-Corporal no doubt realising that at the very least we would have to be able to halt on this our first parade, proceeded to give us a crash course on how to halt correctly there and then in the hut.

He had just satisfied himself that we had more or less mastered the movement when there was a shout of "Stand by your beds!" yelled through the open door at the end of the hut. In marched Sergeant Pearce followed by a fierce looking Corporal standing at least six feet two inches in his stockinged feet. By comparison our Lance-Corporal seemed quite a homely figure.

"This," Said Sergeant Pearce indicating the figure alongside him, is Corporal Harridge, your platoon Corporal who, along with myself and Lance-Corporal Leary, who you have already met, are your platoon N.C.O.s. You will be getting to know us very well during the next six weeks whilst you're doing your basic training," he said with a smirk on his face.

"With regard to your training," he continued, "I've decided to give you the same choice that I give to all new intakes. You can have it the easy way or you can have it the hard way. I don't mind which, it's up to you, it's your choice."

I suddenly warmed to the Sergeant, it seemed very reasonable of him to give us a choice in the matter. In my own mind I had already decided that I would opt for the easy way, when I was interrupted in my line of thought by the Sergeant who was speaking once again.

"Now I must warn you however, that the easy way is not exactly easy, but oh dear me the 'ardway's really 'ard, but as I say the choice is yours. I personally don't mind which way we do it," he cooed in a fatherly tone, with an even more fatherly look on his face.

"Think about it," he smiled.

"Right, we're now going on muster parade on the square. Corporal Harridge here will be our right marker; he'll be standing on the square and we march up to him and halt; then right turn and have your names checked off. Eventually you will be given the order to left turn and be marched back here. Simple, any questions? No! Good! Outside on the road in threes then and we'll be off. Now, not bloody tomorrow," he yelled. "Bloody move." He bellowed.

At this stage the Lance-Corporal, Corporal, and the Sergeant all started yelling at once with the general idea of inducing us to get out on the road in double quick time

Having got out on the road and lined up in three ranks to the general satisfaction of the Sergeant and the two Corporals, we marched off towards the square. On the way Corporal Harridge disappeared to miraculously reappear on the square as our right marker. Our platoon being new boys, was thankfully marched quietly right to the back of the square out of the limelight so to speak, where our many misdemeanours would not be noticed. Between us and the person on the dais at the front of the square, who appeared to be directing the whole affair, were some eight hundred soldiers, who were halting, dressing, and stamping their feet all to the accompaniment of a couple of dozen Corporals and Sergeants who were yelling at the tops of their voices. I just couldn't understand how anyone knew what they were supposed to be doing. And yet out of this apparent chaos a semblance of order was being achieved. To me it was amazing. Even more amazing was the fact that, in a very short time I would, with experience, realise how simple the whole procedure really was.

The roll was duly called; we had a cursory inspection, were dismissed, and were secretly congratulating ourselves on the very good show we had seemingly put up on our first muster parade. Sergeant Pearce halted us outside our billet and proceeded to address the platoon. Apparently we were the biggest bloody shower he had ever seen on the square and if he had his way he'd charge the whole bloody lot of us for such a bloody pathetic display on the muster parade. We were filthy, we were slovenly, we were bloody awful. He was utterly disgusted with us for letting him down. He was so disgusted in fact he didn't want to see any more of us that day and with that he strode off and left us to the tender mercies of messers Corporal Harridge and Lance-Corporal Leary.

Corporal Harridge who was clearly the dominating personality of the two instructed us in his ferocious manner to, "Stand by your beds". A phrase that I was to become very familiar with in the next two years. Our beds being the only permanent feature that we could readily identify ourselves with in the insecure world that we now found ourselves in.

Once we were standing by our beds, he continued, "Sergeant Pearce is a kind and gentle Sergeant who you have just taken advantage of, and I, Corporal Harridge am not going to forget the fact. I consider that Sergeant Pearce has been very lenient indeed in not charging the whole of the fucking platoon for a slovenly display on muster parade this morning. Don't however expect the same lenient treatment from me. I am a hard man and not one to be crossed or upset in any way whatsoever." Thus spake Corporal Harridge.

Lance-Corporal Leary was nodding vigorously in the background.

"Understand"? Corporal Harridge questioned.

Receiving only a murmured response in reply. "Understand?" he roared, his voice reverberating around the hut.

"Yes," we yelled back in unison.

"That's better. Now, the hut," Corporal Harridge continued, glancing around, "Is in a fucking awful condition and as from now I want it in a pristine condition each and every time I come in here. I, Corporal Harridge, will make sure of that. Heaven help any one of you who doesn't believe me. Corporal Leary read out all the room jobs if you please"

Lance-Corporal Leary then proceeded to read out a long list of room and block jobs that had to be carried out each and every morning before muster parade, and the names of those people detailed to carry them out. I was surprised to find that as well as being responsible for keeping our room clean and tidy, we were also responsible for the toilets and washrooms some twenty five yards away, not to mention the corridors in between. A mammoth undertaking when only the most elementary cleaning equipment and materials were available to us with which to carry out these tasks. I remember for instance being expected to clean down the urinals using old razor blades, and other such ridiculous and potentially dangerous undertakings.

As well as the room and block jobs, each person was personally responsible for the cleanliness of his own bed space area. This included his own bed and locker, the floor underneath the bed and the small patch of floor alongside the bed up to the adjacent bed. These tasks were also to be carried out each and every morning prior to going on muster parade at 08:00hrs.

All beds had to be stripped each day and the blankets, sheets and pillows made up into a bed block in the prescribed manner and set out at the head of the bed. One member of our platoon was bold enough to ask the reason behind making up bed blocks each day and was informed that it was to enable the inspecting officer to see whether or not we had "peed" the bed in the night.

Even I could see that by making a bed block one could conceal the said misdemeanour far easier, it was obviously far simpler to whip back the bedclothes of a made up bed to discover a bed wetter. I think that someone somewhere had decided that stripping down the beds each day was good for discipline rather than there be any real purpose behind the order. Besides it looked more military with a whole barrack room with made up bed blocks.

At this stage of the proceedings Corporal Harridge yelled at one of the platoon to strip his bed down in double quick time, quick on its own was never fast enough. Lance-Corporal Leary was then instructed to produce a regulation bed block which he also did in double quick time.

"That," said Corporal Harridge, indicating the finished article, "is how I want the beds made up each and every morning. I also want all of you to find some cardboard to stiffen out the face of the sheets to make them look more soldierly looking. So that's how to make something more soldierly like I thought to myself, stiffen it with cardboard! Would we, I wondered be instructed to stuff ourselves with cardboard, if, after a period of time we still didn't look soldierly enough?

Corporal Harridge then instructed Lance-Corporal Leary to show us how he required our webbing equipment to be set up on the top of our lockers. Once completed Corporal Harridge informed us that that was how he wanted the equipment set up for the room inspection on Monday morning with one small exception, as he put it. All the black brasses on the webbing equipment were required to be shining bright, or else! No one enquired about the "or else", the look on Corporal Harridge's face said it all.

"The rest of the day will be taken up with P.S.O. tests. 'P.S.O.', for your information, standing for Personnel Selection Officer" he informed us

"These tests are devised to find out how intelligent you are, and which jobs in the Army you may or may not be suitable for.

Whether or not you have the right qualifications to be an officer for instance," he said without the slightest sign of emotion on his face whatsoever.

He then proceeded to inspect each one of us individually as we stood by our beds adjusting a beret here and a belt there trying his utmost to make us look like soldiers and in his own mind I am sure realising that he was failing dismally. It would be a long time before we would look like him, six feet two inches in his stockinged feet, ramrod straight, bristling moustache smart as paint, and only about twenty years of age.

Once he was tolerably satisfied with our attire he ordered us to form up in threes on the road outside. "Now" he yelled, "Not fucking tomorrow".

We all charged out through the door of the hut in an attempt to appease the Corporal or at the very least to prevent his not inconsiderable wrath coming down on our heads. When formed up he and Lance-Corporal Leary then marched us over to P.S.O. block. Once there we were herded into a hut which had all the attributes of a classroom, albeit a very austere one. Confronting us at the end of the room adjacent to the blackboard was a Lance-Corporal who, even too my untrained eyes, was looking slightly unsure of himself, as if this was the first time he had ever to deal with a whole platoon of forty people at one time. As different from Corporal Harridge as chalk is from cheese.

The room was set out in a very austere manner with rows of old trestle tables that would take about eight chairs, each facing the blackboard.

"Right, find a chair and sit down," he invited rather than ordered us, still in a slightly unsure manner.

"Right," he continued, I'm passing some forms around which I want you to fill in, when I tell you to and not before." He said with little or no authority in his voice whatsoever. Once he had established that every one of us was in receipt of a form, he was ready to start.

"Right, first of all fill in your name and address." He allowed about a minute for this operation.

"Right, now put down your qualifications." He allowed about thirty seconds for this, it was beginning to look as if time was of the essence, at the rate he was proceeding.

"Right, next," he continued.

"I haven't finished yet Corporal." I called out.

He allowed about another five seconds then called out, "Next," once again

"I'm still not finished Corporal", I protested. Modest as my qualifications were at the time they still took longer than twenty five seconds to put on paper. I was still scribbling away madly when I realised that the Corporal was standing over me.

"What's your bleeding name then, Einstein?" he sniggered, glancing up at the rest of the platoon for reaction which wasn't long in coming in the form of a roar of laughter. With a smirk on his face and clearly satisfied with himself he returned to his desk.

At the time I felt inwardly pleased by the Corporal's remarks, but the longer I was in REME the more I realised how modest my qualifications were in fact, when compared with other National Servicemen I was yet to meet, where if you hadn't a BSc. in Engineering, you were certainly amongst the poor relations.

We had just about completed filling in the form when the

Corporal decided that it was time for the N.A.A.F.I. break.

"Was there anyone amongst us who had been in the Army cadets who was used to marching bodies of men around?" Our one and only ex-Army cadet once again owned up to the fact and was entrusted by the Lance-Corporal to march us across to the N.A.A.F.I. instructing him to have us back in the classroom in exactly thirty minutes time, or else There was that expression again.

I was soon to realise that in the Army everything stopped for N.A.A.F.I. break at 10:30:hrs come hell or high water. In fact I often wondered if it also happened during wartime. "Hold on a moment Jerry it's N.A.A.F.I. break. Back in half an hour." I bet the Jerries didn't reciprocate.

After N.A.A.F.I. break we were marched back to the P.S.O. block and there for the rest of the morning we were engaged on wading through books of tests to presumably establish the level of our intelligence, or incompetence! I never did discover which the Army was really looking for!

The tests started off with a series of simple arithmetical calculations getting progressively harder but nothing too difficult. These were followed by problems such as people rowing up rivers at 4 knots against currents of 3 knots; cows grazing on railway viaducts with trains approaching, which way should they run etc., etc. It gave you a feeling of being back at school again, except that everyone here was wearing khaki.

At 12:30hrs back to the hut, or billet as most people were now beginning to call it, to collect our knife, fork, spoon, and mug, and then be marched down to the cookhouse by the ever obliging ex-Army cadet who I sensed was by this time really enjoying his exalted position. The food was as bad as ever. This time however the meal was accompanied by a bright red coloured lemonade that looked really inviting but tasted of nothing but water. Was this the dreaded bromide we had all heard about? The stuff that was meant to subdue our sexual urges. Mark you judging by some of the sexual exploits that a number of the fellows had already been boasting about, perhaps some of them needed a dose of bromide. A big dose in fact. In spite of all the dosage we were rumoured to have received in those days I find that it is only now having any effect on me!

As far as the cooking was concerned rumour had it that the Army Catering Corps staff in the cookhouse, weren't real cooks at all but only cooks in training. That would certainly account for the atrocious food that was being served up by them.

In the afternoon back to the P.S.O. building for further tests and exercises, which by now were becoming increasingly difficult, to the point of becoming totally incomprehensible to me. It would appear that the Army had discovered my level of competence if no one else's! What bothered me however was that glancing around the classroom I could see that the rest of the platoon were still happily scribbling away at their answers, yet Einstein here was totally perplexed over the last batch of questions. I consoled myself with the thought that they were probably still working on the answers to the first batch of questions, I hoped!

Exercises completed we were marched off this time by the Lance-Corporal to the camp cinema, henceforth to be known as the "Gaff", for what reason I was never able to discover to see a film named "Call Up." I thought that it was going to be the Technicolor film on Venereal Disease that I had heard so much about prior to being called up but this was not to be. In fact it was not to be for the whole period of my National Service. I was never to get to see it though I met plenty of National Servicemen who had seen it and delighted in explaining it to me in all its intimate gory detail.

Then teatime. Thank goodness for a slice of bread and jam, at least I could eat that without feeling as if I wanted to be sick.

Back to the billet where we were informed that we were free for the rest of that evening. We were advised however by Lance-Corporal Leary to spend the time cleaning our webbing and brasses in readiness for our room inspection on Monday.

A quick trip to the N.A.A.F.I. before it closed, enabled most of us to purchase blocks of blanco and tins of Brasso with which to carry out this task. Unfortunately wire-wool or fine emery paper were not available to us to clean the black brasses. Which would have got the job done fairly quickly. The only method available to us at the time was cardboard soaked in Brasso and to rub, and rub, and rub. A very long and laborious business.

It was at this stage that we realised that it was prudent to immediately put your regimental number on all your Army equipment and clothing, if for no other reason than to help prevent it being stolen. If it you had cleaned it and left it out to dry, you could find that it would have had been replaced by someone's equipment that hadn't been cleaned, this would give you many hours of extra work. In fact it helped prevent any of your equipment being stolen for whatever reason. Being in possession of equipment with someone else's number on it was a chargeable offence or so we were told, but then everything appeared to be a chargeable offence if you listened to Corporal Harridge.

As I was laboriously applying my number to all my articles of equipment and clothing it troubled me to think that I had got to remember my number of 23040258. I'd never be able to do it. I must have been living in "cloud cuckoo land." Even today I can remember it more readily than my telephone number, and I use that every day.

That night most of us didn't get to bed until about 02:15hrs after having the lights turned out two or three times by another friendly guard who had been in the Army a whole five weeks.

Next morning we were up bright and early at 05:15hrs, three quarters of an hour prior to the Orderly Sergeant making his official rounds to wake us up, obviating the need for him to bang his pace-stick against the fire bucket, that being one of the least aggressive ways of waking us up. One of the more aggressive being to up end beds and tip people on the floor. By getting up early we certainly made his job easy in those first few days.

We then had three hours in which to strip our beds, to make our bed block, clean our bed space, have breakfast, do our room job, and prepare ourselves for muster parade at 08:00hrs. As at this stage however we didn't know our arm from our elbow there was by nowhere near enough time for us to perform all these operations. Later on, when we had become "veteran" soldiers, we would waltz it in less than an hour, but not at the moment.

In those early days however we soon learnt that, although you could clean your bed space and guard it against all comers, it was pointless doing your block job in say the ablution block until the very last moment, otherwise you would find that all your work had been undone by a late arrival for a wash and shave. There again there was conflict between doing your block job and being ready for muster parade. You could easily get your boots dirtied after cleaning them, by doing your block job. You soon realised that you cleaned your boots and other equipment the night before, and kept them in a safe place out of danger of being marred in any way whatsoever. You then carried out all your chores in your slippers, and put your boots and equipment on at the very last moment just prior to going on muster parade. At this early stage however we were always frightened of being late on parade so we dressed for parade at the very earliest possible time much to our detriment. In time we would learn our lesson.

On muster parade again, where we were once more positioned well away from any prying eyes, it was obvious however that this situation would not carry on for much longer. Sergeant Pearce inspected us once again and informed us that our turn out was better than yesterday but he still wanted further improvement.

This time however we were not just dismissed and marched off the square, we had to carry out various intricate, to me, drill manoeuvres then march past the dais, in column of route, complete with some officer or other taking the salute. Well that was what the Regimental Sergeant Major called it. Somehow or other our platoon marched past the saluting dais without tripping over our own feet too many times and the R.S.M. didn't yell at us too loudly. From this we concluded that our performance was acceptable.

Once we arrived back at the billet Corporal Harridge roared at us to stand by our beds. Sergeant Pearce then entered through the door and gave the room a cursory inspection. Although he considered that the room was still filthy, as it was Saturday morning he didn't feel inclined to charge us that morning, but woe betide us on Monday morning when room inspections would begin in earnest.

"This morning," he explained "You are all going to the tailor for your battle dress fitting. You have two battle dresses, one of them you will choose for best, the other one you will eventually use for your working dress. After the battle dress fittings Corporal Harridge and Lance-Corporal Leary will be giving you foot drill instruction until lunch time so that as from Monday the platoon can stop being a shambles on muster parade. That's an order!" he bellowed.

We were then commanded to get our two sets of battle dress and line up on the road outside in columns of threes. Once formed up we were marched off to the tailor with all three N.C.O.s in attendance, Corporals Harridge, and Leary contributing all the vocals, with Sergeant Pearce clutching a resplendent "silver" topped swagger cane leading the way.

Eventually we were confronted by the tailor, who was a Quartermaster Sergeant of absolutely enormous proportions, weighing I should imagine about twenty stone. We were instructed to produce our two suites of battle dress for his perusal. It was only at this stage of the proceedings that it suddenly occurred to me the enormous variations there were in shades of khaki. It went right across the spectrum from dark brown to almost ginger. The trick was then for the tailor to obtain two suits of battle dress in the correct size and matching shades. In the first instance this was attempted by swopping trousers or blouses with other members of the platoon, when this process wasn't progressing very far the tailor then introduced further suits of battle dress from his store into the equation. It soon became apparent that it was going to be an impossible task for every man to have two battle dresses of both the correct size and matching shades of khaki. The tailor then decided that it was only necessary for us to have our best battle dress in correct size, and matching shades, and that he would settle for our second suit of battle dress just being the correct size, regardless of shade. It now became a matter of opinion whether or not your battle dress blouse and trousers were of matching shades or indeed of the correct size. Judging by some of the decisions made by the tailor I came to the conclusion that he was colour blind as well as being unable to use a tape measure with any accuracy!

After about an hour of this shambles the tailor professed himself satisfied with the mix and match sets that we now had in our possession and bade Corporal Harridge to march us away, Sergeant Pearce having seemingly disappeared. Little did I realise at the time that this process of best battle dress inspection would be carried out regularly for the next two years, or to be more precise for the next 727 days, as I had already picked up the "days to demob" syndrome.

During that time, at intervals of approximately every two months I was to be rebuked by the inspecting officer for having such bad judgement on what was or was not a matching shade when in actual fact I had little or nothing to say in the matter. The first time that I was rebuked over my lack of judgement on shade perception by an inspecting officer I attempted to explain that it hadn't been my judgement but the Quartermaster Sergeant's judgement. That clearly wasn't the information that the officer wished to hear. He wanted to belittle me personally and I resented the fact. Eventually I could let incidents in the Army like that roll off my back like water off a duck but that time was way in the future.

Back to the billet, battle dresses away, "Out on the road in three fucking ranks, fucking quick." We were then marched up to the back of the camp by the inevitable Corporal Harridge and Lance-Corporal Leary.

As we were being marched along by the duo I suddenly realised that they also were all now sporting silver topped swagger canes; most impressive they looked too I might add, marching us along. It was only later that I heard that there was hardly a billiard cue to be found in the junior N.C.O.'s mess and that the silver tops to their swagger canes were in fact "bulled up" aluminium milk tops. From a distance however you could have fooled me though!

By this time it was a fairly hot day and some consideration was given to us, I suppose, by the fact that we were taken into a motor transport shed and drilled in there out of the sun. Mark you, I suspect that this act was as much for the drill instructor's benefit as ours.

After we had been drilled for an hour or so and seemingly getting it all wrong Lance-Corporal Leary suddenly lost his temper with us. With eyes up to heaven and yelling out the words "Jesus fucking Christ," he snapped his swagger cane over his knee and implored us to look at what we had made him do, I assumed that the junior N.C.O.'s mess would be another billiard queue short come the morning. Next he hurled his beret on the ground and seemingly stamped on it with his hob-nailed boots. A closer inspection however I am sure would show that his boots were very skilfully just missing their target each time. Meanwhile Corporal Harridge stood impassively at one side contenting himself by muttering "What a fucking shower". After this display of affection we were marched back to our hut by a pair of seemingly very unhappy N.C.O.s

On arrival we were addressed by Corporal Harrridge. "As punishment for the fucking awful performance on the drill session instead of having the afternoon off, we now had to parade at 14:00 hrs. outside the hut for a gardening session. When we would be required to cut the grass and generally clear the area around the hut."

After lunch, the food was worse than usual clearly the cooks had made a special effort for the weekend, we were duly paraded on the grassed area outside the hut, and for starters were ordered to cut the grass. When one of our number was bold enough to enquire the whereabouts of the grass shears even he realised we couldn't expect a lawn mower from the Army was given the answer. "What do you think your fucking jackknife's for, picking your bleeding nose?"

At this retort we all rushed inside to get our jackknives. The sight of some forty persons cutting a large grassed area with jackknives is a sight which has to be seen to be believed I can assure you. There was a broad grin on Lance-Corporal Leary's face as he watched this spectacular, and I believe that I saw a semblance of a smile on Corporal Harrridge's face also. After an hour, or so of this gardening fiasco, Corporals Harridge and Leary became bored and clearly had other things to do in what was surely their official time off duty. They therefore decided that our punishment had fitted the crime", and that we were now free for the rest of the day, free that is provided we didn't want to go outside the camp , or to do any of the many things that the Army didn't want us to do. We retired to our hut and most of us laid on our beds and fell asleep exhausted from the ramifications of our first two and a half days in the Army. How the hell was I ever going to survive the next two years I wondered?

CHAPTER 3

IN WHICH I AM INTRODUCED TO ARMY DISCIPLINE

As we were apparently not to be called upon to do any more duties that Saturday, after a sleep the majority of us decided to spend the time attempting to get our webbing equipment into some form of order before the impending inspection on Monday morning. I spent until eleven o'clock or so that night, with only a short break for tea, cleaning brasses and blanco-ing equipment and also polishing up my boots. The black brasses were now reasonably bright and the webbing had now taken on a khaki hue thanks to the many applications of "blanco" which was applied by rubbing a wet nail brush on a block of khaki blanco and brushing it onto the webbing. The problem with this process however was the fact that when you applied the blanco you got it on the brasses and when you attempted to clean the brasses you got the Brasso onto the webbing turning it black. A very frustrating business indeed but not however as frustrating as trying to get all the wrinkles out of your boots especially your best ones. We were told by our inscrutable Lance-Corporal that the time honoured method of doing this was to heat up a spoon handle over a candle, then by pressing it hard on the boots attempt to iron out the wrinkles on very small areas at a time, whilst liberally applying boot polish. At first I was very sceptical over this advice and considered it another leg pull from our estimable Lance-Corporal but experience proved however that this was indeed the best method of bulling up your boots. An electric iron would possibly have achieved the job quicker but where was one to obtain an electric iron?

At 11.15 pm, sorry I mean 23:15hrs, I again dropped onto my bed totally exhausted. Hard and uncomfortable as my mattress was I fell asleep instantly in spite of the fact that the lights were still on in the room and that the other occupants of the room were causing quite a lot of noise with their chatter.

No yelling, no shouting, no noisy Orderly Sergeant to wake us up. It was Sunday morning in the Army, all was peace and serenity, I couldn't believe it, even our most enthusiastic members of the platoon were still in bed. At any moment I expected the barrack room door to fly open and the Orderly Sergeant to burst in demanding to know why we were all still in our fucking beds and threatening to put us all on a charge. But no this was Sunday morning and apparently the one day when there were no demands on us for the whole of the day, or so we thought. I got up in a leisurely manner washed, and walked, not marched, to the cookhouse for breakfast, the food unfortunately was as bad as ever, but I was forced to eat it or go hungry. On completion I returned the dirty dishes to the collection point and proceeded towards the exit under the watchful eye of the Orderly Sergeant who was standing in a prominent position in the middle of the cookhouse.

At the exit of the cookhouse was a very large container of scalding hot water where you were expected to wash your knife, fork, spoon, and pint-sized mug. This steel tub was about two feet six inches high and was of about thirty gallons capacity. The trick was to clean your utensils in this tub of water without burning your fingers, and indeed without dropping anything in the tub, where it could sink to the bottom never to be seen again unless you were extremely lucky. You would then be confronted with the cost of replacing the article and, rumour had it, be charged with losing government property. To be caught walking away from the cookhouse with dirty eating utensils was also a chargeable offence, or so we were told, hence the eagerness for everybody to crowd around the tub to clean their eating utensils.

Yes, the Army really was as stupid as that, especially at basic training camps.

Back to the hut, where in view of the fact that I still wasn't happy with the cleanliness of my equipment a day of "bulling" was envisaged. No sooner had I commenced on this operation however than the Orderly Sergeant appeared on the scene and informed us that we had been given the "honour" of being selected as the duty platoon for that Sunday.

Incidentally when we first saw Sergeants walking around camp with a large crimson sash across their right shoulder we quite mistakenly thought that they were colour sergeants not realising that there was no such rank in R.E.M.E. if indeed in the British

Army any more. They were in fact Orderly Sergeants, the sash denoting this fact. They were on duty for a predetermined time and, in conjunction with the Orderly Officer had, in theory at any rate, quite sweeping powers whilst on duty.

We soon found out that although normally we should have been free that Sunday, only a comparative expression you understand? Being duty platoon meant that we would now be far from free! The Orderly Sergeant, the Sergeant with the crimson sash, then proceeded to hand out jobs left right and centre.

I was lucky I was included in a detail that had to go to the gym and clean it up and prepare it for use on Monday morning. I say lucky, because we were released from our job after only about an hour and half an hour, other people were not so lucky and were kept working all day. Such was the luck of the draw.

Dismissed from our work we returned to our hut and continued with our "bulling". At this stage I should explain that the cleaning of the webbing equipment and brasses didn't take place in the barrack room but outside on the newly jack-knife cut grassed areas surrounding the hut. The "bulling up" of the boots did in fact take place in the hut however due to the fact that it was difficult to keep candles alight outside.

Most of this boot "bulling up" took place on the trestle table in the middle of the barrack room. At this early stage of our Army career we were not aware of the "fetish" of the barrack room table and the fact that it was to be regarded as some form of "Icon" to be revered as such and never used, least of all for "bulling up" our boots upon. It was to be kept in snowy white condition for the never ending round of room inspections.

Unfortunately blobs of candle grease and black boot polish adhered to it all too easily and it soon took on the appearance of a large slab of "Spotted Dick". We were to learn to our cost that this was not the way to treat an Army "Icon".

Lunchtime came and went, teatime came and went, and still the majority of us carried on "bulling up" our equipment, the only relief we had from this chore was listening to the hut's rented radio that we had volunteered to take over from the previous occupants of the hut. The Trouble was we could only get one programme on it, the Light programme as far as I recall. On reflection this had probably been arranged on purpose to obviate any argument over which programme to listen to. Mark you there were still arguments over whether or not the radio should be on at all, but as we were all paying for it I think that the majority of us considered that it should always be on regardless of the programme content. When I say always on I only mean in our off-duty periods of an evening and at weekends.

Again I fell into bed at about 23:30 hrs. totally exhausted hoping that I had done enough to my equipment to pass the inspection on the following day.

Reveille was normally at 06:00 hrs., but so keen were we in those early days that most people were up by 05:00 hrs., and by the time the Orderly Sergeant came around at reveille to get us up there was nothing for him to do. Oh how times would change in the future!

A quick wash in the crowded washroom, a hurried breakfast, completion of your room and block jobs, last minute adjustments to your dress then onto the square for muster parade at 08:00 hrs. Roll call and an inspection of the platoon by Sergeant Pearce when there was much yelling and shouting at almost every member of the platoon over some fault or other with their turnout, but no actual punishment handed out at this stage. Then as a grand finale, a march past of the whole battalion in front of someone standing on the saluting dais, who we were informed later by Corporal Harridge was the Regimental Sergeant Major, who acted as if he was God. Much to his disgust, we were always saluting him in those early days when he was wearing a raincoat, due to the fact that no rank is shown on raincoats coupled with the fact that he would insist on wearing a peaked cap in a similar manner to the commissioned officers. By and by however we soon learnt to recognise the difference between a warrant officer's cap and a commissioned officer's cap, and we stopped making this mistake.

I decided that the easiest way of not making this mistake, was to stop saluting anyone, but the Army didn't take very kindly to my solution to the problem, especially the R.S.M.! Funny man.

Back to the barrack room, hasty final adjustments to our equipment, then the expected "stand by your beds" yelled through the open door. A hurried movement of everyone to the foot of their beds and a quick dressing by the right as in marched Sergeant Pearce, pace stick under his arm, closely followed by Corporals Harridge and Leary. His first comment as he entered the room being that the beds had not been dressed in correctly by the right and that they were out of alignment. He ordered that this be corrected immediately.

The execution of this command was carried out by the Sergeant standing at the head of the room with us poor minions pushing and pulling the beds as the Sergeant, aided and abetted by the two Corporals, yelled encouragement to us. "Number three bed back a bit, number five bed forward, steady. Number six bed back a bit, steady," and so on until the Sergeant was happy that each and every one of the beds were in line.

"That," he announced, "Is how I want the beds to look for every future room inspection, or else!" Or else what I thought?

Allowing for this small, in my mind, error, I thought that the room looked pretty impressive with all the beds made up and the webbing equipment laid out on top of the lockers surmounted by our steel helmets, and I was fully expecting that the Sergeant was about to tell us so albeit in a grudging manner. I must have been living in cloud cuckoo land in those days to think that!

Sergeant Pearce commenced his inspection. He stopped in front of each member of the platoon as he came to them, eyed him up and down, then his bed, bed space and locker surmounted by his equipment and made what he thought was an appropriate comment. As he made his way down the line of platoon members his remarks became more and more abrasive regarding the condition of their dress and their equipment. When he reached Private Berry's bed space he strode past him to inspect his equipment and uttering the words, "Fucking disgrace", with one flourish of his pace stick swept Berry's equipment from the top of the locker straight out through the open window onto the ground below.

Stan Berry hearing the commotion behind him turned round to see what was going on. He was immediately commanded to, "Stand still and face the front".

Having clearly executed his platoon inspection party piece Sergeant Pearce carried on his way as if nothing untoward had happened and seemingly without the necessity of having to repeat the performance. He obviously didn't do encores.

Having completed his inspection he stood at the end of the barrack room flanked by his two Corporals and was about to address us when he spotted the table. He exploded!

"Look at my fucking table, Jesus fucking Christ what have you done to it? WHAT HAVE YOU DONE TO IT", he yelled going red in the face. "It's like a fucking spotted dick".

I recall that although I wasn't particularly religious at the time I used to get extremely hot under the collar over the Almighty being referred to in such derogatory terms, I could see no necessity for it and yet it was an expression freely used by all the N.C.O.s at Blandford.

He continued, "In all my born days I have never been so insulted in my life, it is an affront to my rank to be expected to inspect a barrack room that reminds me of a pigsty. No that's insulting pigs, you're worse than pigs! I warn you that if you continue with this attitude you will all find yourselves in serious trouble if you are not already in it".

At this stage I noticed that Stan Berry was still giving sidelong glances out of the open window, trying desperately to see where his equipment had ended up. He was probably thinking that he only wanted to lose that lot and he'd probably be paying for it for the rest of his two years National Service. No wonder a Captain went down with his ship!

Sergeant Pearce composed himself, drew himself to attention, and brought his voice down a decibel or two.

"Tomorrow morning", he continued, "The room inspection will be carried out by your platoon commander Lieutenant Grainger I warn you here and now that he is a very hard person not easy going like me and if he finds the room in the state that I have found it in this morning then I wouldn't like to be in your shoes for all the bloody tea in China."

With a final, "And get that fucking table cleaned", he turned on his heels and strode out of the barrack room.

There was a pregnant pause for a few moments whilst we looked at each other in serious amusement. All except Stan Berry who was still trying to catch sight of his equipment lying somewhere outside on the ground.

"Right", said Corporal Harridge breaking the silence. "Now listen carefully. Today will be taken up with P.S.O interviews. You will all be interviewed by an officer who will decide which trade you are going to follow whilst you are in the Army. This will take up most of the day. Those of you not on interview will remain in the hut, you will not wander around. You will be called to the P.S.O. block when you are required for interview"

So saying he also disappeared with Lance-Corporal Leary once again trailing in his wake.

No sooner had they departed than Stan rushed out of the room and after a pause came staggering back through the door piled up with all his equipment muttering something about, "Stupid bastards." He then proceeded to re-erect his equipment on top of his locker without attempting to clean it in any way whatsoever. When he was asked by a member of the platoon if that was wise? He merely retorted "Sod 'em, if they think I'm going to clean that lot again after they knocked it out of the bloody window, then they're mistaken."

Members of the platoon were coming and going all day attending their P.S.O. interviews, coming back with what I thought were tall stories regarding how the interviews had gone, and which jobs they were going to do whilst in the Army.

Eventually my time came for interview, I was marched over to the P.S.O. block, was ushered into a room in front of an officer, I was then ordered to "Stand at ease", obviously no niceties of sitting down at this interview.

"Right Skinner", said the officer glancing up, "The purpose of this interview is to decide what we are going to do with you whilst you are in R.E.M.E. What trade you are going to take etc. etc. Have you had any thoughts about the subject?" he questioned.

"Yes sir", I replied smartly, "I should like to have a shot at a commission".

There was silence for a few moments whilst he studied the papers before him.

"Hmm! You certainly have the qualifications, yes I think that we can agree to that", he said to me much to my surprise, I was expecting a far longer discussion over the matter.

"In about a week's time then you will be sent from here to No. 2 Training Battalion at Honiton where we put all fellows like you into "D" Company for about eight weeks where we prepare you for W.O.S.B. Do you know about W.O.S.B.?" he asked.

Was it a catch question? Should I say yes when I didn't know. If I said no, would it alter his decision? After all he had already said that he thought that he could agree to my request. If I did say yes he might start questioning me about W.O.S.B. All these thoughts were racing through my mind. I took a chance and made my decision.

"No Sir", I replied smartly.

"Right, well W.O.S.B. stands for War Office Selection Board and the Board is situated at Barton Stacey near Andover. When we think that you are ready we send you there for three days where you will do lots of interesting things and be assessed on your suitability for sending to O.C.T.U." At least I knew what that stood for.

"If successful you will then be sent for approximately six months to Eaton Hall Officer Cadet School, after which you will be commissioned. Any questions?"

"No sir".

"Right, well looking on the black side of things we must consider what we are going to do with you should you fail W.O.S.B. Have you had any thoughts on that," he asked.

"No sir I've not thought about anything beyond gaining a commission".

"Hmm, with a technical background like yours I think that you would be an ideal candidate for an E.C.E, that's Electrician Control Equipment. What do you think?"

Being totally uninterested in anything in the Army other than a commission I answered in a similarly uninterested manner.

"I don't know a thing about electricity or electronics sir", I replied in alarm.

"Oh you'll soon pick it up", he said with what I thought was over optimism." And in any case we send you on a six month course to learn all about the subject anyway".

I would only learn later that boy-soldiers spent three years doing the same course and joined the six month National Service course merely as a refresher course. I was to find out later that the course was only really suitable for people already experienced in electronics.

"Where would this course be sir?" I queried.

"Number Five Training Battalion Arborfield near Reading", he replied.

So in the unlikely event of my failing my commission that was to be my fall-back position.

"Any questions?

"No sir".

"Right attention, about turn, quick march".

I made my way back to the barrack room feeling very pleased with myself. On arrival I found that the only other occupant in the room was Stan Berry, he was lying on his bed hands clasped behind his head blissfully drawing on a cigarette and at the same time admiring his webbing equipment on top of his locker.

"How did you get on cocker?" he asked.

"They're letting me have a crack at a commission", I said with a slightly excited voice".

"Oh good, we'll be going to Honiton together then, I wonder which other buggers will be coming with us? I bet one of them will be that young snotty nosed public school drip, they go for that type at W.O.S.B. you know", he said with some obvious knowledge of the subject.

At first I was taken back that Stan had also been selected to be sent to Honiton, but then I began to warm to Stan and his nonchalant attitude towards the Army, and the way he treated the whole experience as one great joke. If only I could react like him to the situation that I now found myself in. The time was months ahead however before I would learn how to think and act like him. If I had done so at this stage I could have saved myself many months of anguish.

No call was made on me for the rest of the day so I was able to spend all my time on the serious occupation of "bulling up" my kit, while Stan laid on the grass looking on with mild amusement and a twinkle in his eyes, intermittently shaking his head at me, when he thought that I was doing something the wrong way.

The next two days were taken up with trade testing members of the platoon, and this consisted of the recruits nominating an

Army trade parallel to the one that they were working at in *civvy street* and going through the rigours of taking the Army test of competence for that trade. It didn't necessarily mean that they would be carrying out that trade whilst in the Army but it did immediately classify them as a tradesman and entitle them to another 3/6-d (17.5p) a week which would eventually boost their pay from 28/-s (£1.40p) a week to 31/6d (£1.57.5p) per week

Unfortunately being a National Serviceman they wouldn't receive this rise until they had been in the Army six months. If however they were prepared to sign on for three years as a short term regular soldier, not only could they receive this increase immediately but they would also receive a regular's pay, approximately double that of a National Serviceman, This was only one of the many ways that National Servicemen were discriminated against, and yet the longer I remained in the Army the more I realised that the National Serviceman was totally indispensable to the Army and that it could not function without them, as basically the majority of the so- called regular recruits, what I could see of them, with few exceptions, were absolute rubbish. I decided that there was no Army trade that was parallel with the one that I had carried out in *civvy street* and therefore did not take part in any of these trade tests. I later learnt that I would have quite probably passed with ease the mechanical draughtsman's trade test and should have taken it and eventually been in receipt of another 3/6-d per week. As it was, although on the face of it I was earning 28/-s per week, after I had had 10/-s per week marriage allowance deducted, along with national insurance, barrack room damages and other stoppages. I received the princely sum of a 10/-s, one week, and 15/- the next. I just couldn't believe it, 10/-s a week for serving Queen and Country and me a married man of twenty two years. I am certain that the young people of today just would not have stood for it. So why did we?

Next morning it was pouring with rain and we were all hurried off the parade ground before we all got soaking wet. Or was it before the Regimental Sergeant Major got soaking wet?

We sighed a sigh of relief as we made our way back to the barrack room. We had no sooner arrived there however when the now familiar call of "Stand by your beds", came ringing through the open door, and in strolled a very smart but very young looking Second Lieutenant reminiscent of a dummy from the Army and Navy Stores shop window in his brand new barathea uniform. He was closely followed by Messers Pearce, Harridge, and Leary, in that order. Everybody knew their place in the Army.

He turned to Sergeant Pearce who looked old enough to be his father.

"Stand them at ease Sergeant Pearce if you please."

"Room stand at ease".

The dummy then invited us to "stand easy."

"I am Lieutenant Grainger, your Platoon Commander. I want you to be happy whilst you are here, (joke), should you have any problems then just inform Sergeant Pearce that you wish to see me and he will arrange a meeting, if he feels that a meeting is necessary that is of course."

"Now I understand that Sergeant Pearce has informed you that I am going to make a room inspection this morning and that he made one yesterday to let you know what I shall be looking for."

I glanced across at Stan and noted that he had taken the precaution of closing the window adjacent to his locker.

Lieutenant Grainger strolled around the room glancing at this and that but apparently nothing specific, with Sergeant Pearce trailing in his wake whilst the two Corporals stood by the door at the head of the room, looking on expectantly. It looked to me as if Lieutenant Grainger was out of his depth.

He returned to the head of the room and addressed the platoon.

"On the whole I'm quite pleased with your turn out".

I saw the Sergeant grit his teeth whilst the two Corporals stared directly to their front in a non-committal attitude. The Lieutenant seemed to sense the tension in the air and hastily added.

"But we must always seek higher standards so I therefore expect a hundred percent improvement for my inspection tomorrow. Thank you Sergeant Pearce".

"Room, room 'shun", bellowed out Sergeant Pearce, who threw up a very smart salute whilst the two corporals stood rigidly to attention. He received in return a nonchalant wave of the

Second Lieutenant's swagger cane as he made his exit through the door.

There was silence for a few seconds whilst the Sergeant glanced at the two Corporals with a shrug of the shoulders and a look of disbelief on his face.

"Right Corporal Harridge march this shower down to the gymnasium let's see what Staff Ford thinks of them".

We were marched down to the gym by Lance-Corporal Leary. Everything seemed to be delegated in the Army, which usually ended up by the task in hand being given to a Lance-Corporal, very often acting unpaid. Whether or not Lance-Corporal Leary came into the acting unpaid category I had no way of telling.

We were ushered into the gymnasium changing room. No sooner had we arrived when a very loud voice issued from the open door leading into the gym proper, informing us that we had two fucking minutes, in which to get fucking changed and to be standing in two fucking rows in the gym.

Pandemonium broke out as everybody struggled to achieve this order. When at last we were all expectantly standing in the gym we were confronted by a number of tough looking individuals in red and blue striped jumpers and dark blue trousers. At this stage nobody said a word, every- body was waiting expectantly.

After a lapse of a minute or so a tall blonde-headed figure strode out of an office at the far end of the gym. The Physical Training Instructors in the striped jerseys came to attention and called us to attention at the same time. We complied stamping our feet on the gym floor as we had been taught to do out on the square.

"Right," roared the blonde figure." That's the first thing I don't want to see you doing any more in my gym is stamping around and making a lot of fucking noise when you come to attention. In my gym you don't stamp your feet. You slip your right foot into the side of your left foot, softly and silently just like a bridegroom slips in his prick on his wedding night, got it? Good."

He waited for a laugh before proceeding to demonstrate what he meant, with his feet of course, there being no females present.

"Right", he continued. "I'll introduce myself. I'm Staff Ford,

I'm known as the blonde bastard of Blandford, and I am, so be warned. The only person you have to watch out for more than me around these gyms is Sergeant Major Henry, 'e's king around here and don't you forget it!"

"Right run up to the end of the gym, touch the wall and return to your place; last one back is on a charge. Move".

There was a stampede like a herd of elephants with everyone running up to the far end of the gym and returning back to their places again. Staff Ford seemingly selected a man at random as being the last man back to his place and instructed Corporal Green, "to take his name as being idle on parade."

Staff Ford continued, "Now when I say, one hundred up, I want you all running on the spot for a hundred steps just as fast as you can...

"Right, one hundred up", he bellowed.

Forty pairs of feet thundered out a tattoo upon the gymnasium floor in an effort to comply with the given order.

"Corporal Green take that man's name for disobeying a lawful command", he ordered, pointing to the most inoffensive member of our platoon, once we had all finished our hundred ups. "I distinctly saw that he took only ninety nine steps and not one hundred as ordered."

Stan Berry I noticed was smiling gently to himself.

There was silence for a few seconds whilst everybody looked to Staff Ford for a lead, but he clearly wasn't going to be hurried, he seemed to be savouring the atmosphere.

"Right sit on the floor," he suddenly ordered. "Stand up, sit down, stand up, sit down. Come on, come on, jump to it, what the bloody hells wrong with you, deaf or something?"

We all sat down obediently whilst he stalked up and down looking at us upon the floor; we all once again waited expectantly.

"Have we got any Olympic champions amongst you?" he asked.

No response, I don't think he really expected any.

"National Champions?" Again no response.

"Any bloody athletes at all? And I don't mean bloody bedroom athletes, I know there's plenty of them amongst you, there always are. Come on, come on, some of you must have done something".

"I've done some cycle racing, staff", I ventured.

"Get to your feet and stand to attention when you speak to me", he roared, much to my discomfort. I complied with his command.

"Good are you?" he asked once he saw that I was on my feet and standing to attention.

I've ridden a couple of times in the Isle of Man road races, staff".

"Have you", he said. He seemed to have heard of the Isle of Man and appeared suitably impressed. "Get your bike down here and we'll arrange a trial for you for the R.E.M.E. team. Good, sit down. Anyone else?"

After I had broken the ice a number of other people were now prepared to volunteer their athletic prowess. This process went on for another five minutes or so, by which stage the Staff Sergeant decided it was time to put us through the mill once again.

Staff Ford and his merry men put us through agony for the next half an hour, doubling here, doubling there, up the wall bars, down the wall bars, over the vaulting horses, up the ropes, down the ropes. Not that I could climb a rope to save my life but in the melee nobody seemed to notice. In no time at all we were almost fit to drop and were wondering how much longer this was going to go on for, when at last Staff Ford halted us, called us to attention, and dismissed us with the instruction to get changed and get out on the road in three fucking ranks in fucking double quick time.

No sooner had we reached the changing room than we were being vigorously pursued by the P.T.I.s. "To get changed and out on the fucking road, fucking quick." I half dressed and gathered up the rest of my clothes and went out through the single door and finished my dressing outside. Once the majority of the platoon were outside on the road the P.T.I. who was standing out there decided that we hadn't achieved the process fast enough and ordered us back into the changing room.

No sooner had we arrived back in the changing room than we were being pursued by the PTI in there, who ordered us back out on the road again. Eventually both halves of the platoon were being ordered through the single doorway in opposite directions at the same time. It was an impossible situation and a fiasco developed. I noted that the two P.T.I.s, the one inside the building and the one outside the building had eye contact with each other and were quietly roaring with laughter. This incensed me to such a degree that at this stage of the proceedings I decided that I was going to take no further part in this stupidity and stood to one side whilst it continued. Suddenly it registered with the P.T.I. on the outside that I wasn't adding to his amusement and demanded to know, "What the fucking hell I was doing just fucking standing there?"

I replied that once he had made up his mind what he wanted us to do I would do it but meanwhile I had no intention in taking part in these stupid proceedings.

I have since realised that wars have been started by lesser statements than that which I made! My name was taken, I would now be shat upon from a great height, my feet wouldn't touch the ground all the way to the guardroom, I'd be charged with insubordination, and I'd also be charged with disobeying a lawful command. But if I returned immediately to the debacle of trying to get through the single door both ways at the same time the P.T.I. might be inclined to forget what I had said, just this once. I returned to the rugby scrum immediately.

Eventually the two P.T.I.s had had their fill of fun and we were at long last allowed to line up on the road to be marched away to our barrack room by Corporal Leary who had suddenly appeared from nowhere having apparently missed the recent spectacular.

I was extremely relieved to get away from my first dose of Army PT.

CHAPTER 4

IN WHICH I LEAVE FOR HONITON.

That night I walked up to the grandly named Information Centre, studied the times of the trains and buses and came to the conclusion that it was quite possible for Doreen to come down to visit me on Sunday, the only day that we could reasonably be certain of being free of duties. Although judging by last Sunday's experience this was by no means an absolute certainty. I had however made enquiries and the possibility of us being duty platoon two Sundays running was most unlikely. My later experiences of the Army however was that the unlikely was the most likely. I think that it was something to do with confusing the enemy in times of war, and unfortunately the Army didn't seem to be able to get out of the habit. Either that or it didn't realise that there wasn't a war on at this precise moment. I telephoned Doreen and explained that in view of the fact that in the very near future I would be moving even further away from home than I was at Blandford it might be a good idea if she visited me that weekend. She agreed with me. I returned to the barrack room happy in the knowledge that I had something to look forward to in the immediate future.

Before settling down to an evening of "bulling" I decided that I had better collect my socks that I had washed and were drying on the line stretched between our barrack room and the adjacent one. Much to my horror I found that my brand new Army socks had disappeared and were no longer there. Without a moment's hesitation I took two other pairs that were still hanging on the line adjacent to where mine had been. Perhaps I was beginning to get the hang of this Army life after all! Feeling extremely guilty I returned to my barrack room and carried on with my "bulling" until about 23:00hrs, with Stan again instructing me how he would have gone about this "bulling" if he had felt like doing it, which of course he didn't. Instead he was lying on his bed reading a book and smoking a cigarette, only glancing up now and again to give me advice when he thought I was going wrong. How I wished that I had had Stan's relaxed attitude towards the Army in those early days.

Up at 05:30hrs again next morning and with a great frenzy, executed all those duties that had to be carried out before muster parade at 08:00hrs.

In those early days it always appeared that we were going to fall well short of meeting the necessary time schedules but somehow or other we always did meet them, albeit that perhaps we omitted to give sufficient attention to details of our appearance. This fact was confirmed that morning on muster parade when half the platoon had their names taken by Sergeant Pearce who appeared to inspect us more stringently than he had done previously. I was at this stage totally unaware of the consequences of having your name taken on parade. Later, experience would show me that this process could vary from you being put on a charge, with an appearance before the Company Commander, to no action being taken whatsoever. Whether or not action was taken seemed to depend upon the person taking your name, and what he was trying to achieve, and whether or not anyone of consequence was in earshot when the name was taken. In this instance no action seemed to materialise from this particular round of name taking. In view of the total uncertainty of "name taking" however there was always a certain quavering in the boots whenever you heard the words, "Take that man's name", especially if it was directed at you!

After muster parade the platoon was marched down to the M.I room for our inoculations, which if the truth were told we had all heard about before joining the Army and were not looking forward to one little bit to say the least of it.

By now it was pouring with rain which didn't help matters, and we were paraded in front of the M.I. room wearing our waterproof capes, which in view of the fact that they were really ground sheets modified by having a collar sewn into them halfway down one side, hung from us in a very lop-sided and un-military fashion.

An orderly emerged from the M.I. room and bade us to roll up both our shirt sleeves as far as they would go. Once he was satisfied that his order had been carried out he went inside the building and came out with an enamel tray containing two enormous syringes. He was closely followed by what appeared to be a Medical

Officer. The orderly then bade us to bare our right arms and to stick them out from underneath our rain capes. The M.O. then went up the column of men, to give them their inoculations. Two people fainted and fell on the rain soaked ground just as they were about to receive their inoculations. They received their "jabs" last of all with an even blunter needle. Having traversed the platoon member's right arms the orderly then ordered us to "About turn", whereupon the M.O. took out the second syringe and made his way back down the line to his starting point, this time stabbing his new syringe into our left arms as he went merrily on his way.

After the inoculations we were ordered into the M.I. Centre for a dental inspection having first deposited our wet capes on the veranda outside.

We queued up, and as our turn came were thrust into a dentist's chair to have our teeth examined by an Army dentist. I was staggered to hear such statements as, "three extraction's, four fillings, two extraction's, five fillings," being called out as members of the platoon had their teeth checked

My hat I thought, these people don't know what they're doing. I had already made up my mind that I wasn't going to let these morons touch my teeth, when I was thrust into a chair for my examination.

"No work required here. All okay," called out the dentist after a detailed inspection.

"Next."

I slipped out of the chair with relief. Perhaps they did know their job after all. Clearly the other chaps hadn't been seeing their dentists in *civvy street*, in spite of the fact that at the time all dental treatment was free.

We returned to the barrack room where we were informed by Corporal Leary, much to our horror, that Mr Grainger would be carrying out another room inspection in approximately half an hour's time, so we had better jump to it and get the fucking place cleaned up fucking quick. Panic seemed to seize each and every one of us, except Stan. We all rushed around trying to do two or three jobs at the same time and not succeeding in doing any of them efficiently. This time however we did remember to line up the beds and dress them by the right. That ought to impress "Sir" if nothing else did.

Far too soon the "Stand by your beds" order came singing in through the door and in strolled Lieutenant Granger in his immaculate uniform contrasting greatly with our denims which was the only form of uniform we were allowed to wear at this stage of our training. This time he didn't invite us to stand at ease and then to stand easy. This was clearly going to be a serious business. He strolled around the room looking this time in particular at the webbing equipment laid out on top of our lockers. He stopped in front of Stan who was smiling benignly in a manner very reminiscent of Stan Laurel, the old time film star, then walked past him in order to make a very close inspection of his webbing equipment. He then returned to a position facing Stan.

"What's your name soldier?"

"Berry Sir,"

"Well then Berry I have to tell you that your webbing equipment is not up to the standard I require. It requires a far bigger effort than that which you have given it so far." Lieutenant Grainger informed him.

I noted that Sergeant Pearce had a notebook and a pencil in his hand, and a look of anticipation on his face. Before either of them could say or do anything further however Stan, with his head inclined slightly to one side, said.

"I'm sorry Sir I find it ever so hard to clean this webbing, but I do try Sir, I really do, but my equipment was so dirty when I had it issued me that I find the task of getting it up to the standard that you require very difficult, Sir. But I'll try, Sir, I really will."

I thought that Stan was going to overdo it and burst into tears but he stopped just short of that.

"Yes, yes well Berry don't get too upset it's not that bad considering but I still want to see a hundred per cent improvement by the time of my next inspection. Understood?"

"Yes Sir", replied Stan smartly.

Stan's little act seemed to have affected Lieutenant Grainger in some way or other and further criticism of other platoon members' equipment was not forthcoming. He took up his position at the head of the room flanked as usual by Sergeant Pearce and Corporals Harridge and Leary. He then announced that there would be a further room inspection at 14:00hrs and that he would be looking for a one hundred percent improvement over that which he had just seen,

With the now familiar, "Carry on Sergeant Pearce", and the immaculate salute from the Sergeant with the two Corporals standing rigidly to attention, the subaltern gave his customary nonchalant tap of his cap with his swagger cane in return and disappeared out of the door.

Once Lieutenant Grainger had left the room Sergeant Pearce fixed us with a glassy stare.

"A serious problem has been reported to me. You're using too much bog paper. I would remind you that you are allowed three sheets of paper per day. Anyone found contravening this order will be severely dealt with!"

This had to be a joke, The Sergeant couldn't be serious. I put it down to another case of the Army playing games with us. It had to be!

Outside it was still raining cats and dogs, and if we had attempted to carry out drill on the square we would have all got soaking wet, Sergeant Pearce decided therefore that the rest of the morning would best be spent in "bulling up" the room and our equipment for the room inspection at 14:00hrs. Before commencing this work however we were allowed to go through the ritual of the morning N.A.A.F.I. break. A process which even at that early stage of our Army career I looked forward to with eager anticipation each morning, although with only 10/- one week and 12/- the next week I had to be very careful how much I spent at these breaks.

In theory I received 28/- per week but what with having to contribute 10/- per week to Doreen to enable her to receive the 30/- marriage allowance per week , and what with paying National Insurance, barrack room damages and other miscellaneous items that the Army insisted on deducting, that was all I was left with. A pittance compared with my £6.10 per week in *civvy street*, but there it was.

Before we knew it, it was 14.00 hrs. and time for our second room inspection that day had arrived. We had been slaving away for three hours in our endeavour to bring the room and our equipment up to an acceptable standard. Corporal Leary had even been helping us by giving advice on those points that Lieutenant Grainger would be looking for.

The room inspection was carried out and the Lieutenant professed his satisfaction at our one hundred per cent improvement on turn out and even went as far as congratulating Stan on all the work he had put in to improving the standard of his equipment. Stan again smiled benignly knowing that he hadn't laid a finger on his equipment since it had been swept out of the window by Sergeant Pearce , was it really only four days ago?

Room inspection over Lieutenant Grainger disappeared and once again we were left to the tender mercies of Sergeant Pearce and our two estimable Corporals. This time however they seemed reasonably satisfied with our performance and decided that we could spend the rest of the time up to our evening meal "bulling up" our personal equipment. After our meal we were free for the rest of the evening, which in effect meant that we could carry on with our "bulling up". If we knew what was good for us that was!

Next morning I was to witness a strange incident in the washrooms, I had noticed a slow imbecilic looking individual who clearly like us was a new recruit, he appeared however unlike us, to have the full personal attention of his own Lance-Corporal. This Lance-Corporal was extolling him in a very loud voice to, wash faster, to shave faster, and to generally move faster. Every time this individual was ordered to do any of these things however he merely looked at the Lance-Corporal open-mouthed and then froze into inactivity as if he was scared out of his life. This charade continued for over a quarter of an hour until the Lance-Corporal red in the face with shouting, and in sheer desperation by the looks of it, declared the ablution operation at an end and commanded the individual to double away smartly, followed by a staccato left right, left right, left right, which echoed throughout the washrooms. The individual responded by looking at the Lance-Corporal even more open mouthed than previously with an even more vacant expression on his face, by lifting up one foot at a time, about an inch above the floor in an extremely slow fashion. Eventually the yelling Lance-Corporal and his slow motion charge reached the door and disappeared from view.

When I enquired what this was all about from the other onlookers, I was informed that the large individual was a "Loony" who should have never been called up and was awaiting a medical for his discharge from the Army. "Loony" or not this person had a whole barrack room to himself and was left to his own devices all day except for occasions such as that I had just witnessed. When I last saw him he was sitting in the sun on the doorstep of his own personal hut reading a comic, whilst I was staggering along the road on my way to Honiton loaded down with full service marching order and a kitbag across my shoulders. Was he really a "Loony", or was he playing the Army at their own game and apparently winning?

Later that Saturday morning we were marched down to the M.I. centre once again to receive the dreaded T.A.B. inoculation. After being inoculated we were informed that we had been awarded thirty six hours excused duties. I don't believe that it was any coincidence that this period covered the weekend when we would normally be free anyway. After lunch our arms began to swell up like balloons and most of us took to our beds, only rising to go to tea and a quick visit to the N.A.A.F.I. in the evening.

I awoke next morning to find that my arms weren't too painful at all provided that no one bumped into them, so I rose and went to breakfast at about 07:30hrs. If only breakfast was 07:30hrs each morning instead of only on a Sunday this Army life could perhaps be made bearable. I spent the rest of the morning doing the inevitable "bulling," whiling away the time to 14:00hrs when I expected Doreen to arrive."

At approximately 12:45hrs a Company runner arrived to inform me I had a visitor awaiting me at the guardroom. I hurriedly donned my best B.D. and rushed up to the guardroom where I found Doreen gaily chatting away to the Sergeant of the guard clearly making an impression upon him. When the Sergeant asked me to sign the booking out sheet, I informed him that I wasn't allowed out of camp yet as I had only been in the Army ten days. He informed me that in exceptional circumstances these rules could be waved and that this was one of those exceptional circumstances. He was taking responsibility for allowing me out of camp into Blandford with my Wife on the strict understanding that

I reported to him personally on returning to camp that evening.

Not being able to believe my good luck or indeed the power of Doreen's charm, I hastily booked out of camp before the Sergeant changed his mind, and in no time at all the pair of us were walking down the hill towards the town of Blandford. We had a picnic lunch that Doreen had brought with her, then we looked around the town. We ended up standing on the bridge over the river that meandered through the town, watching the antics of the Khaki-clad figures and their female companions in the boats beneath us. I was reminded of that old schoolboy ditty, "The Vicar stood on the bridge at Buckingham", etc., etc.!

All too soon 5 o' clock came around and it was time for Doreen to catch her bus back to Bournemouth where she would catch the train to London. A swift and fond farewell and then the long walk back up the hill to camp. I booked back into camp and reported to the guard commander. I offered my profound thanks to him for letting me out of camp. He dismissed them with a shrug of his shoulders and a, "That's all right think nothing of it ", as if he really meant it. Then glancing at my bare epaulettes, added with a twinkle in his eyes. "If however I'd realised that you weren't wearing your Company flashes I'd never have let you out into town. Improperly dressed that's what you are, don't let it happen again!" I hurried out of the guard room.

For the next two days we were kept fully occupied from dawn to dusk mainly with foot drill instruction interspersed with the inevitable "bulling up", and room inspections. Then early on the Wednesday morning four of us had to report to the Company Office with all our equipment for our impending move to Honiton, the horrors of which were constantly being related to us by the N.C.O.'s.

We reported to the Company Sergeant Major only to find that we were still awaiting the arrival of one other person before we could depart. After waiting a quarter of an hour or so, our missing compatriot eventually arrived on the scene. He turned out to be the Public School type. Stan gave me a knowing glance.

"Where have you been, you 'orrible little man", roared the C.S.M, when the public school type eventually turned up. "You should have been here twenty minutes ago, and to think you're just the type to come back here as an officer in a few months time."

The C.S.M. must have been perceptive as the person referred to passed W.O.S.B. and to the best of my knowledge probably did gain his commission. Whether or not he ever ended up at Blandford however I have no way of telling, I can however just imagine the C.S.M.'s face if he did!

At that moment the C.S.M. stepped into the road and hailed a passing coal lorry, which instantly ground to a halt.

"Morning Charlie," he said to the driver. "Couldn't give these lads a lift to the station could you? They've missed the duty truck and they have to catch the nine o'clock train to Templecombe".

"No problem at all Sergeant Major, jump up on to the back boys."

"Thanks Charlie".

We gingerly climbed up onto the back of the lorry, trying desperately to avoid covering all our equipment and clothing in coal dust. With the C.S.M. standing rigidly to attention Charlie engaged gear with a loud crunching sound and we were on our way to Honiton and the next phase of our training.

CHAPTER 5

IN WHICH I AM INTRODUCED TO "D" COMPANY.

The journey to Honiton by train was uneventful. Although we were self-conscious wearing as we were our full service marching order, which included ammunition pouches, but thankfully, minus rifles, no one took the slightest bit of notice of us. This was due no doubt to the large number of uniformed National Servicemen travelling on the railways in those days.

The four of us arrived at Honiton station to find, much to our surprise, a lorry waiting to take us to the camp, which was some mile and a half away. On arrival at the camp we were signed in at the Company Office and were allocated a timber hut as our accommodation. The hut, being unoccupied we were instructed by a Lance-Corporal to select a bed, deposit our kit upon it, and go down to the cookhouse for lunch. The cookhouse which was a very large affair capable of seating five or six hundred persons at tables of ten or so was a revelation of cleanliness compared to Blandford. It was spotless with a beautifully "bulled" red-painted floor that was unfortunately as slippery as ice. One had to traverse it in hob-nailed boots very carefully indeed not to find oneself sprawled upon its brilliant surface.

I was to find that hardly a mealtime would pass without some poor unfortunate soldier crashing to the floor whilst his food went flying in the air before coming down on top of him.

All this usually to the accompaniment of a great cheer by all those present. On one occasion however this didn't happen. The soldier in question fell on his broken crockery, cutting the artery in his wrist. With blood pumping all over the floor I realised why some enterprising person had painted it red! The Orderly Sergeant came rushing over and grabbed the soldier's wrist to stop the immediate bleeding and had him taken to the MI room for treatment.

Once we had collected our food, which looked appetising for a change, we were directed to an area of the cookhouse that was apparently reserved exclusively for members of "D" Company personnel, the Company we now found ourselves in. We had no sooner sat down to tackle our food when an officer complete with Sam Brown belt and sword, appeared at the end of our table. Anxious to make a good impression at our new camp we went to rise from our seats to be met with a "No, no, don't stand up. Are there any complaints?" We suddenly realised he was referring to the food.

"No Sir, it's fine," we replied

"Good". And he moved on to the next table. After a satisfying lunch we made our way back to our hut. On arrival we were met by our very polite Lance-Corporal, who bade us to follow him to the stores to collect our bedding. The Lance-Corporal explained that there would only be four of us in the hut until tomorrow when the platoon organisation would be finalised.

We chose what we considered were the most comfortable and best bed spaces in the hut, and started to get ourselves organised. The Lance Corporal disclosed that he was billeted in the adjacent hut and that if we had any queries we could find him there. It would appear that there would be no further calls upon us for the rest of the day and he suggested that we use the time to settle in, but he did advise us to ensure that our best BD, boots and gaiters were correctly "bulled up" for our USB which we would have to attend the following day.

With that he bade us farewell and departed. USB? What did he mean by USB? None of us had asked the Lance-Corporal as he clearly assumed we knew what he was talking about. We dismissed the subject from our minds and began to make ourselves as comfortable as one can in the Army in an old dilapidated timber hut.

We took stock of our surroundings and found that we were in a reasonably pleasant area tucked away at the back of the camp adjacent to the main Waterloo to Exeter railway line. The consequence of this location was that the hut seemed to rock gently on its foundations each time a train passed by.

The huts were spaced well apart, with large areas of grass in between them. The hut itself was of the usual Army clapboard construction with slated roof with two small iron chimneys, connected to two diminutive solid fuel stoves situated at either end of the hut. Circumstances would prove that these huts were very cold even in the middle of a July night let alone the winter. I was forever thankful that I didn't have to stay in these huts in winter time with only two potbellied stoves to heat them.

The room which took twenty or so beds, had a plain timber floor, of which we will hear more about later, a painted timber wainscoting with an emulsion-ed fibreboard wall complete with open plan roof trusses above that. This made the process of hanging oneself extremely simple if you got too depressed. I considered that this was very thoughtful on the part of the Army!

After an acceptable tea we were preparing our uniforms and equipment for the impending USB on the morrow; we had discovered by enquiry incidentally that USB stood for Unit Selection Board when we were visited by a group of fellows describing themselves as members of the senior platoon. Strictly speaking we found out later that this wasn't true. They were in fact only the next senior platoon to ourselves, which meant that they had only been at Honiton exactly a fortnight longer than ourselves. They explained that in the superior position that they held, they had the privilege and indeed the duty to "Nig" us that night. "Nig" being an expression we would get used to the longer we were in "D" company. This Nigging they explained to us would take the form of a raiding party visiting our hut at about 01:00 hrs. in the morning, and attempt to carry off some booty. This booty would be in the form of some bedsteads or the like. With their synopsis that it would all be great fun, they departed.

We held a council of war. How could the four of us cope with a platoon raid albeit that the raiding platoon would presumably have to deal with our platoon's other hut as well as ours? We soon decided upon the solution, we pushed all the beds to one end of the hut, thus making a platform some two feet high above the floor. We then collected all the lockers which were about some six feet high and proceeded to make a wall of these across the room in front of our two foot high platform of beds. We then placed all our personal equipment on the beds behind this fortification. Now we felt fairly secure and confident that we were now in a position to repulse the impending raid.

Not bothering to undress for bed we sat down on the mattresses behind the wall of lockers to await events. In spite of doing our utmost to keep awake we must have all dozed off. We were woken by the sound of movement on the other side of the wall of lockers. Peering into the gloom we could see that we were being invaded by a large number of people. At first they appeared to be mystified by finding the hut apparently devoid of all beds and lockers and indeed of occupants.

They then realised that the lockers had been placed in a wall across the centre of the hut, with all the beds behind it.

They gallantly started to assault the wall but we were in a fairly impregnable position being behind a solid wall of steel lockers and also some two feet higher than the attackers. Each time a head appeared above the parapet we whacked it down with our pillows and bolsters in a determined manner,

After five or ten minutes of hectic battling the room, as far as we could determine in the gloom, had taken on the appearance of a winter landscape, as pillow after pillow burst upon an attacker's head and the feathers went everywhere. We didn't think it at the time as we bashed away, that come the morning we would be sweeping up all those feathers and trying to put them back in their burst pillow cases, which we would cobble up with needle and thread from our "housewives". Meanwhile we battled on to repel the boarders with a large degree of success. Eventually the invaders withdrew. We thought we had won and that we were now safe for the rest of the night. Then we realised that standing in the gloom was an individual who was holding a stick with a white handkerchief attached to it. He addressed us in a very serious manner.

"Now look you fellows, it's a good ruse what you have done and all credit to you especially as there only appears to be four of you, but it's tradition for us as senior platoon to carry off some booty from this hut. Now with or without the wall we can do it because we can go away and get more people. If however we do that someone could get hurt and it's more likely to be one of you rather than one of us. Now we think it's terrific what you have done, but we are asking you to take the wall down so that we can get to the beds and take some of them away, and thus carry on the "D" Company tradition. I'll give you five minutes to think about it." And with that he disappeared into the gloom to await our answer.

We held a further Council of War and decided that if it really came to fisticuffs, with odds of twenty or so to four we were likely to come off rather ignominiously. So discretion being the better part of valour, when the emissary returned five minutes later, he found that we had already moved some of the lockers aside to enable him and his compatriots to come through. We then stood aside and watched whilst they removed every single bed from the hut and disappeared in triumph into the darkness of the night. Fortunately they left our personnel equipment alone, they were also kind enough to leave us our own mattresses and bedding on which to sleep out what remained of the night.

This whole incident had been carried out with a considerable amount of noise at about one o'clock in the morning, and yet no one in authority had come to see what was going on. I was soon to find out that "D" Company appeared to be a law unto itself, and that only on extremely rare occasions would anyone come to investigate unusual happenings in our lines. It was as if incidents such as the one to which we had just been subjected, were encouraged and indeed expected in "D" Company by those in authority.

As soon as it was light, at about 04:00hrs, we decide to start searching for our missing beds. We split into two groups and began scouring the camp. It was at this stage that we found that another hut was on the same mission as ourselves and it became a race to retrieve the easier found beds, regardless of which hut they had come from. As well as the more accessible places, one of our beds had been placed on top of the forty feet high concrete water tower that stood guardian over the whole camp. We found out later that it was a point of honour to always put at least one bed on top of this tower. As dangerous as the process was taking a bed up the narrow steel cat ladder, if a platoon didn't manage to achieve this feat they were regarded as second class. Pushing it over the edge of the water tower and hoping for the best was the only way to achieve retrieval of a bed from this position. The best usually meant a very bent bed indeed, that then took many hours of patient repair. Two more of our beds had been placed between the tracks of the railway line, causing us very little trouble of retrieval at that time of morning.

By 06:00hrs we had found all the beds bar one, we just could not find the last one anywhere. We made a last despairing search for it before we went to breakfast with the thought that we were likely to be confronted with a room inspection with a bed missing.

"Room ready for your inspection Sir, well actually there's a bed missing and we don't really know where it is". How much did a bed cost we wondered? Then we found it leaning against the Company Commander's office door. The four of us eagerly snatched up the bed and raced around the drill square with it back to our hut, nearly sweeping an early risen Warrant Officer off his feet in the process. Much to our surprise he didn't even bat an eye lid at us. We came to the conclusion he must have either been sleepwalking or returning from a late night binge in the mess.

We then went happily, if wearily to breakfast where we found, much to our delight that "D" Company was allowed to take breakfast half an hour later than the other Companies. I wondered whether or not this concession was acknowledgement of the fact that members of "D" Company were usually up half the night on some antic or other?

Luckily there was no muster parade for us that morning. Due it would appear, to the fact that No.26 Platoon, of which we would hopefully soon be members, had yet to be officially constituted. We therefore had some spare time in which to carry on clearing up the room from the antics of the night before.

The Lance-Corporal whom we had met the previous day came into the hut, ignored our clearing up process as if he was expecting it, and asked us if we had read last night's orders on the Company notice board to see what was happening today, and whether or not we were personally involved in any way? We had to admit that we hadn't. Then without any swearing or cursing he emphasised that it was absolutely essential that we did this each and every evening. In particular we must study part one standing orders to see what was happening next day and whether or not we were involved in any way. Not to worry, this time he had studied it for us. He then proceeded to give each of us the time that we were to attend the Company Office that morning for our USB's. We quizzed him over the purpose of the USB's.

He explained that although we had been sent to "D" Company from Blandford, the Company Commander Major James always interviewed "D" Company entrants personally to confirm that they were indeed suitable recruits for the Company, failure to pass the USB meant being placed in one of the other Companies at Honiton. By what he could see of us however he was sure that we had nothing to worry about and would all pass our USBs.

"What questions are we likely to be asked at this interview?" I asked anxiously.

"Absolutely anything", he replied, "From questions about your academic qualifications, right across the spectrum to current affairs".

He asked us if we had had the opportunity to study the papers that morning. We said no we hadn't, In fact we hadn't even purchased one. We explained that we had unfortunately been involved in other urgent matters so far that morning.

He looked around the room, smiled and merely said, "I see. Right, I suggest you get back to the cookhouse immediately. Outside you will find a newspaper vendor, he should still be there. Get a newspaper, preferably something like the Telegraph, and if nothing else study the news on the front page. That should give you sufficient information for your first USB.

"First USB" I retorted. How many do we have?"

"As many as it takes is the answer I can give you. It depends entirely on you. Usually however, it's three, one now, one halfway through your training and one prior to you going to W.O.S.B. Should at any stage you fail one, you will be transferred to one of the other Companies at Honiton he told us reassuringly.

With this sobering thought in our minds we hurried off to purchase our newspapers. We returned to the hut and were studying them in earnest when we were interrupted in the process by the sudden appearance of a short, wiry, and very severe looking Sergeant standing in the doorway.

"Room shun", he cried out in a very authoritative tone. We sprang to our feet immediately.

"You there", he said pointing at me "Name rank and number".

"Private Skinner Sir, 23040258, I replied hesitantly, looking down at my towel, on which I had emblazoned my number, for confirmation.

"Remember your number Skinner, you won't always have your towel close by to remind you, and it's a chargeable offence not to be able to give your regimental number to a superior officer. And it's Sergeant not Sir. Sir is for when you are addressing an h'officer. Do you understand?"

"Yes Sir 'er Sergeant". He looked at me, shook his head, then went through the ritual of asking the other members of the hut the same question, which after my bad example they all got it right. He then proceeded to give the hut a cursory inspection. "What are all these feathers doing floating around?" he queried. Been keeping chickens in 'ere? Get them cleared hup I'm Sergeant Suff", he informed us. Your Platoon Sergeant. Right now listen carefully. In approximately two hours' time you will be attending your unit selection board. Interviews in front of the Company Commander Major James. This interview requires you to be dressed in your best BD, boots and gaiters, make sure that they are in good order. You will parade at 11: 00 hrs., for me to inspect you, to satisfy myself that you are in a fit state to attend your USB. Do you understand?" He received only a mumbled response. "Do you understand?" He shouted.

"Yes Sergeant", we replied in unison.

"Good. I'll be back 'ere at 11:00 hrs., then, with that he departed.

I noted that he had spoken in a very forced refined type of voice and definitely had great difficulty in knowing when or when not to put aitches onto words. It was only later that we found out that he was known by one and all as "'Ardy hannual Sr'nt Suff." But I am racing ahead.

We prepared for our interviews both by getting our uniforms and equipment ready and at the same time scanning the newspapers. I was in a state of nervous tension, and even Stan looked mildly agitated.

As good as his word the Sergeant turned up spot on 11:00hrs bade us to stand to attention and critically inspected us. At last after making various adjustments to our dress he professed himself to be reasonably satisfied with our turn out. He then personally marched us down to the Company Office. There he ushered us into a room where we were ordered to sit down with others and wait until called for interview. We sat there in silence in a highly charged atmosphere.

Eventually my name was called and I was ushered into an office by the Company clerk. I found myself standing before a table behind which was sitting a Major, a Captain and full Lieutenant. The Major was speaking to me. "Name rank and number if you please."

"Skinner…. Private…, 203 er 23040258."

"Get it right Skinner, get it right "the Major urged, not doing much for my self-confidence. "You've been in the Army long enough to remember your Army number by now. Right Skinner, stand at ease, stand easy, I am Major James, "D" Company Commander. This he said indicating with his hand is Captain Laurie, and this is Lieutenant Brown. Now the purpose of this interview ", he continued looking me full in the face, "Is for this board to determine whether or not you are capable of staying the pace in "D" Company, whether or not you are the type of person for us to send to W.O.S.B as a representative of REME, understood?"

"Yes Sir".

"Good".

Over the next half an hour there followed a whole host of questions relating to the type of school I had attended, my thoughts on those schooldays, my academic qualifications and career to date, and finally questions on current affairs, a subject in which until that morning I had taken little interest. Luckily due to the Lance-Corporal's earlier advice I had anticipated correctly the subject matter of the majority of the questions.

I was then asked to wait outside. I didn't have long to wait. I was called back into the office and informed by Major James that I had been accepted into "D" Company. He hoped I would find my stay interesting and enjoyable!

I returned to the hut to find our friendly Lance-Corporal waiting for me. He instructed me to gather up my kit and find a bed in the adjacent hut which would be my "home "from now on. Half an hour later, Stan, with the inevitable smile on his face joined me in the new hut. One of the other people who had loyally stuck by us during the previous night's fracas we never saw again. Presumably he had failed his interview. The rest of the day was again taken up by documentation and form filling. All the questions we had answered at Blandford we had to answer all over again, presumably to see if the answers would still be the same as those already given. The day was spent in a fairly relaxed atmosphere. I had a feeling however that the axe was going to fall pretty soon and when it did our training would begin in earnest.

That evening at tea I was surprised to find that the Orderly Officer had dressed for dinner so to speak and appeared in his full dress uniform. He asked us once again if we had any complaints over the food, which after Blandford I certainly hadn't.

After tea we were in our hut "genning up" on our newspapers, just in case further current affairs questions were likely to be in the offing. When a Corporal, who we had not seen before entered the barrack room. And with a very commanding voice wanted to know why we were all relaxing when we had a room inspection at 20:00 hrs. We explained that we knew nothing about a room inspection.

Whether we previously knew about it or not, he informed us, there was to be a room and kit inspection at 20:00hrs by our Platoon Commander who we had yet to meet, the Corporal informed us. The Platoon Commander required us to parade in best BD boots and gaiters, furthermore all kit had to be laid out in the approved manner. Should we not yet be conversant with the manner of a "D" Company kit layout he presented us with a large diagram showing us what was required. Then with a final, "My heavens you're all going to be in trouble by the looks of it". He turned on his heels and departed. Our friendly Lance-Corporal was nowhere to be found, from whom to seek advice. We were on our own it seemed. We were stunned but didn't panic as we might have done at Blandford.

We decided that in the first instance we would all lay out our individual kits on our beds as per the diagram left with us, we then split into separate groups with specific tasks to carry out such as sweeping the floor, dusting the shelves etc. One enterprising fellow even bulled up the stoves with boot polish. He contended that the inspecting Officer would be so pleased with the stove that he would be put off looking for faults elsewhere. Unfortunately we found out to our cost that this thinking was misplaced. We then donned our best battledress, boots, and gaiters.

With five minutes to go to the appointed time, whilst our final preparations were still being carried out in earnest, we noticed a knot of uniformed figures marching up the pathway to our hut. There was a Second Lieutenant, presumably our Platoon Commander along with an Orderly Sergeant or at any rate a Sergeant with a red sash across his shoulders and they were followed by a Corporal and two Lance Corporals.

The extremely smart Orderly Sergeant entered the barrack room and roared out the familiar cry of "Stand by your beds, Officer's inspection. Room, room shun." At the same time throwing up one of the smartest salutes I had seen to date. Then in walked a very superior looking Second Lieutenant. A right bastard by the looks of him. I noted that the three Corporals had stayed outside immediately adjacent to the doorway.

The Lieutenant standing just inside the doorway, announced that he was Lieutenant Frobisher our Platoon Commander. He then peered tentatively around the room.

"Sergeant?"

"Sir".

"Were these men informed that there was to be a room inspection this evening?"

"Yes Sir".

I can't believe it. I'm dumb-founded".

He then confronted the nearest soldier to him,

"You soldier, name rank and number ".

The soldier spat out his name and number in staccato fashion, much to my, and I have no doubt his own relief.

"Well Green", that apparently being the name of the soldier. "Were you informed that there was to be a room inspection this evening?" questioned the officer

"Yes Sir", replied Green.

"Then why haven't you done something about it Green?"

"I have Sir, I've tried very hard Sir".

"Tried, tried, then I suggest that you haven't tried hard enough, any of you," he said looking at the rest of us in the hut.

"Sergeant take this man's name, and have him taken to the guardroom, I'll deal with him in the morning".

"Yes Sir, Name and number demanded the Sergeant.

"Green 23040657", Green replied in a quavering voice.

"Corporal Parker", the Sergeant yelled through the open doorway to one of the waiting Corporals outside. Take this man to the guardroom. My compliments to the guard commander and would he have Green here locked up in the cells overnight. Mr Frobisher will be along later to sign the charge sheet".

"Yes Sergeant".

The last we saw of Green was of him being doubled away to the guardroom by an immaculately dressed Corporal.

The Platoon Commander then turned to address his platoon.

"Lesson number one in "D" Company you never try to do something, you either do it, or you don't do it. You never try to do it. If you don't do a thing, you must have a very good reason for your actions, or else! Understood?" He continued,

"In this instance I would suggest that you haven't indeed done anything about the inspection. An inspection that on your own admission you knew was coming. It's tantamount to disobeying a lawful command. Is that not so Sergeant?"

"Yes Sir".

"So what are your reasons for your actions?" He posed the question generally to all those present in the room. There was no response, but did he really expect any I asked myself?

He then walked around the hut glancing at the kit laid out on the beds. He looked at one individual's kit, picked up his comb, and held it up to the light and minutely inspected it. He then called to the Sergeant.

"Sergeant take this man's name, his comb is filthy dirty. Have him dealt with if you please".

"Yes Sir. Name and number?"

"Brown, 23040632 Sergeant", volunteered a very apprehensive Brown.

"Corporal Sams", the Sergeant called through the doorway, as an even smarter Lance Corporal appeared before us.

"Yes Sergeant".

"Take Brown here away, you know what to do with him".

Another poor unfortunate was doubled away, presumably to the guardroom.

I was beginning to wonder if being a member of "D" Company was such a good idea after all. Maybe the people who had failed their USBs this morning were the lucky ones.

At this stage the Platoon Commander put his swagger cane to his chin and scratched it as if deep in thought.

"Sergeant".

"Sir".

The condition of this room is appalling, absolutely appalling , these men I regret must be taught a lesson they will not forget. I suggest that you take them to a quiet part of the camp and give them half an hour's intensive foot drill and any other drill you consider appropriate. "Understood?" he queried.

"Yes Sir". Replied the Sergeant. "Right outside on the road in three ranks with your rifles. Move.

We rushed outside eager to comply with the command in doing so I noticed that we had generated quite a lot of interest from members of adjacent huts and a large number of people were looking out through windows and others were peering at a distance around the ends of huts. All apparently enjoying the spectacle of seeing us poor unfortunates being put through the hoop. Once the Sergeant was satisfied that we were all smartly drawn up in three ranks outside the hut and that the two Corporals had returned from their trip to the guardroom, he double marched us away to a very quiet part of the camp, near the rifle range. Here the four N.C.O.s drilled us and double marched us until we were fit to drop. I for one realised that I wasn't as fit as I thought I was.

Thankfully, at long last the Sergeant decided that we had had punishment enough and that it was time for us to return to our barrack room.

When we arrived back, our Platoon Commander was standing outside our hut gently tapping his swagger cane against his thigh. "How did they do Sergeant he enquired?"

"Not very well Sir , I've seen better Sir, much better".

"H'm I still think that they could do with a good shake up in the gym do you not agree Sergeant?"

"That's a good idea Sir".

"Right have them change into shorts, vests, and slippers, and get them on the road outside then have Corporal Parker double them down to the gym".

Once we had changed into our gym kit leaving our uniforms on top of our kit layouts on our beds we were doubled down to the gym by Corporal Parker.

On entering the gym I was surprised to find the place swarming with PTI's. I'd never seen so many all at one time. They were clearly awaiting our entry, we were obviously in for "a hot time in the old town tonight". To quote a well-known tune of the time.

Without having time to draw our breath, the PTI's swung into action, for half an hour or more we were put through absolute excruciating agony, far worse than the session we had been subjected to at Blandford. These PTI's knew their job. They were masochists, absolute experts at making people suffer. They were not content with doubling us around and making us execute the most exacting aerobatics until we were fit to drop for the second time that evening. Their piece-de- resistance was to have the whole platoon scramble up onto the wall bars where we were ordered to hang by our arms until ordered to let go. As people dropped from the wall bars they were doubled away to the guardroom for disobeying a lawful command. Well that was the reason given by the senior PTI for the men being doubled away smartly to the guardroom.

At last the grateful order came for us to finish our agonising session, and to line up on the road outside the gym in three ranks. We were then double marched back to our hut. Long before we reached our hut however I had made the decision that I no longer wanted anymore of this treatment and that first thing in the morning I would seek an interview with the Company Commander and request to be released from "D" Company. When we arrived back at the hut we found the Platoon Commander and the Orderly Sergeant awaiting our arrival.

"Have the men stand by their beds Sergeant".

"Yes Sir. Stand by your beds". A slight pause then, "Room,

room shun".

The Platoon Commander paced up and down our ranks looking at each one of us in the face in a quizzical manner.

"Whilst the men have been away Sergeant, I have been looking at the men's mugs, Many of them are filthy, a chargeable offence I believe Sergeant, is that not so?"

"Yes Sir".

Oh no I thought not more trouble. Don't they ever give up?

"I think that a mug inspection is in order Sergeant". Said the Lieutenant.

"Yes Sir".

My heart sunk for the umpteenth time that evening.

"Right", said the Sergeant, "On the order, present mugs, you will all pick up your mug in your right hand and offer it for inspection. "Present mugs," he commanded.

As each member of the platoon reached to pick up his mug with his right hand, some of us tried desperately to clean off tea stains and other marks with our left hands.

"Sergeant," said the Platoon Commander, "Will you please instruct the men not to attempt to clean their mugs, it's too late now. If they are dirty they will have to take the consequences. Let this be a lesson to them, he said with a smirk on his face.

"Don't try and clean your mugs, leave them as they are, roared the Sergeant, and carried on with the semblance of a smile on his face.

What a bastard I thought.

The whole Platoon stood rigidly to attention with their mugs thrust out in front of them for inspection. Even Stan looked slightly perturbed as he thrust out his mug in front of him along with the rest of us.

The Platoon Commander walked towards the nearest member of the Platoon as if about to inspect his mug, but instead looked towards the door of the hut, and called out. "Right you can come in now lads." Out of the gloom of the night air came two men wheeling a trolley surmounted by a tea urn, followed by others carrying trays of sandwiches and cakes. We all stood there mesmerised. What the heck was going on?

The Platoon Commander pushed his cap to the back of his

head with his swagger cane. The Orderly Sergeant and the three Corporals suddenly roared with laughter.

Our Platoon Commander then informed us, "We are members of the senior Platoon and you have all just been "Nigged".

We didn't believe it. We still all stood rigidly to attention, with our mugs held out in front for inspection.

Not until the Platoon Commander took off his cap and sent it spinning across the room to land on one of the beds did we begin to believe that we had had a joke played on us. But after he had sat down on a bed and accepted a mug of tea from the Orderly Sergeant, with a "Thanks Geoff, get stuck in the rest of you," were we finally convinced that the whole evening had indeed been one great joke. For the senior platoon at any rate, but not for us!

By this time all the members of the senior platoon had crowded into the hut and entered into the mild festivities. They then explained to us that although tonight had been a "Nigging" everything that had taken place would in fact be repeated in earnest in the

weeks to come whilst we were in "D" Company. The purpose behind the evening to which we had just been subjected was to prepare us in advance for these happenings. At this stage we realised that all members of our platoon that had been charged had now reappeared along with members of the senior platoon. Far from being taken to the guardroom they had in fact been taken to the senior platoon's hut and held there until the "Nigging" was complete.

Earnest conversation ensued between us, the most junior platoon of "D" Company, and them the most senior. Advice was freely forthcoming regarding all the pitfalls in the "D" Company training that we were about to undertake. The things we must avoid and the things we must keep an eye out for. The best way of cleaning this article and that article, how to avoid being put on show parade.

Show parade what was show parade we asked?

Then with broad smiles on their faces they took obvious delight in explaining to us all about the intricacies of show parade.

The smiles became even broader when they noted the looks of horror on our faces as they explained the system.

Show parade was apparently intended to be "D" Company's" unofficial alternative to an official charge. We were to find out however that Charges were handed out almost as freely as show parade. So basically we could look forward to double trouble in "D" Company.

The big snag about show parades however was that, although not showing on your records in any way, they could be awarded by an N.C.O. in the Company and did not incur the involvement of a commissioned Officer. Consequently they were awarded very freely indeed, in an almost indiscriminate manner in fact. Because it was unofficial it was treated virtually as a joke by awarding N.C.O.s. To the recipient however it was far from a joke; it worked this way or so we were told.

The Platoon Sergeant would be unhappy over the cleanliness of the barrack room table. The person whose room job that day was cleaning the table would be put on one night's show parade. That meant that he would have to present the table for inspection at 19:00hrs that evening to the Company duty clerk. The duty clerk would then inspect the table and might decide that it wasn't good enough and award another night of show parade. The next night he might pass the table but decide that the presenter's cap badge was dirty and award him another day's show parade for that. In this way the original award of one day's show parade had already been extended into three days and had been known to have been extended into weeks. We were assured that it was something to be avoided at all costs, if at all possible.

Our socialising with members of the senior platoon went on until quite late. From our conversations with them we gained the distinct impression that their word held sway in "D" Company. That they in some mystic way acted as a regulating body within "D" Company lines.

We were to find that even the senior platoon changed each fortnight on completion of its training programme, and junior platoons were promoted to take their place, each succeeding platoon taking on the mantle of senior platoon with great pride and expertise. So much so that none of us even with hindsight had the slightest idea that our tormentors for the evening were anything but the genuine article. We congratulated the senior platoon on their excellent performance and asked how on earth had they obtained the necessary uniforms for the night's "Nigging". We were surprised to be told that their Platoon Commander had obtained them for the miscreants on the understanding that they made a good job of the proceedings. Which in our opinion they had.

At that stage we were unable to envisage ourselves giving a similar performance in approximately eight weeks' time when we were informed it would be our duty to do the "Nigging". We were assured however that in seven weeks' time we would have become experts in the subject the same as every platoon before us. With that the senior platoon departed, leaving us with the feeling that we had become members of an elite organisation.

CHAPTER 6

LIFE IN "D" COMPANY

The next morning in spite of the fact that reveille wasn't until 0:600hrs there was feverish activity in the hut from 05:00hrs onwards by certain individuals, as if in some misguided way (in my opinion) this action would be taken as a sign of initiative. By 05.30hrs or so the noise in the hut had become so intensive that even I decided to rise from my bed and get dressed. By the time the Orderly Sergeant came round at 06.00hrs to rouse us we were all up and dressed and busy at work all bar a resolute few who were determined to stay in bed until the last moment.

Naturally one of these people was Stan. Getting up early did have one small consolation however and that was the fact that there was still hot water in the wash rooms.

After ablutions the first task was to strip your bed and make it up into a bed block. This procedure consisted of folding the blankets and sheets into approximately 30" squares, with the sheets inserted between two blankets, and the third blanket wrapped round the outside of these to hold them together. This block was then placed at the head of the bed surmounted by the two pillows. We were soon to discover that the only way these bed blocks would satisfy inspecting Officers and N.C.O.s for smartness was to stiffen the face of sheets and blankets with cardboard.

Your Housewife (the soldier's clothing repair outfit), along with your non-issue washing kit was then placed upon the bed block. The under blanket then had to be drawn taut across the mattress, a towel placed on it at the foot of the bed with your knife, fork, spoon and mug placed thereon guarded by a pair of spare leather laces neatly rolled into circles. The bed had to be left like this ready for inspection each day until the end of the working day at about 1700hrs. Effectively it meant that you couldn't even sit on your bed until that hour without fear of retribution. And as there were no chairs in the barrack room this, in effect, meant that you couldn't sit down until 17:00hrs each day.

Although in reality this whole ritual was enforced in the name of discipline, the bed blocks we were told were to enable any inspecting officer to see at a glance who the bed-wetters were! Not that I ever recall any being found.

Just when we thought that we had completed all our chores and could safely go to breakfast, our Lance-Corporal appeared as if by magic and detailed people off to carry out room and ablution block jobs, informing us that these jobs had to be carried out each and every morning before muster parade until told otherwise. I was astounded. I just couldn't see at that stage how we could do all the tasks we were apparently expected to, go to breakfast and then be ready for muster parade at 08:00hrs. Least of all carry out everything to the satisfaction of the hierarchy, bearing in mind that the hierarchy consisted of anyone with one stripe on his sleeve upwards in rank. When we did eventually reach the dining hall for breakfast, we found that not only were we allowed to go in half an hour later than the other Companies we were actually expected to do so. A hurried breakfast over I prepared for my first muster parade at Honiton with great trepidation. I think that we were all relieved to find that we were marched onto the square at the back of the battalion, where we hoped we would not be noticed for our obvious lack of experience in drill procedure. In part I think our rearguard position was really due to the fact that we had still to be issued with rifles and from that respect were a little bit of an oddity on that parade. Immediately after muster parade, this oddity was put right by us being marched down to the armoury and each issued with a Lee-Enfield rifle. We really felt like soldiers now even if we didn't look it, and we didn't.

After the issue of rifles we were marched back to the barrack room and instructed on the intricacies of cleaning the rifle and informed of the dire consequences of being in possession of a dirty rifle. We were then shown the bracket at the side of our bed where the rifle was to be stored with the strict order that the bolt must never be left in the rifle but hidden elsewhere amongst our kit. Any rifle found unattended with the bolt still in it was a chargeable offence for the owner. Even in those days precautions had to be taken against the stealing of rifles by anyone, but in particular by the IRA. Not that the threat of a charge for this offence worried us unduly as we were beginning to realise that anything whatsoever we did in the Army could apparently be construed as a chargeable offence if the Army so decided. It appeared to be a case of "Heads, the Army wins, tails, you lose" in whatever we did. The longer I was in the Army the more I realised how true this was.

This instruction was given to us by Sergeant Suff and our Lance- Corporal under the stern and watchful eye of our very young Platoon Commander, Second Lieutenant Hopkins to whom we had just been introduced; who standing there with very large ears protruding from beneath his nice new shiny flat cap, was henceforth referred to by us as "Flopper".

After the ritual of the N.A.A.F.I. break, which as far as I recall was the only Army ritual I thoroughly approved of, we were marched off, complete with our newly acquired rifles, to the firing range which was situated outside the camp confines. Once there we were given a demonstration of Lee-Enfield rifle fire power by a group of very able marksmen indeed. We were reminded, by our Platoon Commander, that when the Germans first came up against the B.E.F, in the First World War armed with these rifles they thought they were up against a force armed with machine guns, such was the rapidity of fire in the hands of experts. Considering that the Lee-Enfield was only a manually operated bolt-action ten round magazine rifle this was some deception.

That demonstration was the first inkling that I received, rather than just being given basic training we were being treated more as students of warfare, a theme that was to become more and more apparent as our training in D Company progressed.

After the demonstration we were hurried back to camp for lunch after which we changed into our best B.D.s and had our platoon photograph taken with "Flopper" taking pride of place in the front row. Being tallish, I was as usual placed in the back row. Photo-session over it was back to the barrack hut and change into our denim uniforms which was to be our normal working dress whilst at Honiton. We were then shown by our Lance-Corporal, all other authority seemingly having disappear-ed, how to lay out our beds, lockers and equipment in the approved manner. He emphasised that everything had to be to be constantly up to inspection standard as inspections could take place at any time whether or not we were in the hut. The problem was how to achieve this end when all the equipment was constantly in use. Through bitter experience we were to find that as soon as we had finished with the equipment we had to clean it prior to putting it on display once again. Consequently we spent the majority of our "spare time" cleaning equipment and indeed washing clothes as all clothes laid out in the lockers were expected to be clean ones. We had some help as far as washing was concerned in as much that we could send clothes to the laundry each week free of charge but they took a week to wash, which meant that you had a lot of washing to do yourself. Many an enterprising young man who had more money available than I, got over the problem by procuring for himself, by fair means or foul, spare items of equipment, thereby leaving one set of equipment completely unused for inspections.

In theory and also in practice this action brought retribution on the head of the beholder if he was found out, as in some warped way of thinking the Army expected you to use your equipment but still retain it in pristine condition for spot inspections. The Army called it discipline, I called it ridiculous.

After the departure of the Lance-Corporal we all set too to "bull up" our equipment in an attempt to bring it up to the standard that it had been intimated was required in "D" company We were in bed late that night.

It might be of interest at this stage to list the amount of clothing and equipment that was in fact issued to us National Servicemen.

Two pairs of boots, in my case, one pair second hand. One pair to be designated "Best" and be kept in pristine condition, and in the main not used. Two suits of battle dress, consisting of blouse and trousers in heavy khaki serge. Although both of the same quality we had to decide which suit would be designated "Best" for our two year sentence.

Two suits of denims, consisting of blouse and trousers similar in design to the battle dress, to be used for working dress and fatigues etc.

One Greatcoat which only seemed to come in two sizes, large and extra large, which when worn gave a very fair imitation of a bell tent.

One black beret complete with one REME cap badge.

One pair of knitted gloves and one jersey pullover.

Three khaki flannel shirts complete with one khaki woollen tie.

Three pairs of khaki under-draws, which nobody seemed to wear as they were so terrible, people preferring to provide their own.

Two P.T. vests, one red and one blue. Two pairs of P.T. shorts, and one pair of plimsolls.

Two pairs of pyjamas and three white towels.

Three pairs of heavy grey woollen socks.

No under vests were issued and it was a chargeable offence, or so we were told, to wear a P.T. vest other than for P.T. It is interesting to note however that it wasn't a chargeable offence to wear our own non-issue underwear, as if the Army were acknowledging that we had to wear suitable underwear but they weren't going to provide it!

As far as webbing equipment was concerned we were issued with a large pack, a small pack, two ammunition pouches, one belt, a bayonet frog, and two cross straps to hold the whole lot together and one gas mask.

We were also issued with a very old second hand belt, which I rarely wore as it would never pass even the most rudimental inspection.

Two pairs of anklets and a ground sheet that also doubled as a waterproof cape, that when worn adopted a lopsided attitude in a totally un-military fashion.

A set of Billy cans (to be kept highly polished at all times and not to be used).

A jack-knife, and a "housewife" which was a linen wallet containing needles and cotton along with spare buttons etc.

And one kitbag. The general idea being that you could pack all your official issue gear in your large pack, small pack and kitbag. There was no consideration taken into account for personal items, even though a personal holdall was not forbidden. The sheer problem of moving all your official equipment on its own, meant that personal holdalls were to be avoided when you knew you were to move camps.

Finally, one AB64 Pay Book and Identity Card which "must

be carried at all times", in your top right hand breast pocket. All that lot had to last you for two years and if in poor condition at the end of that time had to be paid for. The reason given for this little gem was that the Army allowed you something like three pence a week clothing allowance with which you were required to replace any worn-out kit within your period of National Service. You were also expected to provide soap, shaving soap, face flannels, and razor with this three pence a week along with any article the Army could think up. To safeguard against loss, all equipment and clothing had to have your regimental number emblazoned thereon. It being a chargeable offence to be in possession of articles belonging to someone else, or so we were told!

The following weekend, to keep us occupied no doubt, it was decided to organise a map reading exercise for the Company. We were split into groups of four persons, and handed our first clue then sent off out of camp at something like two minute intervals. The clue once solved, would lead us to the second clue which would be hidden under a bush or something similar somewhere in the countryside. This clue would then lead us to the next clue and so on and so forth. We carried on until we reached something like the fourth clue, after which we couldn't find any subsequent clues they just didn't seem to be around and we all caught up with each other and wandered around the countryside in a great gaggle of people.

Now whether or not the whole scheme had been dreamt up to keep us occupied on a Saturday afternoon usually our time off, I will never know. But keep us occupied for the whole of that Saturday afternoon it certainly did, in spite of the fact that there were other things that we would much rather be doing, such as lying on our beds fast asleep! This was to make up for all the sleep lost in the week, carrying out night exercises etc.

We all eventually arrived back at camp tired out and weary hours past the projected time, to find that we had only been beaten by one other group. A group that had got fed up with the map reading side of things and who we found out later had decided to catch a train back to camp, they had unfortunately miss-timed everything and had arrived back at camp first before anyone else instead of last as they had anticipated. There was an inquest over what had gone wrong with the exercise, but no real answers were forthcoming and, after all we were only National Servicemen that the powers to be were trying to keep occupied for two years so did it matter anyway? And the whole thing was soon forgotten. So much for map reading.

The next day being a Sunday we did have a rest and spent it sleeping on our beds, recovering from the exertions of the previous day. If the truth were told, I suppose, none of us were as fit as we thought we were, or would like to have been! But with time we would be, or so we thought!

CHAPTER 7

IN WHICH WE LEARN THAT "D" COMPANY IS THE SHOWPIECE OF R.E.M.E.

At 0:500hrs next day the same morning ritual was enacted by the same enthusiastic few. This few was soon turned into the many. However, when we were reminded that this morning was going to be a CO's parade and that this time we would be required to parade with rifles along with the rest of the battalion, jumping out of bed we dressed and rushed through our room jobs, our block jobs, our breakfast and prepared for our first parade of any consequence in "D" company.

This first important parade taught me that it was very unwise to get dressed in your parade uniform until the very last moment. You rose, dressed in denims, carried out all your chores, went to breakfast, came back did final preparations to your equipment, including a last "pull through" of your rifle, and then re-dressed in the designated parade uniform. All this preparation took as long as it sounds, although as time went on we did initiate short cuts to the system.

Even at this stage some opportunists in the hut decided that the best way to gain more time for themselves was not to do their room jobs, or at best to do them very hurriedly and consequently very badly. Their actions bringing swift retribution down on the hut members as a whole in the way of extra cleaning and extra inspections. It is interesting to reflect that these people who had little or no regard for the trouble they brought upon their colleagues were usually the ones to pass W.O.S.B and to come back as officers. The ones that tended to work as a team with their fellow inmates, with few exceptions, failed.

All too soon the Platoon Sergeant appeared and brought to an end our frenzied preparations for the forthcoming parade, along with our last minute adjustments to our kit laid out for inspection. We were bade to get "Fell In" on the area outside the hut and were marched off towards the parade square.

Even with the passage of time. I still recall my first CO's parade. The scene that met my eye as we approached the square was, to me, truly impressive with over a thousand men being marched onto the square from all directions in what appeared to me to be in an indiscriminate manner. It wasn't of course an indiscriminate manner, as each platoon or body of men was being marched onto a right marker, in our case being our missing Lance-Corporal. This time instead of being at the back of the parade we were at the front along with the rest of "D" company with a very smart body of men with white discs behind their cap badges taking up the position to the extreme right of the parade. I was later to learn that this body of men was composed entirely of men from "D" company personnel who had passed W.O.S.B. and were awaiting posting to officer cadet school.

The parade at this stage was being orchestrated by the Regimental Sergeant Major. Not until he was entirely satisfied that his parade was as perfect as he could make it, would he hand it over to his Commanding Officer. I noted with some surprise that a very smart drum and bugle band had marched onto the square and taken up a position alongside the saluting dais.

The R.S.M. eventually handed over the parade to the CO who then took up a position on the saluting dais. The officers, who had been marching up and down at the side of the square, were then ordered to "Take Post" by marching up to their platoon and taking up a prominent position to the front of it.

We were then ordered to execute one or two drill manoeuvres which if the truth were told were executed rather badly by our platoon, after which it was time for the inspections to begin. With the band striking up a march in slow time, the C.O. climbed down from his dais and accompanied by the R.S.M. headed for a part of the battalion far away from us. Each platoon was then inspected by either the C.O. and the R.S.M., the Company Commander and the C.S.M., or if you were lucky by your own Platoon Commander, who although very critical was usually the lesser of the three evils.

This morning we had the lesser of the three evils and "Flopper" inspected us, even so he was obviously out to make an impression upon us. He was extremely critical, quietly pulling each and every one of us apart and bade the platoon Sergeant to take six person's names. They were all subsequently put on show parade. Inspections over, the C.O. beat a retreat to his dais, the band changed from slow time to quick time, the whole of the Battalion marched past the dais with the C.O. taking the salute. After which we were marched off the square back to our hut where our Sergeant informed us that we had incurred the displeasure of our Platoon Commander and that he had been ordered to give us extra drill instruction for the rest of the morning in order to attempt to bring us up to a standard that wouldn't embarrass him ever again in front of the whole of the Company or indeed the Battalion. All this however was to take place after the ritual of N.A.A.F.I. break, which would give us time to change into our denims for the drill instruction.

After an hour and a half of intensive foot and rifle drill, by which time I think that the majority of us were totally confused, the Sergeant with the Lance-Corporal standing by his side, addressed us thus.

"Normally you are free from 12:00hrs on a Saturday until Monday morning but not this weekend, not because your drill is bad, which it is, but because you are all improperly dressed on parade," he said this with a smile on his face. "You will therefore parade here outside your hut at 14:00hrs to be addressed by Mr Hopkins. When I give the order to dismiss, you will turn to the right count three and march away smartly into your hut. "Dismiss".

Back in the hut we queried with the Lance-Corporal what was meant when the Sergeant informed us that we were all improperly dressed on parade.

"If you had all read Company orders you would have seen that in "D" Company we don't polish our second best boots but dubbin them, none of you picked up this point, consequently the Sergeant considers that you were all improperly dressed on parade. The Sergeant catches out each new intake over this point, it's his little joke.

"So just because of that," I retorted, "we're going to have to work this afternoon."

"Believe me," replied the Corporal with a shrug of the shoulders, "No new intake in "D" Company ever gets their first Saturday off. If it hadn't been the boots it would have been something else."

We were to discover that our Lance-Corporal was in fact

a "D" Company member who had been deferred by the War Office Selection Board and was waiting to be called for his second interview. In the meantime he had been given a stripe, acting and unpaid no doubt, and had been seconded to the training staff of "D" Company. He was a very nice chap and very quiet so much so that we soon referred to him, very irreverently as "Creeping Jesus". A more unlikely drill instructor you would never meet.

Dead on 14:00hrs we paraded outside the hut to be addressed by our Platoon Commander.

"I am extremely disappointed to find that in the very short period that you have been in "D" company you have allowed the cleanliness of your hut to deteriorate to an alarming extent. I refer in particular to the state of the floor". With the semblance of a smile on his face he continued. "Saturday afternoons as you are aware are normally free of duties but not today, due as much as anything to your poor showing on parade this morning. I require each of you to hunt around the camp and find a house brick together with a bucket of sharp sand. I then require you to spend the afternoon with the aid of a little water sanding the floor of your hut until it comes up whiter than white. I shall be back at 16:00 hrs. to see what type of job you are making of it. Should I not be satisfied you will continue the work tomorrow until I am. And I don't want any wag telling me that Sunday is a day of rest. Not in this man's Army! Dismiss the men Sergeant and set them to work if you please."

We then hunted around the camp, found our house bricks and sand and set to work sanding the floor. We collectively made sure that there were no absentees or shirkers and all beavered away for the next couple of hours under the watchful eye of our Lance-Corporal, by which time the floor looked a complete mess.

Spot on 16:00hrs we espied Lieutenant Hopkins coming up the path with the Sergeant, who went through the usual "Room, room shun" ritual, as if we were being visited by royalty, we all stood to attention, some with bricks in hand, which were dripping with water, and all smothered in sand. The Lieutenant stepped gingerly into the room doing his utmost to ensure that none of his personage touched any of the mess that was all around him. With a very cursory glance at the mess that had once been defined as a floor, he declared himself satisfied with the work carried out and informed us that there would be no necessity for us to do

further work to the floor on the morrow and with a parting, "Don't be naughty boys again," disappeared very quickly out of the hut.

The Sergeant, who was left standing in the middle of the room surveying the mess that was all around him had a perplexed look upon his face. Still standing to attention we looked at him expectantly. There was a pregnant pause until it was broken by the Sergeant.

"Yes, well you heard Mr Hopkins, he's happy with the floor and there's no need for you to work on it tomorrow. I suggest however that you clear up this mess before I inspect the room on Monday," and with that he disappeared out of the room with a broad grin on his face. It appeared that we were free now until reveille on Monday morning.

Next day much to our surprise we were indeed left alone to our own devices, though much of the time was spent in clearing up the mess that we had caused the day before. By this time we suspected that there had been nothing particularly wrong with the floor. The whole episode had been organised just to show us that the Army held all the trump cards. Though in truth we knew that already. Once the floor had been cleared up some of the unperturbed fellows stretched themselves out on the grass around the hut and sunbathed whilst the majority of us set to and bulled up our equipment in an attempt to bring it up to the very high standard that was seemingly expected in "D" company.

In no time at all however we found ourselves once again at 05:00hrs Monday morning when the whole irritating routine started all over again for another week.

I soon got into the routine of life in "D" Company, I can't say settled into it, because I don't believe that, in the whole of my two years National Service, I ever settled into Army routine. Settled in my mind implies a certain amount of contentedness and I was never contented in the Army.

Life in "D" Company was hard, make no mistake about that, I recently saw a film on television about present day discipline in Colchester military prison and in my opinion it was very similar to the discipline we lived under at Honiton in those far off days, and yet the inmates of Colchester were there for punishment for the crimes they had committed whilst in the Army and we weren't. The accommodation was also far superior for the criminals, to that which we had to live in.

We were soon to find out that "D" Company was the showpiece of REME. Here were concentrated their best National Servicemen, in theory if not in fact, whose members, provided they passed their USBs would be sent to W.O.S.B., where a decision would be made as to whether or not they were potential officer material, if they were they would then be posted to Officer Cadet School and gain the Queen's Commission. If they weren't!! they could look forward to the Scrapheap, though we didn't know this at the time. There was no in-between apparently..............

In the meantime Major James, "D" Company's C. O. was determined that his men would be an example to the rest of the Battalion, they would be smarter, fitter, better marksmen, and all round better soldiers than men from other Companies, and above all they would act as gentlemen. All these pre- requisites entailed us in taking anything that was thrown at us without batting an eyelid, anyone who didn't come up to his high expectations was thrown out of "D" Company though in my experience few were. He tended to run the Company on the lines of a strictly disciplined University. Indeed, he even had members of the Universities OTCs. spend their summer camp with us. In their sand-coloured webbing, outlandish cap badges and, in some instances, outlandish uniforms, they stood out like sore thumbs from the rest of us, but it appeared that the Major wouldn't have it otherwise.

Our dress for each day was always battle order, even if we were only attending lectures. Consequently all our equipment had to be cleaned at the end of each day ready for any spot inspection that could be imposed upon us at a moment's notice. We were doubled around the camp at the high port, and on the few occasions that we marched, we marched at the light infantry rate of 145 paces to the minute, thanks to Sergeant Suff who had been in the light infantry himself, the Green Howards. Bearing in mind that the light infantry marched at the trail and we were marching at the slope this could be a very tricky operation indeed for us, especially when it came to halting!

Sometimes the platoon Sergeant, who as I say, had been in the Green Howard's Light Infantry , would have us marching at such a high rate of knots, he hadn't time to call out the usual Left right, Left right, but only left, left, left. He thought it a great joke as we did our best to keep up with his timing. We in turn considered it a point of honour to try and make his joke backfire. The penalty for slipping in our hobnailed boots when brought to a halt after galloping along at this fantastic rate was show parade. The crime? Not obeying a lawful command when ordered to do so. Or so the Sergeant said.

Show parades and charges seemed to flutter down upon us as snowflakes in a blizzard. I recall being on a working parade feeling in pristine condition when I had my beret unceremoniously whipped off my head, and the back of my cap badge minutely inspected and declared filthy dirty and finding myself on show parade that night.

Worse was the fate of an old Etonian member of the platoon who forgot to put the bolt back into his rifle prior to rushing to a period of rifle drill in one of the drill sheds. Our keen-eyed Sergeant soon spotted his omission but instead of awarding him show parade decided that the offence was so serious that the person should be charged with "conduct prejudicial to military discipline". Amazingly enough Major James, the Company Commander dismissed the person with a warning. Unfortunately for the miscreant as he was leaving the Company office, the Sergeant noticed a small speck of boot polish on the man's neck, he was immediately wheeled back before the Major for a second time and charged with being dirty on parade. This time he was awarded three days C.B.

In return for all this hard discipline we were exempt from carrying out any guard duties, cookhouse fatigues, fire pickets or any other menial tasks outside or inside "D" company's lines. High jinx within Company lines appeared to be the order of the day and nobody seemed to interfere with what we did, not even the guard patrols. Major James, the Company Commander did not expect us to swear and indeed he did not allow his N.C.O' to swear at us, incredible as it may seem in basic training.

As time progressed we realised that all the points that the senior platoon had drawn our attention to on that second night in "D" Company were coming to pass, thereafter we proceeded with our training with an increased lookout for all potential pitfalls.

Basically our eight week or so programme was intended to prepare us specifically for W.O.S.B. but as well as rehearsing all the activities that we would have to perform there we were still put through the normal basic training programme with the addition of an infantry weapons course.

Basic training consisted of the usual foot drill of left and right turns, halting, saluting etc., and rifle drill consisting of slope arms, order arms, present arms etc. as well as instruction on firing our rifles on the 25 yd. range. The latter ideally ending with attainment of at least one 2" grouping of five shots with the Lee Enfield rifle and be designated a first-class shot. In addition we were expected to be proficient with the Bren Gun, Sten Gun and the .38 Revolver, not forgetting the Hand Grenade. All this was not so far removed from normal basic training that every National Serviceman received. Where our training did differ however was on those matters that we would be examined on at W.O.S.B. command tasks, current affairs, and exercise appraisals.

The command tasks took on two forms. One where you were in charge of a group of say six men, and given a specific task to overcome. You and you alone directed the group to execute the task. Should the group fail to carry out the task you were the person responsible for that failure. Only limited help was given you by other members of the group, as clearly when their turn came to direct they wanted to show that they could do it better than you. The variation on this theme was when a group of six people were detailed to solve a problem and through discussion and direction a leader emerged to take command. This form of command task was definitely not for the quiet unassuming personage!

A task usually consisted of a problem such as bridging an artificial chasm, or crossing a make-believe river, where at first glance the equipment provided appeared to be totally inadequate for solving the problem. A detailed analysis would always prove, however, that the equipment was just adequate for completing the task in one particular way. It was for you to find that way. Unfortunately a time limit was put on all command tasks so you couldn't spend all day looking for the solution.

Our Current Affairs lectures were usually given by civilian instructors. Due to the fact that we were perpetually tired in view of our eighteen hour working day, these lectures gave us an opportunity to relax. Consequently the lecturer was often confronted with a whole class of soldiers fast asleep.

Unperturbed the lecturer would carry on as if we were all wide awake until he had delivered his lecture in full, at which time he would wake us up so that we could depart to our next training session. I am sure that an Army personnel lecturer would not have been so considerate.

The exercise appraisals were quite interesting, we would be given a problem, such as a breach in a sea wall or a railway accident, or some such disaster, and limited resources in man power and equipment with which to tackle the problem. We would then be required to write a treatise on how to deal with the problem. After which we would have group analysis on the best solution to the problem.

At this stage of my Army career the various problems and disappointments I encountered were there to be overcome. I had as my goal W.O.S.B., followed by the strong possibility of O.C.T.U., and a commission. This above all made me grit my teeth and get on with the job in hand, which if the truth were told I didn't whole-heartedly believe in or enjoy.

We all attempted to shine brighter than our fellow hut mates. If we were individually perturbed or worried over a particular matter we did our utmost not to show it. We considered that to do so would be a sign of weakness on our part and entered as a black mark against us somewhere on our records. Days were long, up at 05:00hrs, hard work until 23:00hrs. If during the day there was time to relax you fell asleep. Going out of the camp for a little relaxation was out of the question, for me at any rate, in those early days there was just too much work to get through. In any case there was the guardroom inspection to pass when booking out of camp. Guard commanders were no exception in requiring a higher standard of dress from "D" company personnel than members from the rest of the battalion. Going out of camp just didn't seem worth the bother.

Great relief from the tedium of camp life could be experienced by arrival of a food parcel from home. Unfortunately even receiving one of these had its problems. Any parcel had to be picked up from the post room, where the post room Lance-Corporal, who I hasten to add was not from "D" company, was an absolute moron. He took great delight in refusing to serve you for such misdemeanours as being improperly dressed, without specifying the nature of the offence, or putting you to the end of the queue merely because you were in "D" Company. I even heard tales of people having to hand over items from their parcel before being able to take it away. Although he was clearly a very unsavoury character he was on the permanent staff of the camp and you just didn't argue with those people. Getting a parcel out of the post room was indeed a very tiresome process.

Eventually we had been in the Army for four weeks and we were told that we could now apply for a thirty-six hour pass to go home at the weekend, for many of us that caused quite an excitement and something to look forward to.

Having written out and submitted our applications, we were duly paraded on Saturday morning outside the Company Office to collect our passes, or so we thought. "Flopper" emerged from the building, waved the passes in the air and asked us if these were what we wanted. We naturally chorused back that they were.

He then informed us that as we had been bad boys it had been decided that we couldn't be granted leave that weekend. He then proceeded to tear the passes up in front of us.

To say that we were disappointed would be an understatement. My own feelings were indescribable I just couldn't believe that the Army could be so childish. It went through the charade of getting us to put in for leave passes, which someone in the Army knew we weren't going to get, then it held a parade to inform us that we couldn't have them.

A very disgruntled platoon was marched back to their hut where we prepared to spend the weekend in camp, reflecting on what might have been.

My enthusiasm for the Army sank to zero once again.

CHAPTER 8

IN WHICH WE PREPARE FOR W.O.S.B.

Much to my surprise I found that on Wednesday afternoons all military training ceased, to be replaced with recreational training if you were in an official team you took part in that sport, if you were not you took part in one of the many ad-hoc events that were going on. I decided to take part in a game of baseball, and almost immediately sprained my ankle whilst running over rough ground. The ankle ballooned up alarmingly and I had to hobble away and sit down.

By next morning I could still only painfully limp around so I was ordered by the Platoon Sergeant to report sick, which I duly did. Reporting sick I soon discovered was no simple matter. To do so one had to parade outside Company Office with your small pack containing specific items such as, pyjamas, clean shirt, clean underwear, towel, washing gear, and plimsolls on the assumption that the medical officer might decide to send you to hospital, so you had to be ready therefore for that eventuality.

On having our names checked off by the Company Clerk we were marched off to the MI Room, with me hobbling along as best I could. When my turn came to be seen by the Medical Officer he examined my ankle and gave me seven days light duties whatever that meant. Clutching my seven days' light duties chit I made my way back to the hut to rejoin the platoon, thankfully too late to go on muster parade. Unwittingly I had discovered at a very early stage that if you reported sick it automatically prevented you from going on muster parade as both events took place at the same time. I remembered this fact for future reference!

At first I was embarrassed over my injury and my inability to keep up with the rest of the platoon in our training. Next morning however my embarrassment left me when I realised that being on light duties meant hobbling on to the square at the back of the Battalion merely to have your name taken and to be dismissed almost immediately, after only a cursory inspection. Perhaps reporting sick and being put on light duties wasn't such a bad proposition after all!

My elation was short lived however, later that day I was called before Major James to be informed that if my incapacity caused me to drop behind with my training programme I would at the best be back-coursed, and if my incapacity persisted, posted away from "D" Company. That little talk as I am sure it was intended to, was enough to make me grin and bear the problem of my painful ankle and keep up with the others, though I gladly excepted early dismissal from muster parade for seven mornings, especially the CO's parade on the following Saturday morning.

On this C.Os parade instead of the normal strict inspection reserved for such occasions, Major James announced that it was such a nice morning that it called for a stroll through the countryside and promptly took the Company for a six mile route march, which in new boots and best BDs couldn't have been much fun on that very hot morning

It was generally accepted that this little jaunt into the countryside was in retaliation for the production of "Decoy" a very well-produced "D" Company magazine that had recently been distributed within Company lines and eagerly purchased at sixpence a copy. Whilst in no way treasonable some of the cartoons were a trifle pointed. In spite of this factor however we got the distinct impression that the Major thought it great piece of initiative. That his men, his gentlemen? had produced a magazine with virtually no resources of to speak of. At a later date I would contribute an article to this illustrious publication.

Rising from the back of the camp to approximately five hundred feet was Gittisham Hill, at the top was an area of common and scrubland, upon which we spent a lot of our time playing soldiers. With such games as seeing who could camouflage themselves effectively, or who could approach silently without noise or appearing on the skyline and other such military matters.

Up there, on top of the hill away from the confines of the camp, the atmosphere was slightly more relaxed, even "Flopper" would occasionally let down his guard, much to the apparent disapproval of Sergeant Suff. Often giving us a ten minute break, long enough in fact for us to relax and take stock of the quietness that was all around us up there on the hill, time to look down in the quiet air, upon Honiton and the camp of No.2. Training

Battalion situated as it was at the far end of town nestling in the valley below, with the A30 and the railway snaking its way up to London and home.

When "Flopper" wasn't with us the Sergeant would march us up the steep road to the top of Gittisham Hill at his usual ferocious pace. Leading from the front he would try his utmost to leave us behind, which considering we were all in battle order with rifles and he was carrying nothing but himself, should have been an easy task, but when he arrived at the top of the hill, although many would have fallen by the wayside on the climb up, there was always a small group of stalwarts one respectful step behind him. He had always threatened that anyone overtaking him would be put on a charge, and although we all thought he was joking no one was willing to put the point to the test. I think that if the truth were but told his age was catching up with him and he announced this caveat to save his embarrassment! This was probably a correct assessment of the situation, because soon after this, he disappeared to be replaced by a much younger Sergeant, who appeared to be a National Serviceman.

One of the most interesting activities carried out from our vantage point on the hill, was taking compass bearings on various land marks we could see in the distance and plotting them on the map of the area. This entailed taking at least two independent bearings and I recall on one occasion, when we were walking in the very long grass from one point to another, one of our number stumbled heavily and quite spontaneously called out, "Oops, sorry Madam", whereby we all looked up with great interest, to hear him further call out, "Oh, good morning Padre", at the same time throwing up a smart salute. Even our new Sergeant had the semblance of a smile on his face.

From time to time we would make our way up Gittisham Hill at dusk for the purpose of night observation courses on various subjects. Sometimes the woods would have to be traversed without activating the trip wire flares that had been set up by our estimable Company Commander earlier in the day. At other times the platoon would be split into two, each half starting at opposite ends of the common with the order to advance towards each other with the object of "capturing" members of the opposition as they were discovered. Each time we attempted this exercise however, the two halves of the platoon would arrive at their destination without "capturing" any of the opposition having seemingly passed within inches of each other without detection. So much for night observation!

It would usually be after midnight before we were ready to make our way wearily back down the hill to camp to find, surprisingly for me, that "Flopper" had laid on a meal for us in the cookhouse of something like, egg, bacon, fried bread and the inevitable baked beans. I must admit this was very considerate of him. What wasn't considerate however was the fact that after having devoured our meal we would then have to clean all our equipment ready for the following morning, or later that morning I should say.

On such occasions we didn't usually manage to climb into our beds until about 02:00 hrs. with the knowledge that we would have to vacate them three hours later ready to start another day.

Nearly every other Saturday there was a passing out parade at Honiton, of soldiers who had finished their basic training. Quite a fuss was made of these parades by the Army, and parents were encouraged to visit the camp for this event. These days were in fact referred to as "Parent's Day". The Army always seemed reluctant to recognise the fact that a large number of National Servicemen were married and that these days would be more appropriately termed "Relatives Day," or even "Open Day".

"Parents Day" fuelled the feeling amongst us that we were being treated as schoolboys, as indeed we were.

When I informed Doreen of the forthcoming "Parent's Day", after first assuring me she didn't qualify, and wasn't likely to in the foreseeable future, she jumped at the opportunity of coming down to stay for a few days, until in fact our promised five days recess leave that would commence the Wednesday after.

I eagerly went out of camp that night in order to book accommodation at a local house for Doreen's forthcoming visit. It was my first venture out of Camp

It was about 08:30hrs on the Saturday morning of the passing out parade and I was eagerly anticipating the time later in the morning when I would meet Doreen, when I was informed by a Sergeant that my Wife was in camp looking for me. Finding this hard to believe I dashed off in search of her and found her wandering through the camp. Apparently she had been looking over the wire when a Sergeant inquired if he could help her. When she explained who she was and was trying to catch sight of me, he invited her in to make further inquiries

Up to that time, other than the consideration shown to me by the guard commander at Blandford in my first few days of service, it hadn't appeared to me that anyone in the Army was any- where near to being human. But here was I proved wrong. It wasn't however going to happen to me very often whilst in the Army.

After a few moments of conversation Doreen hurried off to breakfast. She then made her official entry into camp at about 10:00hrs along with the first of the many other visitors. We had coffee in the N.A.A.F.I. We then wandered around the camp with me showing her where the various events of torture took place.

After witnessing the passing out parade we stayed in camp just long enough to have lunch and for me to procure my 36 hour pass, then we disappeared from the confines of the camp as quickly as possible. Even outside the camp I couldn't completely cast off the shackles of the Army as I hadn't any civilian clothes with me to change into, as we weren't allowed to wear civilian clothes until we had been in the Army for six months.

Having participated of tea at the Heathfield Café in Honiton, which by tradition "D" company had seemingly turned into something relating to their own club, we made our way to a very interesting old time country fair being held on the outskirts of the town. After looking around the fairground for a while we eventually made our way into a large boxing booth marquee, where some rather battered and down at heel boxers were challenging all comers to go three rounds with them. Five pounds was offered to anyone who was still on their feet at the end of three rounds. A not inconsiderable sum of money at that time.

A great cheer went up from the Army contingent in the audience when a REME member climbed into the ring to challenge. He was invited to select one of the three boxers that he wished to fight and not unnaturally picked the oldest and in my mind the most decrepit looking boxer as his choice. He left the ring to get changed whilst the selected boxer went through the motions of shadow boxing in preparation for his contest. Another roar from the crowd announced the return of the challenger, and for the second time he climbed into the ring.

As it appeared to me that we had a person here who had been out with his compatriots, got "jugged up", and had now been persuaded to challenge one of the boxers out of bravado, I expected a massacre, and a massacre is what we got. The only thing wrong with my thinking was that it was the REME man that did the massacring. He hammered the fair booth boxer unmercifully for three rounds and knocked him down twice. When the end of the third round came and the REME man was given the five pounds for still being on his feet he refused to accept the money wishing instead to go on for a knockout. Which judging by the condition of the fair booth boxer was likely to have come to pass in the very next round. A roar of support went up from the REME personnel in the crowd of onlookers.

A swift consultation took place in the ring between the promoter and his boxer and then he announced that the contest that we had just witnessed had been for three rounds only and that it wasn't in either of the contestant's interests for the bout to carry on for a knockout. This he announced amidst a tirade of boos coming principally from the REME contingent, including Doreen and myself.

The promoter with both arms in the air to quieten the crowd then further announced that in response to obvious public demand, next Saturday night there would be a rematch between the two contestants with a bout of six three minute rounds with a prize of ten pounds to the winner. I felt sorry for the fair booth boxer. He looked old enough to be my father and I felt certain that next Saturday he was going to receive the hammering of his life. Fortunately or unfortunately I would be on leave the following Saturday and would be unable to see the rematch. I was told later however that the REME man walked the contest, as I anticipated he would.

After the fair we walked back to our accommodation for the night, which happened to be a house near the camp, with the anticipation of another pleasant day on the morrow. Unfortunately however the next day was a very wet and miserable one but nevertheless we took the train to Exeter for the day, arriving back at Honiton at about 10:00 hrs., Doreen to go back to her "Digs" for the night and me back to camp.

Next morning we were up at 05:45 hrs. which to me was an improvement upon the previous 05:00 hrs., this later rising time was brought about by the fact that we were managing to get through our pre-muster parade chores much quicker now that we were becoming more experienced in how to do them.

After muster parade, which went without a hitch as far as I was concerned, I launched myself into the day's training programme with a will, in the knowledge that, that evening I would be meeting Doreen. I didn't partake of the Army tea, instead I hurried out to meet her at the camp entrance and we went along to the Heathfield Café for tea. I was surprised to find that it was fairly full with members of "D" Company personnel also having tea. It was at this stage that I realised that there were a number of "D" Company personnel who were more affluent than I who used to go to the Heathfield Café each night for tea rather than dine in the cookhouse back at the camp. I have no doubt that after tea they moved on to a pub for the evening. Oh what it must have been to have some spare cash around your person in those far off days!

After tea we went for a walk in the adjoining countryside and met a gardener at a very large country house who in the absence of his employer showed us around the house and gardens. The pleasant evening passed all too quickly however and it was time for me to return to camp and Doreen to her "digs". After having been out for the evening I then had to set to and bull up my equipment for the following days muster parade, consequently I didn't get to bed until after midnight.

Next night I was late in getting out of camp due to the fact that I was put on show parade for being in charge of a dirty hut table! Cleaning the table being my room job for that particular week. Unfortunately some kind person had put his boots on it after I had cleaned it. Consequently instead of meeting Doreen at 17:00hrs I had to prepare the table for a 19:00hrs show parade to be inspected by the Company Duty N.C.O. along with all the other miscreants of the day. Unfortunately on such an occasion it wouldn't only be the table that the N.C.O. would inspect but also the two people bringing it. The chances of having further show parade penalties awarded were therefore trebled.

It so happened that in this instance the duty N.C.O. was satisfied with what he saw and we rushed the table back to the hut before he changed his mind. This action was then followed by me hurrying out of camp to be with Doreen for what was left of the evening.

With regard to show parades it is interesting to note that a film I saw on television recently (in the 1990's) about Colchester Military Prison confirmed that show parades were used there very extensively. It is a matter for interesting speculation therefore whether "D" Company borrowed the idea from Colchester or Colchester from "D" Company.

Next day we were put through the hoop quite ferociously by our new Sergeant until lunch time, at which time we were allowed to down tools, hand in our rifles to the armoury, collect our leave passes, pack and rush off to catch our respective trains and buses for our five days' leave.

I was making my way to the guard room prior to leaving the camp when a yell of, "Skinner," brought me out of my day-dream of the pleasant time I was promising myself for the next five days. I looked up to see that it was our new Sergeant who had called out, my heart sunk into my boots.

"What an earth are you trying to conceal in your map pocket?"

"It's a camera Sergeant," I said looking down at the large suspicious bulge in my uniform.

"You don't have to keep it in your map pocket as if you're trying to steal some military secret; it's quite in order for you to carry it over your shoulder in uniform. Looks smarter anyway."

"Yes Sergeant, thank you, Sergeant," I said as I tugged the camera out of my pocket and swung it over my shoulder.

"Have a good leave." he called out.

I nearly dropped dead in my tracks, so he was human after all under that hard veneer of his. I joined the queue to sign out of camp for my eagerly anticipated leave. I met Doreen we caught the

4:00pm train from Honiton and arrived home at about 9:45pm. Home at that time being a room in my parent's house.

My first impulse on arrival home, was to change out of my uniform into civvies, even that little action made me feel that the Army was a thousand miles away, and so it would be for the next five days at any rate. I must confess however that I did put my uniform on just once more the next morning for my trip to the office where I used to work, in order to let them know that I was still alive. Why I wore my uniform I don't know. Bravado? Perhaps.

My immediate reaction to the visit was how on earth did I manage to do such a boring job? I left the office, not looking forward one little bit to going back there after National Service. It occurred to me that perhaps inwardly I was enjoying Army life more than I was prepared to admit outwardly, or more than I realised!

The five days leave that I had looked forward to so enthusiastically seemed to flash by with the speed of light and before I realised it I was sitting on a Honiton bound train travelling back to the "bull", the discipline and the inevitable heartache. On reflection I realised that for the next two years I was going to lead two lives. One when I was in the Army, which to me was going to be purgatory, and the other when I was on leave in an atmosphere of happiness. I could see that I was going to find it difficult to come to terms with this type of life.

After a very pleasant five days at home the camp seemed to be even worse than I recalled before going on leave. My only consolation was the fact that I kidded myself that things would improve when I had completed my training. Little did I realise at the time that I still had over a year's further training in front of me.

One consolation about being back in camp however, was the fact that after initial teething problems hut 26 of No.10 Platoon now worked as a team. We now looked after each other, we helped each other, the comradeship was great. If I had to be in the Army I couldn't have wished to be with a better group of men. Not like the early days when I recall there was an argument in the hut over a trifling affair and one of our number received bad cuts around the eyes from an unprovoked attack.

That evening the perpetrator of the attack had come back to

the hut after a visit to the N.A.A.F.I. with his clothes in his arms and his unmentionables boot blacked. The Senior Platoon had its own inevitable way of dealing with problems, when it heard of them. Even that person was now a reasonable member of the team.

Next morning was Thursday. Even if I didn't feel too happy about the Army, every other Thursday I was cheered by the sight of the new intake arriving to start their National Service. Nobody, but nobody could look as lost and dejected as that group of people. The arrival of these unhappy individuals also acted as a reminder of the fact that that day we had moved up a point in the matter of Platoon seniority in "D" Company and were also a fortnight closer to going to W.O.S.B. which at that time was the extent of my future planning in the Army. The point at which my Army career was going to be determined one way or the other, for better or for worse.

Thursday was also the day, by the way that we got paid, at that time I was paid 10/-s one week and 12/-s the next.

"Never in the field of human conflict had so many waited for so long for so little!"

Although I had just returned from leave I toyed with the idea of applying for a 36 hour leave pass for the weekend, then looked at my 10/- and decided I couldn't afford it.

With a sigh of relief we reached mid-day Saturday and were with a bit of luck free until Monday morning. Weekends spent in camp however were absolutely boring, a lot of the time was spent reading and even more time spent sleeping, we hadn't even the benefit of a radio to listen to as I recall. The boredom was normally only relieved by a visit to the N.A.A.F.I. for a cup of tea and perhaps a game of table tennis.

That Saturday however I was persuaded to accompany a group of the lads on a visit to a local cider house. We had a jolly evening playing darts and drinking the odd mug of cider. On leaving the establishment however the cool air hit me and I fell flat on my face, to a howl of laughter from the others. They dragged me to my feet and we made our way back to camp with me in a near drunken stupor. As we neared the guard room I sobered up and managed to sign back in under the watchful eye of the guard commander, thankfully for me without trouble. We hurried back to our billet and I gratefully climbed into bed, pulling my cape over the blankets for additional warmth, for even in the summer I found that three blankets were not enough to keep me warm. The problem with using our capes however was the fact that they "sweated" and by morning my blankets would be quite wet and they didn't dry out by being made into a bed block for the day.

Most of Sunday was spent in bulling up equipment in preparation for another hectic week, commencing with muster parade the following morning. And continuing throughout the week with the usual dosage of bull, drill, discipline, and of course the inevitable best BD inspections. These best BD inspections were usually carried out by the Company Commander ably supported by the QMS tailor. The first consideration to be given to a best BD was whether or not it fitted correctly, followed by whether or not the blouse and trousers were of the same shade of khaki, of which there appeared to be dozens. No sooner had it been decided that the BD was of the right size then someone would decide that the two halves were not of a matching shade. A hunt would then be made to see if a match could be made within the platoon as there appeared to be a reluctance to fetch more uniforms from the stores, from thereon for an hour or so the BDs were passed around the platoon like "Ring a Ring A Roses, by which time no one was much better off than when they started. At this stage "Flopper" the Platoon Commander, would profess himself satisfied and would depart from the scene.

At the next best BD parade the process would start all over again. I was to find that best BD inspections would be held at least once a month throughout my two years in the Army.

In a very unwise and rash moment, after listening to some ex-boy soldiers I was advised that the only way to get really sharp creases in my BD trousers was to shave the creases prior to pressing. I carried out this process with disastrous results. The next best BD inspection was held by the Company Commander Major James and as usual he was taking no prisoners so to speak. He took one look at my beautiful creases and roared out in a deafening voice, "You soldier have scorched your trousers, Sergeant take that man's name and see that he buys a new pair, immediately."

"Come over here soldier," called out the CQMS and looking at my trousers, said, "What the hell have you been doing to them?" I shrugged my shoulders in despair, a new pair of trousers would cost me a least two weeks' pay.

"Here try these on," he said quietly, throwing a pair across to me. "If they fit I can exchange them for your scorched ones without charge. He winked knowingly at me.

I tried them on but showed him that they were far too big for me.

"Ah, they're alright you take 'em son and save yourself some money, they'll get changed at the next BD inspection, I'll see to that." And he was as good as his word. I was beginning to realise that when some of these senior N.C.O.'s let their guard down they were human after all. The whole episode taught me a lesson. I never touched my BD with a razor ever again.

Before I knew it the time had arrived for another passing out parade and another "Parent's Day". Doreen as enthusiastic as ever but still not a parent at this moment in time thank goodness, decided to come down for the occasion. By this time I had become friendly with a chap in the Officer Cadet School Platoon and Doreen had been corresponding with his wife. The four of us spent most of the weekend together. Geoff, the OCS member had been selected as one of the two stick orderlies for the passing out parade. This entailed marching in slow time between the ranks of soldiers preceding the inspecting retinue. It was the highest honour that could be bestowed upon any one in "D" Company and I gladly basked in the reflected glory that shone upon me by being with Geoff during the day.

Perhaps I should explain here that the passing out parade also entailed the participation of a large portion of the battalion in addition to those actually passing out.

"D" company as well as providing the two Stick Orderlies also fielded the Officer Cadet School Platoon, those people who had passed War Office Selection Board and were awaiting posting to Officer Cadet Training Unit. They usually stole the show for smartness of drill and tended to overshadow all others on parade, no doubt to the gratification of Major James, but not the other Company Commanders. The parade which lasted approximately half an hour consisted of all the drill movements that had been learnt at basic training, culminating in a march past with fixed bayonets, the CO taking the salute.

"D" Company personnel never passed out as such, they either passed W.O.S.B. and carried onto O.C.T.U., or failed and immediately fell from prominence in the Company until finally posted for trade training. The latter always seemed to me a rather ignominious end to eight or nine weeks of very strenuous and specialised training.

We had lunch in the cookhouse, Geoff by this time resplendent in his blazer and flannels, a privilege reserved for persons having passed W.O.S.B. That evening we four went into Exeter to the cinema by train. The next day we spent a very pleasant time on the beach at Sidmouth, ending up with the usual tea at the Heathfield Café, after which it was time for me to return to camp, and Doreen to return home on the morrow.

The next week we had the obligatory platoon dinner at the London Hotel, Ottery St. Mary. The Army surprisingly enough supplying a lorry to transport us to and from the venue. This would be the last function that we held as a platoon, from here on in we would be attending W.O.S.B. and returning to be designated success or failure and never to meet again on equal terms.

After the dinner, Second Lieutenant Hopkins, in a very merry mood, related to a receptive audience, a very long and drawn out tale about a man with constipation who eventually relieved himself on a vision at the bottom of a well. The vision turned out to be a likeness of Second Lieutenant Hopkins, intimating that everybody relieved themselves on him. I give the polite version of the story.

As merry as I was that evening I realised that I wasn't the only person in the Army with a persecution complex. Perhaps it was contagious.

The dinner incidentally cost us twice as much as it should have done, the treasurer, our one and only University OTC platoon member, had all the money stolen just before the dinner, or so he said. I think he took us for a ride and I don't mean in the lorry!

The day after our platoon dinner we reached the dizzy height of senior platoon and were now therefore eligible to "Nig" the junior platoon. That night we raided the junior platoon's hut, at about one o'clock in the morning and purloined all their beds in a similar manner to that which we had been subjected, was it really only eight weeks before? Then the next night a select few of our number with uniforms borrowed off our platoon commander and other supernumerary N.C.O.'s set off towards the Nig platoon huts. Not wishing to be left out of such an evening, I pleaded with Creeping Jesus, our own Lance- Corporal to loan me his uniform, which after a little reluctance he did. I hurriedly pulled it on and sped off to catch the others up.

We put the Nig platoon through pure hell, both on inspections, drill, and in the gym. We had learnt a lot in our short time at Honiton I excelled myself to such a degree when drilling a group of men that I had a sleepy looking Sergeant open the window of his quarters in a quiet part of the camp, and call me over to him.

"If I ever hear you yelling at your men like that again Corporal I shall make sure that you lose that stripe of yours." he informed me, "Now bugger off somewhere else and let me get some sleep!"

If only you knew I thought, hurriedly moving the body of men off to an even remoter part of the camp. I had unwittingly drilled them by the Sergeants' sleeping quarters.

Later on in the evening I had just deposited a mystified looking Nig in the N.A.A.F.I. instead of the guard room as ordered by the "Platoon Commander", with instructions to stay there until called for, when I was involved in a tricky incident.

"Just a moment Corporal," I heard a voice call out from behind me as I was walking away from the N.A.A.F.I.

I turned to see a Corporal from "B" company standing with hands on hips facing me.

"Yes".

"Are you sure that you're entitled to be wearing that uniform?"

"Pardon?" I queried.

"I said, are you sure that you are entitled to be wearing that uniform?" he repeated.

"What an earth do you mean by that?" I replied feeling myself going red in the face.

"I mean I don't think that you're a Lance-Corporal, Lance-Corporal."

"So what do you think I am?" I queried.

"I think that you're wearing someone else's uniform for some prank or other that you're having in "D" Company."

"If you think that I suggest that you check with "D" Company Office in the morning. I should think that Major James will be delighted to hear your theory. Smiths the name by the way, Corporal."

And with that I turned on my heels and marched off in as smart manner as possible, before he had a chance to ask any further questions.

I don't think that I convinced him by any means, I just don't think he knew what else to do about the situation though. Perhaps I should have asked him to accompany me to explain his misgivings to my Platoon Commander who was nearby. And I do believe that our Platoon Commander for the night could have carried it off, he was excellent. In fact the other platoons congratulated all of us for an excellent Nigging. All except some of the nigged platoon who said they realised it was a joke all the time. Those who said so however couldn't explain why they still complied with our orders, or indeed why they planned to "do" me when they got me in an alley one dark night for being such a bastard to them, if it wasn't for the fact that they believed that we were the genuine article.

All in all they didn't seem to take much heed of the advice we gave them that evening and I had a feeling they were going to be in for a difficult time in "D" company.

Incidentally we had to buy our Sergeant an extra pint for loan of his uniform, our imitator wore the Orderly Sergeant's sash over the wrong shoulder and the mistake was spotted by him on the evening, which made us speculate on how many of those in authority actually watched the nigging?

Having aspired to the dizzy height of senior platoon meant that our W.O.S.B. postings were now imminent. To celebrate this fact coupled with our successful nigging, a couple of nights later we decided to hold an impromptu dinner in the hut. All persons attending, as well as contributing to the consumables, had to dress for dinner. This dress it was decreed would consist of pyjama trousers and webbing belt, khaki jumper, khaki bow tie, with a white towel across the shoulder in the form of a bandolier, complete with beret worn back to front. The Scottish members amongst us decided to substitute the trousers for a towel kilt, with a small shovel as a sporran, and a blanket across the shoulder in the form of a folded cloak.

After an enjoyable "dinner" composed of the remnants of our parcels from home plus bits and pieces bought from the N.A.A.F.I., someone decided that as senior platoon we should carry out an inspection of "D" Company lines. Jock Martin was nominated the inspecting officer, General McMuddle of the White watch. One of the chaps immediately converted himself to become the "General's" girlfriend, others rushed out and returned surprisingly with javelins, where they found the javelins heaven only knows, to become his personal bodyguard. The rest of us stuck our bayonets into our belts. We were ready to inspect the Company.

Each and every hut was inspected in turn with the personal bodyguard entering the hut first, calling it to attention, the "General" and his "Girlfriend" entering under crossed javelins, the rest of us eagerly following and helping with the inspection. All in all we created absolute chaos within the Company, and sparked off a night of raids and counter raids between huts. Amazingly enough though no one dared to attempt a raid on our hut. The senior platoon it seemed was absolutely sacrosanct.

We went to bed late that night, or rather early next morning, thoroughly satisfied with our night's work.

This event was very soon followed by another in "D" Company, which caused quite a stir at the time but with the benefit of hindsight now seems insignificant and even amusing.

After muster parade one bright and sunny morning, instead of being dismissed and marched back to our hut we were paraded outside the Company office and held waiting there for a long time whilst Major James was clearly conferring with his Platoon Commanders inside. He eventually appeared, called us to attention and unusual for him didn't stand us at ease whilst he addressed us.

"I would hope that I could address you as gentlemen and potential officers," he began, "But this morning I have to address you as potential gentlemen and potential officers due to an event that has taken place involving "D" Company personnel, the details of which I am sure you are all aware. I would inform you that the men concerned have already been dismissed from my Company in disgrace, as will anyone else who finds the incident amusing. I am ashamed, disgusted and disappointed with you. That is all I have to say to you. Carry on Sergeant Major."

With that he turned and disappeared very quickly into his office.

Many of us glanced at our neighbours with raised eyebrows.

"Stand still, face the front," roared out the CSM and we immediately complied with his order.

"Platoon Sergeants march your men away."

We were marched back to our hut and launched into our training programme and it wasn't until N.A.A.F.I. break that I had the opportunity to ask around the platoon the reason for Major James's outburst. I was then told the story. Apparently three or four nights earlier a group of "D" Company personnel had visited the N.A.A.F.I. to buy some cakes, when the cakes were pushed across the counter it was asked if they could be put into a bag.

"Ain't got no bags," was the reply from the N.A.A.F.I. girl serving them.

"You must be joking, we can see plenty from where we're standing,"

This remark was followed by raucous laughter from the rest of the party. The inference being that the N.A.A.F.I. girls only wore knickers to keep their ankles warm.

The soldiers picked up their cakes and departed from the N.A.A.F.I.

The N.A.A.F.I. girls reported the matter to their manageress who in turn reported the matter to the Provost Sergeant. The group were now marked men. Immediately they next appeared in the N.A.A.F.I. the Provost Sergeant was called and they were hauled before Major James who without a second thought threw them out of the Company. Bang went their chances of W.O.S.B., and their chances of a commission, slim as they might have been anyway.

Call a N.A.A.F.I. girl a bag and you didn't get to W.O.S.B. But pass W.O.S.B. and get to O.C.T.U, then the only thing that would stop you getting your commission was putting the Commandant's wife in a family way, or so it was fondly believed at the time. Such was the way of the Army as we saw it.

CHAPTER 9

IN WHICH I ATTEND
THE WAR OFFICE SELECTION BOARD.

The N.A.A.F.I. girls' event was however soon dismissed from our minds by the forthcoming visit to the battalion of the Director of Mechanical Engineering, who was" top cat" in R.E.M.E. The whole of the camp was, at the drop of a hat, put in a state of high tension. Whereby, amongst other things, gravel paths were swept, insignificant stones painted white, windows cleaned, grass cut, fire points painted red, and of course our equipment" bulled" up time and time again.

Two of our number finding themselves in possession of a tin of red paint and a brush, presumably acquired when the painters of the fire points were looking the other way, took it upon themselves to climb up on the roof of our hut and paint the two chimneys bright red.

The incident inspired our C.S.M. when walking up the path to our hut to exclaim in anticipation, "What have we here then lads a knocking shop?"

"Wish that it was Sir."

"I don't think that the D.M.E. will appreciate what you have done to one of his hut's chimneys lads", get them painted black."

"Black Sir, but we've only just painted them red Sir. Where do we get black paint from?"

"Same place you got the red paint from no doubt", he replied with a twinkle in his eye.

That weekend, much to everyone's annoyance, all leave was cancelled and we were all confined to camp to enable the frantic preparations for the impending visit to continue. By this time everything that didn't move was being painted and everything that did was being saluted just in case it happened to be the D.M.E. doing a sneak preview.

At last the day of the inspection arrived.

Just before going on parade, "Flopper" enquired, if by chance the D.M.E. should stop at the platoon to have a chat, had we any celebrities in our ranks that he could tell him about? Any titled gentlemen, film stars, Members of Parliament, etc. etc., he called out in a jocular manner.

No response was forthcoming

"Just as I thought, a pretty un-interesting lot aren't you".

Silence, then.

The D.M.E. is Omerod's uncle, if that's of any interest Sir", called out one of our number.

"Oh yes pull the other one".

"No it's true Sir, Omerod is the D.M.E's nephew".

"Is this true Omerod? Queried "Flopper" becoming visibly excited.

"Yes Sir, but I've never met him and he probably doesn't even know I exist".

"Flopper" was by now really excited. "So what's your first name "and where is your home town, and you're his nephew you say?"

If "Flopper" had had his way I am sure that he intended to make any meeting between the two as historical as Stanley meeting Livingstone. In the event the D.M.E .came nowhere near our platoon during the whole of the day much to "Flopper's" disappointment, but to our immense relief.

This annual inspection was held to give the D.M.E. a snapshot of the proficiency of the battalion...

The annual Admin Inspection was another reason for any camp to be thrown into a state of utter confusion, and was as far as I am aware carried out to investigate the battalion in far greater detail. I used to ask questions about these inspections, but never did build up a clear picture of their true intentions, which led me to wonder whether or not anyone really knew their true intention. In my experience all they appeared to do was to spread panic throughout the unit to be inspected.

These D.M.E'.s inspections as all other inspections were regarded by the National Servicemen merely as one more nuisance the Army had dreamt up for their discomfort, rather than something that was really necessary . An event that was not to be taken too seriously, attended to at the time, and then forgotten about. After all we were only going to be in the Army for two years. *Only two years!*

The regular soldier on the other hand, from the Colonel down to the lowest private appeared to take these inspections very seriously indeed. A bad report could bring retribution upon the permanent staff as a whole for a long time to come, whereas we National Servicemen would be moving on in the very near future and with any luck would probably miss the main thrust of this retribution. I suspect that this difference in outlook between the Regular Soldier and the National Serviceman was the cause of much of the friction that was evident between these two bodies of men from time to time.

The D.M.E.'s parade commenced at 10:30 hrs. and although the parade itself was not too strenuous as such, the two hours of standing under a hot sun was, especially as long periods of this time were spent standing perfectly still, the only movement possible being a slight swaying from the ball of the foot to the heel to prevent cramp setting in. One or two of the old lags often decided to faint rather than put up with this discomfort. These men were immediately removed from the parade square on stretchers by medics on duty for such an event. It was rumoured that all men fainting on parade and not hurting themselves were put on a charge as malingerers. Those who impaled themselves on their bayonets when doing so were not, as these cases were considered genuine!

As I say, much to "Flopper's" disappointment, but not to ours, the DME did not wish to inspect his platoon. We just had to stand on the square awaiting the usual grand finale of any parade, the battalion march past, with the salute being taken, of course by the D.ME.

After lunch the D.M.E. again took the salute, this time at the passing out parade of "B" Company. A great honour, or so we were told, I doubt however that "B" Company saw it that way, but I could be wrong.

Next morning it was on orders for me to attend my final U.S.B. for a decision to be given on whether or not I was considered a suitable candidate to attend W.O.S.B, as a representative of R.E.M.E. Dressed in my best B.D, boots, belt, and gaiters I attended the Company office with great trepidation. I was immediately ushered into Major James's office, who was seated behind his desk looking at the papers before him. He was flanked by two officers that I didn't recognise.

I saluted as smartly as I knew how.

"Stand at ease Skinner".

I complied with his order, which for once sounded more in the nature of a request, rather than an order.

"I've been looking at your record whilst here in "D" company and am happy with your progress and am pleased to confirm your W.O.S.B. posting ". This latter he said looking up and smiling.

"Thank you Sir".

"Well done, go to W.O.S.B. and be successful as I am sure that you will be. I have no further comment to make.

"Thank you Sir".

"Right dismiss Skinner and good luck".

I threw up another smart salute, about turned and exited the office in a trance. I couldn't believe the briefness of the interview. Some interviews I under-stood could be very prolonged indeed and even then ended in disappointment for the interviewee.

A few days later I found myself Barton Stacey bound on the 07:00hrs train from Honiton, in company with seven of my "D" company compatriots. We arrived at Andover station along with other Army personnel to be greeted by a very polite Sergeant.

"If you gentlemen are bound for Barton Stacey would you be good enough to climb aboard the lorry please and then we will be on our way".

I looked around to see if he was really speaking to me, he was. In a state of disbelief I climbed onto the lorry with the others. I had a feeling that I was going to enjoy my stay at Barton Stacey.

A ten minute drive through the countryside brought us to a camp that announced itself as 'War Office Selection Board, Barton Stacey.

We swept through the gates and halted at a building which was labelled 'Reception'.

The Sergeant appeared at the back of the lorry and invited us "gentlemen" to disembark and assemble in the reception building.

I was definitely going to enjoy my stay.

Let's hope I can make this treatment permanent I thought to myself.

We entered the building and found ourselves in a large open plan area furnished with a number of arm chairs, most of which were already occupied by personnel who looked up expectantly as we entered. There was an officer standing at the far end of the room, who as far as I recall was a major.

"Please come in gentlemen and find yourself a seat," he requested. He then went on to call out a list of names presumably to satisfy himself that all who were required to be present were indeed present. He then began.

"Right gentlemen, as you are aware the purpose of your presence here is for you to be assessed to see if you have the necessary attributes to receive training for a commission in the Army. I will inform you quite categorically that there is a commission awaiting all of you that measure up to the required standards. What are those standards you ask me? Well whilst here you will undergo certain tests and exercises all designed to see if you have the abilities that we are looking for.

Contrary to the tales that you have heard about W.O.S.B, we do not play tricks on you whilst you are here. We do not have special mats that are whipped away from under your feet and when you fall on your backside we listen to hear whether you exclaim "oh bother" or, "oh fuck it". Your reaction to such an incident is of no interest to us whatsoever. Nor do we have spies in the dining room to see if you eat your peas off your fork or your knife. You will only be assessed here on your ability to make decisions, and your fitness to lead men, and other various military matters. No other factors will be taken into consideration.

I am sure that you are all aware that whilst you are here on course gentlemen only overalls will be worn, and that no badges of rank, or indeed of regiments will be displayed at any time. That means no headgear will be worn. Instead each of you will be given a tie on numbered pullover, upon which will be displayed your W.O.S.B number. This number must be worn at all times. You will only be referred to by that number by the course observers and all other personnel whilst you are here. From now on neither your rank or your regiment are of any interest to us. You all start on a level playing field so to speak.

Your programme will commence immediately after lunch

with a series of written intelligence tests, which I believe you will find interesting, followed by an essay or two. Then tomorrow will be taken up with command tasks, group discussions and an interview with the selection board. Friday morning you will perform your agility tests down in the wooded area and later that morning you will be given your results."

Many years later I turned on my car radio to immediately recognised the self-same introductory speech still being handed out to W.O.S.B. candidates. It was a programme about the "modern" British Army!

"As far as accommodation and messing arrangements are concerned", he continued, "you will be allocated two to a room and messing is in the dining room for everybody. Breakfast is between 07:30 hrs. and 08:00 hrs., other meal times will depend your various course activities but you will be kept posted of these times. I require a prompt 08:30 hrs. start on course each morning gentlemen. Please do not be late.

Captain Forsythe here will allocate you your room and W.O.S.B. number. Thank you gentlemen."

Whilst the Major had been talking to us I had been anxiously glancing around the room trying to assess the competence of the other candidates. I was a trifle unsettled to note that over fifty percent of them were N.C.O.s, up to and including the rank of W.O.1. Hell I thought what is going to happen when I start ordering them about? I began to attempt to memorise the faces of the more senior ranks amongst us but ceased to do so when I decided that it would be better for me not to know their rank if it came for me to order them around.

It was then my turn to be allocated a number and a room. I found myself sharing it with a regular private from Honiton, a most unusual situation. I was led to believe that personnel from the same unit were usually segregated at W.O.S.B. apparently to prevent the possibility of them helping one another or so I had been told!

We changed into our overalls, donned our speedway rider style numbers and went to lunch. I was pleasantly surprised to find that the dining room was very well furnished, the tables covered with snow-white linen table cloths and that we were served by orderlies who addressed us as 'Sir'. My immediate reaction to this type of treatment was that I could get used to it if I really tried, and I felt that I really could try.

Lunch over, we were directed to a classroom type block of buildings, where for the rest of the afternoon, we were subjected to an immense number of intelligence tests that required written answers. I recall that we had to work ourselves through books of questions. These questions became progressively more difficult until, if the truth were told, it was difficult to understand what the question was, let alone come up with the answer.

In the second part of the afternoon we were given a disaster type problem to deal with, the problem that I was given related to an East Coast area where breaches had been made in the seawall defences and further ones were anticipated. Basically I had to deal with evacuating civilians from the area, safeguarding the properties against looting, and setting about repairing the breaches. At the same time I had to anticipate where further breaches would occur. To cope with this disaster I was allocated a specific sized military workforce along with certain equipment and plant.

The type of problem presented to me was particularly relevant as the year before there had indeed been serious breaches in the east coast defences, causing widespread damage.

The intelligence tests and the exercise essay were very interesting. Under normal circumstances they would have been amusing to tackle, but given that, in this instance, on the answers given, depended whether or not I progressed towards a commission, I could not but help feel the tension building up in me whilst I was formulating my answers.

Afternoon session over we went to tea in the pleasant atmosphere of the dining room.

We were free in the evening and I took the opportunity to telephone Doreen to give her a résumé of the first day's proceedings. I didn't think it had gone too badly for me. At any rate I certainly didn't think that I had dropped any unholy clangers.

Next morning we were woken by a knock on the door at about 0:700hrs by an orderly, informing us that "Breakfast will be served at 7.30 hrs., Sirs". Confirming that we were awake he passed on to the next room. This is the life for me, I thought.

After a wash in a very pleasant washroom, where we were not required to carry out any cleaning tasks as at Honiton, I went to breakfast.

After being served a well-cooked breakfast, we all made our way to the command task area where, if my memory serves me correctly, we were divided up into groups of six people. This time the powers to be made absolutely certain that no two people from the same unit were in the same group.

Although we had to practise at carrying out command tasks at Honiton, the tasks at W.O.S.B. were far more complex and better constructed than those we had been used to solving. The general principles remained the same however. As usual at first glance it appeared impossible to overcome the problem before you with the materials and apparatus at your disposal. There was however one way and one way only in which the problem could be solved and it was up to you to find that way.

Each member of our group was in turn put in command of the group and given a task to solve. This they did with varying degrees of success in the time at their disposal. Eventually I was put in command of the group and taken to my command task, and I couldn't believe my eyes. I had before me one of the tasks that had been discussed at Honiton by returning W.O.S.B.'ites and I knew precisely how to solve the problem. I just couldn't believe my good fortune. My first reaction was to jump in with both feet and carry out the task in record time. I then realised that that would look suspicious to the observing officers.

Basically the task before me consisted of a Boy Scout type two wheeled limber placed on a timber platform in the middle of a grassed area which was surrounded by a barrier of scaffold tubes. The problem was to get the limber off the platform and out of the compound without the limber touching either the grass or the scaffold tube barrier. I can't remember exactly the apparatus at my disposal for carrying out the task but it certainly appeared totally inadequate for the purpose in hand. Trying desperately to suppress my excitement, I stalked around the compound viewing the limber from all angles as if trying to assess in an intelligent manner a solution to the problem, when all the time I knew the solution. I suppressed my desire to start directing my team immediately in the execution of the solution.

After I considered that sufficient time had elapsed for any intelligent person who didn't know the solution to have worked it out, I called my group together and expounded my solution in a very loud and authoritative voice whilst the observing officers looked on with interest. The group under my instruction picked up the limber from the platform and placed it outside the compound without a hitch in double quick time. I was very pleased with myself. The fact that, in a way, I had cheated by having prior knowledge of the solution didn't enter my head.

From the individual command tasks we progressed to the group command tasks where it was up to the individual to impose his dominance upon the group, and by his perseverance take command of the group. These tasks were certainly not for the shy retiring types but then nor was W.O.S.B. Even these tasks I consider I handled with some credit.

After lunch when once again we were treated to the luxury of white table cloths and waiter service. We were taken to the classroom area. Here we proceeded to take part in a series of group discussions. Once again we were under the watchful eye of two or three observers, who like the officers who watched us carrying out our command tasks, were making copious notes of the proceedings.

Whilst these discussions were taking place, individuals were being detailed off to attend their interviews before a board of officers. The format of these interviews was a little obscure to me, as surprisingly we had had little preparation for them at Honiton. We were only told that they would be similar to the U.S.B. interviews. In my case this turned out to be a complete understatement of the situation.

Eventually I was called for interview. I knocked on the door of the room, was ordered to enter, and found myself in a small sparsely furnished room with a table at one end behind which were sitting a colonel, flanked by two other officers. I marched in and stood rigidly to attention facing my potential inquisitors. I resisted the temptation to salute which would have been totally wrong standing there as I was without a beret on. It is an interesting fact that no saluting took place at W.O.S.B. between candidates and observing officers due to this absence of headgear.

"Good morning 76 please sit down".

A nervous 76 sat down.

I had already decided that I would answer all the questions with absolute frankness, that way I considered I couldn't be caught out.

If I made any untrue statements I felt certain that sooner or later I would be tripped up in the interview. I had heard some of my compatriots say that when it came to their interview, they were going to give the answers they thought the Army would wish to hear rather than give the true facts of the case. I thought that this would be the wrong route to take. With hindsight however I now know that they were right and I was wrong. The longer I was in the Army the more convinced I became that most people in authority were only playing a game with us and not dealing with reality. I should have realised this fact much sooner than I did, and reciprocated accordingly at an early stage.

The interview which was more akin to a grilling than an interview, lasted for nearly an hour. Questions ranged from ones over my school days, further education, sporting activities, and work, to one's over my religious beliefs and marriage. We then covered the books and papers I read, and many other subjects including current affairs. Finally I was asked what I thought of the Army so far and that if I gained a commission would I "sign on", to which I replied that, I was enjoying my service so far very much and that if I gained a commission, I would indeed "sign on" neither of which were totally true, but I believed that I had started playing the game too late in the interview.

Eventually the interview came to an end and I marched out of the room as smartly as I could, dressed as I was in ill-fitting overalls. I came away from the interview undecided as to whether it had gone well or badly. I rejoined my discussion group but couldn't concentrate. I kept finding myself returning to the interview and ruminating on the answers I had given to the Board.

That evening I went with my Honiton compatriots to the camp "Gaff" but I just couldn't enjoy the films. I found myself turning over in my own mind the events of the past two days, trying to decide how I had performed and what result I was going to receive the next day.

I was still trying to sum up the situation as I was lying in bed that night with sleep evading me. I eventually came to the conclusion that although I didn't think that I had dropped any undue clangers, I had the feeling that I hadn't passed. The reason I came to this conclusion was that I considered that passing W.O.S.B. was a very important event and you had to be impressive to pass and I just didn't think that I had been as impressive as I could have been.

The next morning I was up at 0.7:00hrs as usual. After breakfast we were directed to the wooded area where we found various obstacles constructed, both on the ground and up in the trees. We had to undertake what were called agility tests under the eyes of the usual band of observing officers. The general idea was that each of us, within a specified time limit, had to gain as many points as possible by tackling as many obstacles as we could within the time allowed.

The obstacles varied in degrees of difficulty and their points' value reflected this fact. The choice was yours to tackle them in any order you thought fit. You could, if you wished, ignore the difficult ones and only tackle the easy ones repeatedly in an attempt to amass your points. I considered that this exercise was not so much an agility test as a psychological one to evaluate our perseverance factor, i.e. did a person go for the easy or the hard tasks?

These tests however were only a diversion from the main event of the morning; that of all personnel being given their result by the Board.

From time to time people would be taken from their antics amongst the trees and detailed off to attend their final interview. Eventually my turn came to attend.

I knocked on the door of the office and was bade to enter. Once again I found myself looking at a Board of three officers. The interview was very brief and to the point.

"Number 76 the Board has decided not to recommend that you proceed to officer cadet school. That is all, dismiss."

"Yes Sir, thank you Sir."

I executed an about turn and walked out of the room. I

was utterly and completely crestfallen. Although I thought that that was going to be the result I was likely to receive, I had hoped upon hope that it wouldn't be so. At that precise moment I felt that the bottom had dropped out of my world, everything that I had worked for over the past three months had come to nothing, as far as I was concerned my time in the Army to date had been completely wasted.

I returned to my room a dejected person. All that remained now was for me to pack, have a quick lunch and return to Honiton with my compatriots. On exchanging notes with the people I had come with I discovered that four out of the eight had passed, an average result apparently.

For me it was a miserable journey back to Honiton with four of our number being elated by their success and the other four deflated by their failure.

I brightened up slightly on arrival back at camp however when I found that the D.M.E's inspection had been so satisfactory that the whole camp had been given a forty eight hour leave pass for the weekend, and that our passes were waiting for us at the Company office . By 20:00 hrs. I was on my way home in the company of Gwyn, one of the W.O.S.B. successes. In view of the fact that we had missed the last train from Honiton we started to hitch-hike to London, the best part of two hundred miles away and with darkness starting to fall.

Being totally inexperienced in the art of hitch hiking we got onto the first lorry that stopped for us regardless of where it was heading for as long as it was going eastwards, a fatal mistake made by most "Nig" hitch hikers. Future experience was to teach me that you decide upon your route and religiously stuck to it. You didn't accept lifts from vehicles proceeding along another route in the hope that you could turn it to your advantage somehow or other at a later stage of your journey.

The lorry took us away from our best route to London and dropped us off in a lane on the outskirts of Taunton. We walked into Taunton without gaining a further lift, found that there was a train for London at 2:00am and decided to wait for it. So ended my first attempt at hitch-hiking.

I eventually arrived home at 7:00 am, managed to break into

the house and woke Doreen up, much to her surprise. The look on her face was worth all the trials and tribulations of the night journey. If the truth were told however the pleasure of being home was completely overshadowed by my disappointment at failing W.O.S.B.

All too soon the weekend flew by and once again I found myself on the 6:00 pm train out of Waterloo, Honiton bound.

The very next morning I found that I was subjected to the discrimination that befalls a failed W.O.S.B. man on his return to Honiton. The failures were immediately segregated and placed in the Holdees' platoon and I found myself on full-time fatigues pending my posting to trade training at Arborfield. Instead of being served at snowy white table-clothed tables by orderlies as of a few days ago, I found myself washing and cleaning in the Sergeant's mess, and other equally delectable jobs. Oh how the mighty had fallen!

The W.O.S.B. successes on the other hand were required to place a white disk behind their cap badge, don their best B.D. They were then detailed to help the permanent staff train the new intakes to "D" Company whilst awaiting their posting to O.C.S. As far as I could see there was no reason why the failures could not have helped in this task also and at least have left Honiton with some dignity. As it was the discrimination between the two groups could not have been more complete. People that you had been working cheek by jowl with for the past three months appeared to be encouraged to ignore you. To compound my failure at W.O.S.B, I felt that I was being kicked by the Army for that failure.

On assessing the circumstances of those of our number that had passed and those that had failed W.O.S.B. I began to analyse my own failure in some detail. I came to the conclusion that I had attended W.O.S.B. under some major disadvantages. One, I was married; two, I had been to work; three, I had not already "signed on" for an extra year (that in some eyes would have made me a regular soldier); and four I had attended a Grammar School not a Public School.

I don't think that the latter would have mattered too much if they hadn't been combined with the other three factors. Finally I came to the conclusion that I, like others in similar circumstances, had failed W.O.S.B. before I even got there. It could be that I was making excuses for my failure but I don't think so.

Even Omerod the relative of the DME failed W.O.S.B. I often wonder what would have happened if he had let it be known that he was related to the D.M.E.? He said that he wasn't interested in obtaining a commission that way. I admire him for that! The foolish fellow.

One glimmer of consolation in all this gloom was the fact that the "Holdees" platoon was commanded by Captain Warren, a Korean War veteran. He appeared to sense this inequality between the two groups of personnel and did his best to lessen the blow for us W.O.S.B. failures for our remaining time at Honiton. He decided for instance to pull a group of us out of the general fatigue pool and put us on constructing command tasks that were more akin to those to be experienced at W.O.S.B. With our recent experience he considered that we were the ideal people to design and construct such tasks.

We would have a conference with him, he would give us an outline of what he wanted, he would then leave the rest to entirely to us, only occasionally visiting us to see how we were progressing. If anyone queried the work we were doing and attempted to put us on other jobs we were to refer them to him. Under no circumstances whatsoever were we to stop the work in hand. I have respectful memories of Captain Warren, at least he realised that we were reasonably intelligent people capable of working on our own initiative in spite of having failed W.O.S.B.

We had even greater respect for him when we found out that whilst in the Korean War, his "home" for two years had been a packing case, albeit a large one!

There is one further incident which took place prior to my leaving Honiton which is worth relating.

In the execution of our command tasks we required the use of a hatchet. I knew there was one in our hut, so I went to get it. On my way back to our working party I was hailed by a Major who wanted to know what I was doing taking an axe away from a fire point? Up until that point I hadn't noticed that the axe had a red handle and could be construed as being part of a fire point. I attempted to explain the situation but him being a Major and me a mere Private he wasn't going to listen to me. He took my name and number, confiscated the axe, and informed me that he was putting me on a charge for taking an axe away from a fire point, a very serious misdemeanour or so he informed me.

So on top of failing W.O.S.B. it now appeared that I was about to be charged! When I got back to the others and explained why I hadn't got the axe with me, they thought it a great joke. The axe it appeared was nothing to do with a fire point, it was the "Holdees" own personal equipment for chopping up firewood. The fact that it was painted red was merely one of those things they informed me, which probably meant that it was the only colour paint that they had been able to scrounge! On hearing the good news I decided to go to the Company Office to find Captain Warren. Not finding him there, in trepidation I explained the situation to the C.S.M. instead.

He smiled quite broadly, "What was the name of this Major, Skinner?" he enquired.

"Major Brown, Sir" I replied.

"Hm, "B" Company. Right wait here Skinner," he ordered, and reaching for his polished pace stick, marched smartly out of the office.

Within five minutes he was back again, complete with the red handled axe.

"There we are Skinner," he said handing the axe over to me. "Your axe I believe?"

"Yes Sir, thank you Sir. Am I still going to be charged Sir?"

"No of course not, forget it. It was all a mistake. Mark you it would help matters if you painted the bloody thing a different colour. Better get back to work now otherwise you will have Captain Warren chasing you."

As I left the office I heard the C.S.M. muttering, " I wish that bloody Major would get things right just once in a while."

The last fortnight spent at Honiton before being posted to Arborfield was, in spite of Captain Warren's reasonable attitude towards us one of the most distasteful periods of my Army service. I felt as if I was being treated like a second class citizen. As indeed I was. Any enthusiasm that I may have had for the Army drained from me entirely. Henceforth I sat down to count with ever increasing dread the days to my demobilisation, in six hundred and forty days' time. Even a further forty eight hour weekend leave instigated for our group by Captain Warren in recognition of our good work did little to cheer me up.

Eventually my posting went up on orders. On September 22, I was up at 05:00 hrs. to catch the 07:00 hrs. train from Honiton along with five others en-route to No's 3 and 5 Training Battalions at Arborfield, near Reading, for trade training me as an "ECE", whatever that was.

On arrival at Waterloo station where we had to change trains I telephoned Doreen at work. At least I now felt a little nearer to home than I did at Honiton.

CHAPTER 10

IN WHICH I ARRIVE AT
NO.5 TRAINING BATTALION, ABORFIELD

Eventually after picking up some more personnel from other units on the way half a dozen or so of us arrived at Wokingham station to find the duty truck waiting to whisk us off to Arborfield, some destined for No.3. Training Battalion and some for No.5. Training Battalion. The duty truck driver, who was from No.3 Battalion, took great delight in extolling the easygoing atmosphere at No.3 compared with the "Bullshit" conditions that prevailed at No.5. I shrugged my shoulders with indifference, meaning that I would wait and see.

After about a ten-minute journey we arrived at the entrance to Hazebrouck barracks, home of No. 5 Battalion

"Here we are lads, No.5 Training Battalion", called out the driver.

Cyril, a compatriot from Honiton, and I, tumbled out from the back of the lorry whilst the others very helpfully handed out our kit to us.

"Good luck", said the driver. "By God you'll need it there", he retorted.

"Cheerio", the rest called out in unison from the back of the lorry.

"Come down and see us sometime, if they'll let you. If it's as bad as the driver says it is you'll need the rest!" Roars of laughter came from the rear of the vehicle as it drove off down the road to No.3 Battalion, the apparent Utopia camp.

We gathered up our gear and found ourselves at the entrance of a very impressive looking barracks indeed. All our other camps had been a collection of timber shacks, but what confronted us now really looked very comfortable indeed. In the immediate vicinity, however, we were confronted by the usual swing-pole barrier across the road with a fairly smart regimental policeman standing outside an adjacent sentry box. Behind him was the inevitable guardroom and opposite him on the other side of the road, was a further building that we later found out to be the battalion armoury.

We gathered up our equipment and approached the sentry. He viewed our approach with indifference.

"Yes?" he queried.

"We've been posted here from Honiton", I replied.

"Report to the Provost Sergeant in the guardroom", he ordered.

We entered and found the Sergeant sitting behind a bare trestle table in a room that was decorated in the usual cream painted brick walls and doors. On the Sergeant's far right we caught sight of the iron bars of the cells.

"Stand to attention in the guardroom", he rasped, without even looking up. "Names?" he queried.

"Skinner and Smith from Honiton Sergeant".

"Right", he said, consulting a list on the table in front of him. "You've both been posted to "B" Company. Out of the guard room, turn left, turn left again at the square, "B" Company office is the second office on the left. And march there don't amble. Understand?"

"Yes Sergeant."

"Right, on your way." We hurried out from the chilly atmosphere of the guardroom. We didn't know it at the time but we had just met Sergeant Gill, who along with his son, Corporal Gill and the regimental police, ruled the camp with a veritable rod of iron.

We found "B" Company office on the edge of a huge drill square, which we viewed with dismay, we thought that we had left "square bashing" behind us at Honiton. Clearly we were wrong. After reporting to the Company office we were allocated accommodation in barrack room No.28 in an impressive brick built barrack block on the other side of the square. First however, we had to go to the stores to draw out our bedding and to endure the first of many kit checks that appeared to be a feature of Arborfield and the Army in general.

On being subjected to my kit check it was discovered that I was missing a pair of pyjama trousers. Where I had lost them was beyond me. As any short fall of equipment had to be made good immediately by the purchase of new by the loser at his own expense, I was very dismayed by this discovery. It would mean the loss of about ten shillings (50p), or a week's wages, to me. In this instance however, a very understanding Quarter Master Sergeant invited me to look through a pile of clothing he had in a corner to see if anything suited. I found a virtually brand new pair of pyjama trousers.

"These fit Sergeant."

"Good."

"What do I owe you for them Sergeant?" I queried.

"If they fit you can have them, but don't lose anything else. I might not feel so generous in future.

"Now run off before I change my mind."

"Thank you Sergeant."

His last instruction was easier said than done, in view of the fact that I had to gather up all my equipment before I could even stagger off, let alone run. Eventually however, Cyril and I did manage to lurch off in the general direction of the barrack block in F.S.M.O. with our kitbags across our shoulders and our bedding tucked under our arms. It was fortuitous that we only had a couple of hundred yards to negotiate, as even in that short distance we kept dropping various items as we made our unsteady way towards our designated accommodation, passing well manicured lawns and neat flower beds on our way!

The barrack block was a revelation in comfort compared with the timber huts we had just left behind at Honiton. The building that we now entered was three stories high, brick built, with bathrooms and toilets on each floor and eventually even boasted a library on the ground floor. The whole was in pristine condition. I should have realised there and then who kept it so. It was, I learnt later, only built in 1941.

Barrack room 28 turned out to be one of the largest in the complex and had accommodation for approximately 15 people and was situated on the first floor.

Judging by the rolled up mattresses only half the beds appeared to be occupied. At that time of day there was only one person in the room sitting on his bed, who it transpired, was only at Arborfield on a short two week course on Bofors guns.

In the absence of the Room Corporal, he suggested that

we chose whichever empty beds took our fancy. I wasn't too sure about this arrangement and although I chose a bed I didn't intend to unpack until I had checked it with the Corporal, who it turned out to be an easy going half-caste person on the permanent staff, whom I was to find never seemed to be around when required, and took little interest in anything that went on in the room. His main interests were birds, the human type, and his membership of the battalion rugby team, in that order. Whenever he was missing he was on rugby training, or so he said, and no one ever appeared to query it.

I sat on the bed and took stock. The room was well decorated, with painted walls and woodwork, and a highly "bulled!" hardwood floor. There were even shades on the electric light bulbs. At first the absence of heating bothered me. It was later that I discovered that the central heating was in fact electric heating coils embedded in the concrete floors.

In between each bed was a varnished clothes locker, and at the foot of each bed was a green painted bed box. On top of the lockers was the usual layout of personal webbing equipment surmounted by the steel helmet. In one corner I noted a heavy looking floor "bumper" with a tin of polish alongside. Clearly there were no housemaids here.

In one direction the room overlooked the drill square with a good view of the camp's timber offices. In another, a view of the rugby pitch framed in the distance by a collection of tatty Nissen huts and other buildings, which turned out to be the classrooms, and the so-called laboratories, along with the predictor shed. These poor looking buildings were all in great contrast to the one in which I was now sitting.

I was on "Orders" that night to attend an interview with the R.S.M. the following morning. That evening however, I sampled the camp N.A.A.F.I, which in addition to the normal refreshment facilities on the ground floor, boasted table tennis and snooker tables, and television on the first floor. My first impressions of the camp as a whole were very favourable indeed.

The next morning I resisted my overwhelming desire to go on muster parade that was held on the square, and instead watched the shenanigans from the barrack room. There appeared to be a lot of bullshit for a trade training camp.

At 10:.00hrs, Cyril and I paraded outside the R.S.M's office for interview. He turned out to be a portly middle-aged person who made it quite clear to us, in a very short time, that he ran a very tight ship indeed at No.5 Battalion. He went on to say that, "Anyone transgressing battalion discipline will be dealt with very severely". He then stared at us for a moment or two before speaking again.

"And you can start by having your sideboards shaved off immediately. I will not tolerate sideboards in my battalion."

"Sideboards Sir?" I queried in surprise. I never considered that I had any.

"Sideboards. You know what sideboards are lad; they're any hair in front and below the top of the ear. You've both got them. Get them shaved off immediately. Understood?" he rasped.

"Yes Sir." we replied.

"Good."

I was also to find out in very quick time, that amongst many other facets, he wouldn't tolerate was any hair on the back of the neck, below the top of the ear.

I got the distinct impression that he thought he was running a battalion in the brigade of guards, rather than a training battalion in R.E.M.E. He went on to say that we couldn't wear civilian clothes until we had been in the Army for six months and were in possession of our permanent passes. And that he would deal very severely with anyone contravening this order.

Finally the R.S.M. informed us that we would be on course AA46 which started next Thursday. The course would last for approximately six months. In the intervening time we would be on fatigues under the general control of the Provost Sergeant. I left his office with the impression that he was another person playing a game with us, a game which he clearly enjoyed playing. The trouble was that he had enormous power for someone who was only playing a game. This factor became more and more evident the longer I was at Arborfield until we had our day!

We reported to the Provost Sergeant and were directed to report to the Staff Sergeant in the gun shed, where we would work until our course started, carrying out various odd jobs, but in the main skiving as there wasn't really a real job of work to do.

We gleaned the information that people not yet on a course could apply for a forty-eight hour pass for their first weekend at Arborfield. We tackled the Provost Sergeant on this point, and in an unenthusiastic manner said he had to apply for them for us and would do so as soon as he had a moment to spare. We had little confidence that he would pursue the subject, so as a double indemnity, so to speak, we applied directly to the Company office for them ourselves. We therefore worked all day Friday on tender hooks, speculating on whether or not there would be passes waiting for us at the end of the day. When at 05:00 hrs. we ventured into the Company office to make enquiries, we were both surprised to find the passes waiting for us. It was then a matter of scrambling down to Wokingham railway station, and home, where I arrived at about 8:00pm that evening.

Once again that weekend, I experienced the total pleasure of being at home and making decisions for myself, instead of being constantly dictated to with no right of reply. Even the simple act of wearing civilian clothes was an enormous pleasure to me. All too soon however the weekend came to an end and I found myself making tracks for Waterloo station. This time however, I didn't have to leave home until about 9:00pm as opposed to 5:00pm when I was returning to Honiton. Unfortunately, when I arrived at Wood Green tube station, I found that I had missed the last tube train to central London. Without hesitation I stepped into the road and hailed a car for a lift. In no time at all I was speeding into London, such was the sympathy shown by the majority of the public towards we National Servicemen in those days.

An unusual scene confronted me however when I arrived at Waterloo station. The platform for Wokingham departures was intriguingly empty except for a great gaggle of people halfway down the platform. When the train arrived, even more intriguingly, they insisted in cramming themselves into that part of the train closest to them, whilst the rest of it remained relatively empty. I couldn't understand why they did this, and I chose a compartment in the empty part of the train for my journey back to Wokingham giving the matter no further thought. I then settled down for an hour's doze.

When we arrived at Wokingham station there was an astounding frantic rush of personnel to get off the train and out of the station. It was then I realised the reason for personnel concentrating themselves in the middle part of the train. It was this part of the train that stopped more or less opposite the exit to the platform, thereby giving these people a quick getaway from the platform. I waited for the crowd to clear, then strolled past the ticket collectors and out of the station. Outside I found that two coaches that ran a shuttle service between the station and Arborfield were now full and about to depart. This was clearly what the rush was all about. I was now confronted with walking the three or four miles back to camp, or waiting for the coaches to return from their first run. I decided on the latter course and was eventually in bed just after midnight.

I subsequently found that there was a mark chalked on the platform at Waterloo station that denoted the position of the exit at Wokingham station and that to ensure a seat on the coaches for their first run back to camp it was essential that you occupied a compartment as close to this spot as possible. Sometimes British Rail, very unsportingly, put the corridor side of the coach adjacent to the platform. With only three or four doors in the whole of the coach side, getting out of it quickly therefore became critical. The moment the train entered the station it was an amazing spectacle to see personnel bailing out of the coach doors as it swept along the platform, in a similar manner to that of paratroopers exiting an aircraft, being helped on their way by the efforts of the people still behind them. Experts could judge the distance to an inch, they would jump from the coach with feet flailing at tremendous rate, fly through the exit gate, handing their ticket, or an authentic looking substitute, to a startled looking ticket collector, on their migratory passage to the waiting coaches on the road outside.

Once I had got the hang of the situation I never failed to gain a seat on the first run of the coaches, with one exception. The exception was the night that I, and a large group of fellow travellers, jumped off the train paratrooper fashion, as it drew level with the platform, rushed to the exit to find it boarded up. We were stopped dead in our tracks, with all the other travellers pressing from behind. What the hell was happening? Then we heard the dulcet tones of the R.S.M. calling out above the hubbub.

"Will all troops form a column against the wall and let the civilians off the platform first. You're not a civilian Green, get over there against the wall." This, to an unfortunate Green, who was trying to sneak off the platform with the only two civilians that were on the train. I looked around the platform in the gloom and realised that as well as the C.S.Ms of "A" and "B" Company, the platform was swarming with Military Police, presumable brought in from Aldershot. Everyone appeared to be yelling and shouting instructions at the same time, much to our confusion...

The R.S.M. took command of the situation. "Quiet," his voice roared out in the night air. "An exit has been established at the far end of the platform. All personnel will approach it one at a time. The ticket collector will take your tickets and the Military Police will check all passes.

Some anxious people looked around for an escape route, to find that the Military Police were guarding them all. For once the Army had got organised and executed an efficient plan, unfortunately for us.

I wasn't worried though. I had a ticket, and I hadn't sold any duties that weekend, I was fireproof. There were some of us, however, who weren't, mostly for not being in possession of a valid ticket. It took over an hour to clear the platform and I didn't get to bed until after one o'clock in the morning. Many people ended up on a charge that night, coupled with a possible civilian action for travelling without a ticket.

It transpired that the reason for this heavy handed action was that the previous weekend, one of our illustrious "paratroopers", on leaping off the train, had misjudged his timing completely and had gone straight through a plate glass window alongside the doorway. British Rail was upset by his action, and to add insult to injury, the person was minus a valid ticket. British Rail decided to act and consulted the Army over appropriate action. The result is what I have just described. A Sunday night spectacular at Wokingham station.

Life prior to starting on the course at Arborfield wasn't too bad. No muster parades, a little light work in the gun shed from 08:30hrs until 12:30hrs, with a mid-morning N.A.A.F.I. break of half an hour. An hour for lunch, then an afternoon from 13:30hrs until 16:15hrs. when we were finished for the day. Not being on course appeared to mean not being on a duty roster either. Halcyon days.

A very welcome fact was that there was no booking in and out of camp, which bearing in mind that over fifty percent of the camp perimeter lacked a fence was not surprising. What was surprising, however, and typically Army, was the fact that it was forbidden to exit or enter the camp other than past the guardroom, one of the few places where there was a fence. This was a rule that was naturally flagrantly disobeyed by all and sundry.

CHAPTER 11

IN WHICH I START ON COURSE

The following Thursday I started on course. I immediately found that I was way out of my depth on the subject of electrical engineering and electronics. Most people around me appeared to have at least a Higher National Certificate in the appropriate subject, and many had a degree. As far as I could establish, I was the odd one out with an H.N.C. in Building.

I arrived at my first D.C. theory class to find that the lecturer was a National Serviceman Lance-Corporal.

"Now clearly," he explained, "I don't want to bore all of you by starting from scratch and going over stuff that you all know, so I'll start off by putting a few problems on the board for you to solve. We'll see how you get on with them and from that we'll decide at which level of DC theory we need to start at. Okay? Good?"

The Lance-Corporal, probably acting unpaid, proceeded to draw some diagrams on the blackboard. Everyone around me immediately set about solving the problems, I being the exception. I looked at the hieroglyphics on the board with bemusement.

"Excuse me Corporal," I queried, "what is that swirly thing you have shown there?"

That's a coil," he replied. "Oh, I'm sorry I've drawn it very badly." He proceeded to rub it out and redraw it, this time a little more clearly.

"Okay?" he queried.

I shrugged my shoulders. "Well what's that thing that looks like two W's joined together?"

"That's a 16 ohm resistor," he explained.

"Oh. And what's that other thing next to it?" I asked.

"That's a capacitor. You probably know of it as a condenser."

"I probably don't know of it as either," I explained...

At this point I noticed that most people in the classroom were looking up from their work and smiling at me. The Corporal deducing, incorrectly, that he was being set up, came charging over to me.

"You trying to take the piss out of me?" he demanded.

"No, Corporal, of course not."

"Well it bloody well looks to me as if you are." He then looked at the blackboard from where I was sitting. "It all looks clear enough to me. What the hell's the matter?"

"Well Corporal, apart from the fact that I don't know what a resistor is, I don't know what a coil is, and I certainly don't know what a condenser or a capacitor is, there's no problem at all."

"What do you mean you don't know what they are. I understand that you have a Higher National Certificate, with distinction in fact." He was remarkably well informed I thought.

"Yes Corporal, I have."

"Well, what's the problem?" he queried

"My Higher National happens to be in building studies. My civilian job is a reinforced concrete detailer I explained."

"What!" he exclaimed. "Well what the hell are you doing here then?"

"Better ask the Army that, not me Corporal."

By this time everybody in the classroom had stopped working. Mainly, no doubt, because they had completed the simple, to them, exercises and were now listening intently to the conversation that was taking place between myself and the Corporal. All had broad grins on their faces.

Clearly the Corporal was used to having a class of people who knew the subject inside out and at the worst was merely called upon to refresh some people's memories on the first principles that had perhaps been long since forgotten by them. In my case, however, he was actually going to have to teach me the subject. Something that in subsequent days I was to find he was not equipped to do. He could talk about the subject, but he was unable to teach it. As time went on, I was to find this particular inadequacy in many of the so called lecturers I was to encounter on the course. This inadequacy did not apply to the many Staff Sergeant lecturers however, who were often very good, if indeed a trifle terse. This first lecture was mercifully, for me, brought to an end by the N.A.A.F.I. break.

After the N.A.A.F.I. break we assembled in the camp cinema where we were entertained by a film on the V2 rocket. The film, whilst being very interesting, seemed to bear no connection whatsoever to the course in hand. Subsequently I was to find that whenever we were scheduled to be shown a film on, say AC or DC theory, Servos, or indeed any other subject associated with the course, we always ended up seeing this film of the V2 rocket. Now whether or not the projectionist, for reasons best known to himself, didn't wish to show the relevant film and preferred to show the V2 film, or whether he had lost, or more likely sold the films in question and didn't want to tell anyone, I shall never know. All I do know is that after we had seen the film for the second or third time, we knew it inside out, and all entered into the little game the projectionist was playing with us, and gratefully used the opportunity to have half an hour's sleep, which was extremely useful if one had been on guard the night before.

Friday the first of October was the R.E.M.E. birthday. In the morning there was a parade on the square at which I was thankfully only a spectator. From a spectator's point of view I was reasonably impressed. After lunch, in theory at any rate, the time was set aside for sports. Being a newcomer to the battalion, and not knowing the ropes, much to my disgust I was gripped for fatigues for the afternoon. Then to add insult to injury, I was posted on orders for Wokingham Town Patrol that evening from 20:00hrs until 24:00hrs. For this duty I had to parade at the guardroom in best BD, boots, and gaiters, and with another private, was handed a nice blue armband ,with the letters "RP" (Regimental Police) emblazoned thereon in crimson, by the patrol Sergeant who invited me to slip it on my right arm and join him in the duty truck. The three of us were then driven down to Wokingham town centre.

The general idea of the patrol, I discovered, was for the three of us to keep law and order in the town by preventing any hell raising activities that members of the Arborfield Garrison might attempt to start, in order that the good citizens of Wokingham could sleep easy in their beds that night.

After being dropped off from the lorry we made our way to the police station and presented ourselves to the Station Sergeant, informed him that his estimable force was being reinforced for that night at any rate, by our three-man commando force, and as nothing was likely to happen until the pubs turned out at 22:30hrs, would it be in order for us in the meantime, to retire to the social club at the back of the station and play a few games of snooker first? The Police Sergeant readily agreed to this suggestion.

At about 22:30hrs, after having lost every game of snooker that I played, and having made my half pint of shandy last all evening we went out on patrol. My vision of the three of us, aided and abetted of course by constables of the local constabulary, fighting with hordes of drunken squaddies, thankfully never materialised. In the event we found the town extremely peaceful and we didn't in fact meet a single person in uniform, drunk or otherwise. As the town clock struck midnight, the duty truck rolled into the town square to pick us up and take us back to camp, where our Sergeant entered a "no incident" report at the guardroom. I then made my way back to the barrack room where I attempted to get into bed without waking anyone up, a virtually impossible task.

I was led to believe that there was never any trouble in Wokingham from garrison personnel and that the Wokingham town patrol was completely unnecessary and a waste of time and resources. The same could be said over the Arborfield road patrol and the Reading town patrol. I have a sneaking feeling however that somewhere the "powers that Be" thought that these needless patrols were good for discipline.

I think it is worth noting that when on these patrols, other than the diminutive "RP" arm band, we had nothing to denote the fact that we were on police duty and yet I was led to believe, that in theory at any rate, we had similar powers to the Military Police. Perhaps if we had been issued with white cross belts and a revolver on the hip, loaded or not, we may have felt, and been able to act, the part. As it was I always felt something of a joke when detailed for these patrols.

The next morning the whole of the Company paraded outside the Company Office and was detailed off for fatigues. The work for the whole of the morning was designated technical cleaning, and consisted of cleaning out and polishing all of the classrooms. If the work had been organised efficiently, we could have been finished inside the hour. But as it was decreed that we were on fatigues for the whole of the morning, the work had to take the whole of the morning. Army logic!

Came 12:30hrs I skipped lunch and hitchhiked into Reading to meet Doreen. Due to the fact that I was on guard on Sunday, we had decided to spend Saturday afternoon together as some consolation for not getting home for the weekend.

On these occasions we would usually have lunch, take a walk down by the river, have some tea and then go to the cinema. By the time we came out, it would be time for Doreen to catch a train back to London, and for me to hitchhike back to Arborfield, having spent just over eight hours together. If this sounds romantic, remember we had only been married just over six months.

Next morning at 07:45hrs, I paraded in best BD, belt and gaiters for guard mounting. Sunday guard mounting was the only day when one complete guard of eighteen persons was relieved by another guard of eighteen persons. At all other times a guard commander handed over to the Regimental Police, which was merely a matter of signing a book. Sunday mornings were a different matter however. The R.S.M. had taken the opportunity for instigating a guard mounting ceremony outside the guardroom at the entrance to the barracks. If we had been carrying rifles it might have been of interest to passers-by but as we weren't I considered that the ceremony fell flat on its face. Nevertheless we had to go through the motions of the ceremony as the R.S.M. lived in the house opposite the entrance and there was always the possibility that he was watching the performance through the net curtains of his bedroom window.

It had been rumoured that he had a mirror rigged up to enable him to watch the proceedings whilst lying in bed, but I found this hard to believe.

Our ceremony over, we settled down to twenty three hours of absolute boredom. Basically the guard consisted of a Sergeant or Staff Sergeant Guard Commander, a Corporal deputy, and a guard of sixteen other ranks. The guard was divided into two groups of six and one of four. The two groups of six would patrol separate areas of the camp in pairs, with two hours on duty and four hours off. The group of four would, in turn, stand sentry in the box at the entrance gate for two hours, with six hours off.

The extra two hours off duty was, I believe, to recompense for the utter boredom of this particular duty. The off duty hours, night and day, had to be spent in the guard room and as there was no accommodation for such a large guard, this necessitated spending the off duty hours in the cells usually reserved for prisoners. No undressing was allowed as the guard was liable to be called out at any time by the Orderly Officer, usually in the middle of the night. A decent Orderly Officer however would tip the wink to the Guard Commander as to the time he would be coming to turn out the guard. A not so decent Orderly Officer would also do this but then turn up at a different time just to try and catch everyone out! In any event it was up to the sentry at the gate to keep a weather eye out for the approach of the Orderly Officer and warn the guard commander accordingly through the buzzer connecting the sentry box to the guardroom.

As soon as the sentry saw the Orderly Officer approaching he would "buzz" a pre-arranged signal to the guardroom. This would be the signal for frantic activity within as people were woken up and hastily prepared for the forthcoming inspection. The officer would ask the sentry to "turn out the guard", who in turn would yell out "stand to the guard", he would then wait as long as he dare with the officer breathing down his neck before uttering "guard turn out." The longer the sentry delayed the more time the guard had to prepare themselves before turning out, which was crucial, as if the turnout was, in the Orderly Officer's eyes, slow, he would declare himself dissatisfied and inform the guard commander that he would return and call out the guard for a second time later that night. Or if he didn't do that, at the very least when he inspected the turned out guard he would find some minor fault with the guard's uniform, which seeing that they had been slept in wasn't very difficult. He would then have the individual in question charged for being improperly dressed on parade, or some such charge.

The guard, in theory, was supposed to be armed with pick handles, but for some unknown reason these had long since disappeared but nobody thought it worthwhile reporting the fact. In the meantime these pick-handles were signed for each time there was a change of guard even though everyone knew they didn't exist. We therefore went on guard totally unarmed, whether on patrol or as a gate sentry.

If you were gate sentry there was no chance whatsoever of you skiving off your duty as you were in the full glare of publicity standing at the barrack entrance, immediately outside the guardroom, where at night the sentry box was floodlit. If on the other hand you were on patrol around the camp things were different. You had the opportunity of breaking into a classroom and keeping one of the coke stoves going for warmth. Or you had the possibility of creeping back to the barrack room for a couple of hours in bed. Either of which could be very welcome on a cold night with six inches of snow on the ground. In this latter instance however you needed an alarm clock to wake you up much to the annoyance of the other occupants of the room to enable you to get back to the guard room at the appropriate time in order to wake up your succeeding patrolmen happily sleeping away in the cells, to take over from you.

Clearly any skiving off should not have taken place. I put forward the excuse however that the people on guard may have had an exam to take the following day and wished to get some sleep to enable them to be fresh for that exam. Even if they hadn't exams to take, they would have lectures to attend that they wanted to stay awake for. Nevertheless these people were around the camp even if they spent some of their time in a classroom or barrack room. Another point is that, in theory, the patrols were meant to be relieved away from the guardroom at a pre-determined place. This was meant to obviate the possibility of all the guard being in the guardroom at the same time. It was a security measure that to my knowledge was very rarely adhered to by those in charge. In general terms the guard duties at Arborfield were carried out in a lax manner. I believe that it is unfair to lay the reason for this problem at the feet of the National Servicemen for their indifferent attitude towards the Army, as was so often inferred whenever a problem was encountered. In matters such as guards we only took a lead from our regular counterparts who were far more experienced than us over such matters, or at any rate should have been, if they were any good!

I consider the fact that the Army authorities insisting on

personnel combining a fairly tough course of study with full regimental duties was the cause of most of the ills at Arborfield, including the one of indifferent or lax guards.

Duties at Arborfield were carried out by "A" and "B" companies on alternative weeks which in theory at least meant that every other week you should have been free from duties. This rarely happened however as supernumerary duties, such as, Heath Fire Piquet, etc., were often given to the "Off Duty" Company. But more on the subject of duties later on when the whole subject blew up in the Army's face sufficient to say at this stage, that most people found the duties imposed upon them at Arborfield iniquitous

If I found myself with a weekend duty then I would "sell it" to someone who didn't wish to go home for one reason or the other. This person would have to impersonate me on whichever duty he was standing in for me. The usual price for a Sunday guard was about £1.10s (£1. 50p) which to me was three weeks' pay at the time. Quite a price to pay for going home for a weekend, a price that I thought well worth paying.

When carrying out a duty for someone else, it wasn't unusual for the person concerned to forget the name of the person he was substituting for, which often caused some amusement when the roll call was being called in the guardroom. The guard commander having called out say "Green" three times without response, would when he got a response at the fourth time of asking, walk up to the individual concerned and ask him if he was sure that his name was "Green"? When he got the reply "Oh yes Sergeant, sorry Sergeant, I didn't hear you. The Sergeant would walk away shaking his head in disbelief, Knowing full well he hadn't got the genuine Green before him. Rarely however would a guard commander take any further action he would play the game along with everyone else, as long as he had got the right number of personnel he wasn't too worried, why should he be? Or so we asked ourselves.

This myriad of duties that we were called upon to perform at Arborfield soon caused me to lose my initial enthusiasm for the camp. I came to the same conclusion as the majority of the people at Arborfield, that No.5 Training Battalion was a pretty unpleasant place to spend your National Service.

The only factor which that helped me get through the week was the thought that with any luck, at mid-day Saturday I would be free to go home. This factor coupled with a forty eight hour leave pass every fourth weekend and a long leave pass of seven or fourteen days every so often were the only events that made my days at Arborfield bearable,

Relief from this overbearing tedium however came from a very unexpected quarter. I was spending a 36 hr. leave one weekend at our newly acquired rented flat in Wellington Road, when I was suddenly taken ill, Doreen called our doctor. A very old friend and neighbour of the family, who with a twinkle in his eye , decided that I was too ill to return to camp that night, directed me to bed and issued me with a sick certificate to be sent to the Army authorities. "Sick of the Army", I would have thought would have been the appropriate diagnosis. My illness lasted for three amazing weeks, our doctor issuing certificates at the appropriate time for me to send back to camp.

To this day I am sure that he certified me sick to give me a break from the Army. Having served four years as an officer himself in the war he probably had some sympathy for my situation. Or perhaps I really was ill and didn't realise it. Either way it was three weeks that I should have enjoyed, unfortunately it was a period of mild terror for me. I never really believed that the certificates that I was sending back to camp made me fireproof, every time I glanced out of the window I fully expected to see a pair of military policemen marching up the front path with the intention of arresting me for desertion or some such charge. I even had bad dreams of it happening to me.

This worry was totally unfounded because at the end of the three weeks when I eventually returned to camp and with much trepidation and reported my return to the C.S.M, he looked me full in the face and merely retorted, "Oh so you've decided to come back to us have you Skinner? As I thought that we might not see you again I had your bedding and equipment put into the stores, you'd better go down there and collect it before it closes otherwise you will be sleeping on bare springs tonight and that will never do, will it?. Oh and you'll have to report sick in the morning for the M.O. to give you the once over, alright?"

"Yes Sir, thank you Sir." I replied and hurried away out of his sight in double quick time.

Had I realised when I was at home that this was the only reception I was going to get on my return to camp, not only would I have enjoyed my three weeks, and I would have done my best to have had my stay extended. The only real consequence of my three weeks at home was that in view of the tuition I had missed it was decided to "back course" me onto Course AA48. This was the start of my prolonged stay at Arborfield.

CHAPTER 13

THE IRA STRIKE AT ARBORFIELD

On the night of 12th/13th August 1955, the battalion achieved national prominence when the guard room and armoury were attacked by six armed raiders belonging to the Irish Republican Army. I read this news in the newspaper sitting in bed in Cambridge Military Hospital, Aldershot, where I was spending a period of time having my ankle examined after I had damaged it for a second time in the Army. This time on a concrete block whilst running to the "Gaff" (cinema) one night.

Apparently the guard of eighteen men had been overpowered by six armed IRA men and locked in the cells; remember the guard was totally unarmed, the raiders then eventually forced an entry into the arms store and magazine. I found out, years later when reading a book on the subject, that they removed 3 rifles, 10 Bren-guns, 35 Sten-guns and 80,000 rounds of ammunition. The civilian police later apprehended two of the raiders on the 16th August and recovered all the arms and ammunition from premises in the Caledonian Road, London.

The immediate over-reaction of authority was to put a Company of armed soldiers, approximately 120 men, on guard each night, which meant that most personnel were on guard every other night. As well as the usual guard of eighteen soldiers in the guardroom, other ad hoc patrols were instigated around the camp, some even on bicycles. Dress for these ad hoc patrols was, surprisingly enough, denims and plimsolls. No bull, all guards were issued with five rounds of ammunition and allowed to actually load their rifles! The lads loved this real life situation and entered into the game with spirit even if in their eyes it was a case of closing the stable door after the horse had bolted. In spite of the relative seriousness of the situation some idiotic Orderly Officers immediately started playing games with us by attempting to creep up on guards with the intention of taking their rifles away from them. After an Orderly Officer, acting in such a clandestine manner was shot at by one of the guards who said he thought he was in danger of being attacked by a member of the I.R.A.; the whole question of guards was reviewed and revised.

The ad hoc guards were immediately abandoned but the guard room guard remained but now increased to forty per night and armed with rifles and live ammunition. I returned from hospital to find this the situation at Arborfield. Due to my hospitalisation however I had to report sick and was awarded 14 days light duties which thankfully precluded me from being available for guard duty.

I then gradually gleaned the real story of what happened on the night of the 12th/13th August.

It was early in the morning when the gate sentry was approached by a person in overalls and sporting a beret who levelled something resembling a revolver at him and instructed him, in a strong Irish accent, to "put his hands up". Thinking he was a soldier returning from a late night drinking spree, the guard suggested that he stopped playing silly buggers and went to bed. Then out of the corner of his eye the guard noticed that other men were coming up behind him out of the shadows. He took another look at what they were holding in their hands and realised that they really were holding revolvers and put his hands up. He was then directed to precede the group of armed men into the guard room, where the guard, being totally unarmed, were easily overpowered and locked in the cells. As the patrolling guards came into the guard room to be relieved they also were placed in the cells. The armed raiders then set about obtaining the keys of the armoury from the guard commander, who was incidentally an ex-Enfield Grammar schoolboy. After knocking him about and still not obtaining the keys anyway, they went across to the armoury and easily forced the lock. They then emptied the contents of the armoury into a waiting van and drove off.

After an hour or so the guards managed to free themselves and sound the alarm, which at Arborfield consisted of hitting empty shell cases situated at strategic points around the camp, with a steel rod. The battalion assembled on the drill square as required in such a situation. When they were told by the guard commander that they had been raided by the IRA I don't think that anyone on parade believed him. They just thought that it was a ruse to get them all up in the middle of the night. After an hour had passed by and no one in authority had turned up to explain the situation people became bored and wandered off back to bed.

It was subsequently rumoured that when the Orderly Officer was woken to be told that the IRA had raided the camp he took no notice, thought it a hoax and went back to sleep. Was his face red in the morning when he found that there really had been a raid and that he had ignored the message given him. He didn't get any "jankers" however only an increase in Orderly Officer duties!

There was an official inquiry. Amongst other things it was rumoured that the guard commander was to be court martialled for not reporting the missing pick handles, the ones that had been missing for some years. As if pick handles would have been effective against revolvers anyway! The gate sentry, a National Serviceman, was censored for not pressing the warning buzzer. When asked why he hadn't done so, his reply was that he hadn't wished to be a hero least of all a dead one. Sensible man, he spoke for all of us. We all felt the same way, we weren't prepared to die for 28/-per week. The court martial never materialised, I believe that was because there would have been too many red faces in high places. The guard commander was merely posted to another unit.

Eventually we reverted back to a nightly guard of eighteen. persons as before the raid, the difference being that we now stood guard with rifles and ammunition, well kind of! We paraded with rifles at guard mounting and were inspected with such, when we entered the guard room we were even issued with five rounds of ammunition which we were ordered to put in our map pocket and only load into our rifles when told to do so. If we had been raided again it was the general consensus of opinion amongst the chaps that we wouldn't wait for an order to load our rifles. But at least we felt a little more like soldiers, and safer, with a rifle and five rounds in our possession whilst in the guard room. I say whilst in the guard room, for when it was our turn to actually go on guard, either on patrol, or as sentry at the gate, we had to hand in our rifle, our five rounds of ammunition, and our bayonet, which were then ceremoniously locked in one of the cells by the guard commander. In their stead the gate sentry was issued a short truncheon, and the pairs on patrol were handed either a whistle or a truncheon, with the strict instruction that the man with the truncheon must walk

25 yards in front of the one with the whistle. If the guard with the truncheon was attacked, the second guard was to blow his whistle, to what purpose we weren't sure. In any case, needless to say, it was extremely difficult to keep your eye on a person 25 yards in front of you on a dark night!

When one or two "Wags" amongst us asked the guard commander what we were to do if the guard with the whistle was attacked first, we were told not ask such bloody stupid questions. Clearly that contingency hadn't been thought through. And no there wasn't any possibility of us all having a truncheon and a whistle each. Again on asking why we were going on guard with a whistle or truncheon rather than our rifles we were informed that it was because, that way it would then be murder if we were killed by the IRA, whereas if we were armed with rifles it wouldn't be. The majority of us considered that we would far rather take our chance with a loaded rifle rather than a whistle or a truncheon, murder or no murder. Naturally we were overruled. Talk about "lions led by donkeys"! On the other hand when we pointed out that the guard, rifles or no rifles, when called out in the middle of the night, was extremely vulnerable to attack, lined up outside the guardroom under floodlights, the "donkeys" did appear to take notice of what we had to say and the procedure was changed. Now after the guard mounting ceremony, the procedure on entering the guard room was that we were issued with a numbered disc. The numbers referred to defensive positions marked on a plan of the guard room hanging on the wall, we were to adopt these positions when alerted by the gate sentry instead of lining up outside the guard room, a reasonably rational idea. The positions allocated were all fairly sensible as well, such as guarding a window or doorway, all lights having first been doused both inside the guard room as well as those outside.

If the call out was a routine inspection by the Orderly Officer he would content himself by inspecting us in our defensive positions. A far more sensible procedure than that previously called for. We were still very unhappy however about going on patrol or gate sentry with only a whistle or truncheon. Eventually the arrested IRA men were put on trial at Reading Court and it was strongly rumoured that the IRA intended to bomb our camp as a show of strength whilst the trial was on. Over the period of the trial in particular, I took guard duty very seriously indeed. It was at this period in time that I got quite a reputation for being a right bastard whilst on gate sentry, all identity cards had to be shown by everyone on entering camp, and I made sure that they did with no exceptions and so did most other people.

One Sunday morning the R.S.M. went to stroll into camp.

"May I see your identity card please Sir?" asked the sentry.

"Don't you recognise your own R.S.M.?"

"Yes sir, you certainly look like him to me Sir, if I see your identity card it will prove it Sir."

"Damn it man I don't have to show my identity card to enter my own camp."

"I'm afraid you do Sir, I have orders to check the identity of everyone entering camp Sir."

"What if I refuse on the grounds that you obviously know who I am."

"Then I'll have to call out the guard Sir."

"You'd do that?"

"Yes Sir."

"Well done soldier," said the R.S.M. pulling out his identity card for scrutiny by the sentry. "Well done."

These were the idiotic farces we had to endure in our everyday life at Arborfield.

Whilst all these farces were going on however we were still having to continue with the main reason that we were at Arborfield, our studies to qualify as Electrician Control Equipment technicians. I was still finding the course extremely difficult to comprehend, truth to tell however, I wasn't prepared to study in the evenings as some of the chaps were doing. I considered that the amount of work I would have to do in my own time to keep up with the course just could not be remedied by studying in the evenings for the few hours that were at our disposal bearing in mind all the duties that we were now expected to carry out in parallel with our studies. It was not unusual for instance for half the class to be asleep during a lecture due to the fact that they had all been on guard the previous night. It would mean another lecture that had to be made up in your own time and as I say I was not prepared to do this. I considered that if the Army wanted technicians then it should have cut down on the duties to enable us to study.

In my defence however it is worth noting that at this stage of the course I had passed the technical drawing and workshop practice exams at the first time of asking. The former exam consisting of drawing simple mechanical items and the latter of making items out of metal by soldering and various other means. I had also passed at the second and in some instances the third attempt exams in, maths, AC theory, DC theory, electronics, machines, servos, and test gear. Other than maths all the subjects were related to electrics or electronics, all subjects were split between theory and practical. The theory side consisting of lectures and note taking, the practical side consisting of using the theory knowledge to make up electrical circuits in the laboratories to run various pieces of equipment, and as we progressed, actually making up the pieces of equipment as well. Most of the practical sessions were carried out in groups of three or four persons and as I usually found myself in a group where the others knew the subject so well that they had the circuit or piece of equipment made up and working before I had time to blink I didn't learn too much at these sessions. Lectures were usually of an hour or so in length and given in the cold and dreary Nissan huts with only a coke fired stove to heat them. We sat on hard wooden fold-up seats at six feet long trestle tables. One way of bringing a boring lecture to an end was by kicking at the stays of the table in front and thereby bringing it crashing to the floor. The practical sessions were carried out in brick built laboratories, so called I suppose because they housed quite a lot of equipment. These laboratories were warmer than the Nissan huts and were better furnished with laboratory style benches and high stools. Lecturers were split between what appeared to be civilians, and Army personnel.

The Army lecturers varied from National Service Lance-Corporals up to Captains in rank, and varied in quality from hopeless to very good, all were reasonably informal. Even the officers would usually enter the classroom and sit on the table out front, with a cheery, "Morning lads, don't stand up," followed by such banter as to how many people he could expect to fall asleep in his lecture that morning due to the fact that they had been on guard the previous night? He would eventually decide it was time we got cracking and launch into his lecture.

I say he, because the lecturers always were male until that particular morning when a W.R.A.C officer walked in. Female starved as we were in camp, even we could see that she looked like the back of a bus so she didn't have the impact upon us as she might have done had she been attractive. We waited for the cheery, "Morning lads, don't stand up," routine that we were used to. Instead she just stood there in a pregnant silence.

"Well," she said.

Well what, we thought.

"Don't you stand up when an Officer comes into the room?" she demanded.

We all reluctantly clambered to our feet.

"Well," she said for a second time,

We looked at each other mystified.

"When an Officer enters the room surely you say good morning sir or ma'am as the case may be," she said by way of explanation.

She was wearing a skirt so it was probably ma'am in this case.

"Good morning ma'am," we sang out in unison, and sat down.

"Stand up," she screamed, "You only sit down when I tell you to."

We stood up once again and received a ten minute lecture on manners mixed with a smattering of Army regulations.

Eventually she gave the order for us to sit, which we did.

Suddenly, much to my surprise, everyone in the classroom appeared to be as ignorant as I was on the subject under discussion and the lecture was interrupted every few moments by complicated questions. It soon became evident that "ma'am" was out of her depth and I believe that she was very thankful when the time came for her to bring the lecture to an end. That female officer never delivered any further lectures to our class. We were a wicked lot of buggers at heart!

From the classrooms we graduated into the searchlight and gun sheds where we were let loose upon and learnt about some of the equipment we might encounter in our service life, once we were qualified and posted to an operational unit. I even managed to struggle through both the theory and practical exams connected with these items of equipment and at last I found myself in the hallowed halls of the predictor shed. The specialised equipment that only E.C.E.'s were trained to work on. The particular predictor I was called upon to train with was the No.10. Predictor, a British invention.

I had always been aware of the "Sword of Damocles" that had hung over me all the time I had been on course. If I failed the E.C.Es course at Arborfield I was likely to be sent on a vehicle electrician's course at Great Malvern, something I didn't want as it was too far from home. Consequently every so often I would make an effort and pass an exam just to try and stay near home at Arborfield. It was a very fine line that I was treading and on more than one occasion I was called before the course officer to explain my failures. After which I would surprisingly be left on course, or at the worst be back coursed. But at last I was on the final stage of my journey, I was actually in the predictor shed. At this point however, fate intervened in the form of Major Toombes the Company Commander. I was ordered to appear before him to explain my dismal performance to date at exams whilst on course.

"You have been called before me Skinner because Captain Wild, (the course officer), informs me that you aren't trying on your course. What have you got to say for yourself?"

"I find it extremely difficult to understand the subject matter of the course sir."

Which was very true. I was no electronics specialist, and never likely to be.

"Nonsense" you're not trying."

"No sir, I find it difficult to understand the subjects."

"Nonsense, you're not trying. You're a well educated person. You could do it if you wanted to, you're not trying I say."

Then his piece de resistance!

"Do you know how much it costs the tax payer to keep you on this course Skinner?"

"No sir."

"I'll tell you. Twenty five pounds a week. That's a lot of money!"

My piece de resistance!

"Does that include my twenty eight shillings a week pay Sir?"

He went purple in the face and exploded. I got the distinct impression that I had said the wrong thing. I only have vague memories of what happened next. After a severe dressing down I was eventually dismissed. As I left his office, I thought: Great Malvern here I come. Perhaps it's for the best anyway. But no, much to my utter amazement I was only back coursed to AA52. I was to be given one last chance to redeem myself. My, the Army must have really been short of control equipment electricians!

Consequently I reviewed my situation. I had just two further exams to take, predictor theory and predictor practical, and I had seven weeks to prepare for them. I decided to give it my best shot and prove to both the Army and myself that I could have coped with the course all along if I had wanted to. It's just that I hadn't wanted to.

When however, I opened up the back of the No.10. Predictor for the first time and saw the mass of wires, valves and other equipment inside, I knew I had a fight on my hands. In passing it is interesting to note that boy soldiers spent three years covering the self-same course as the National Servicemen and on entry into "man" service, came on our seven month course as a refresher before being passed out. Even so they always came bottom of the class – except for me of course. Was I ashamed of myself? Yes, I suppose I was really, but then they intended to make a career of the Army, I didn't. These seventeen or eighteen year old Boy soldiers were a curious mixture of pomposity and bravado gained from their boy service but often lacking in adult type thinking. I recall two such boy soldiers who joined us, who started throwing their weight around from day one. They were quick to inform us that one of them had been an R.S.M. and the other a C.S.M. in boy service, they swaggered around as if they still held these exalted positions.

In my inevitable way I informed them that they may have held those ranks in boy service but they were now in the real Army, amongst men, it would be as well if they forgot about their ranks in boy service. They took no notice and still attempted to throw their weight around much to everyone's amusement. I took every opportunity to bait the pair of them, more so as they were never seen apart.

One evening I was sitting in the barrack room writing home, with only a tough "Brummager" called Bill Farmer in the room, when in walked the ex-boy R.S.M. accompanied by half a dozen ex-boy soldiers. I smelt trouble.

"Okay chaps this is the bloke we want, let's get him," said the "R.S.M." nodding towards me at the table.

"What's this all about then," I queried in a calm voice I didn't feel.

"We're fed up with all the remarks you're making about us and we intend to deal with you."

"I see, this is what happens in boy service is it, eight against one?"

"Come on let's get on with it lads.

"At this stage I was extremely surprised and disappointed to see Bill Farmer, gradually making his way to the door where he eventually sat on an adjacent bed watching the proceedings with interest, presumably with the intent of making a quick getaway if things got too hot. On reflection I couldn't blame him, the problem before me was after all of my own making. He wasn't really involved.

"Hold on a minute. So you're going to do his dirty work for him are you?" I said addressing the rest of the group, who were now sitting on beds around the barrack room.

"You're about the same size as me," I said addressing the "R.S.M", if you're so intent on getting me how about you doing it? "Just you and me, alone?"

"Oh come on lads let's get on with what we came to do."

"Let him do his own dirty work." I interjected, "I'm quite prepared to have a set to with him hut I've no argument with the rest of you." and with that I returned to my writing with a show of bravado I didn't feel.

"Let's get him lads, don't let him put us off." He spoke to a group of now not so enthusiastic ex-boy soldiers.

I carried on with my writing and pretended to ignore the conversation that was going on between the "R.S.M." and his compatriots.

Sensing this rising lack of enthusiasm amongst the "R.S.M's" followers, I looked up from my writing with a little more confidence and addressed the group.

"Don't get involved with something that doesn't concern you."

I pointed to the "R.S.M". "I'm quite prepared to settle any differences with him, here and now, surely he's big enough and ugly enough to look after himself without requiring your help."

The group almost nodded in agreement. I'd won them over.

"Now get on with it, or bugger off before I get cross," I said quietly to the "R.S.M.".

He was about to appeal to the group one last time, saw their lack of enthusiasm and instead said. "If we have any more problems with you we'll be back. Come on lads let's go." And with that they all made their way out of the room,

I sighed a sigh of relief and looked across at Bill.

"Cor' I thought we were going to have some fun there," said Bill.

"Fun, and you ready to bunk out of the door."

"Bunk out of the door! what do you mean?" he said with a hurt look on his face, "I was ready to lock the door to stop the buggers getting away," he retorted, producing the barrack room door key in the palm of his hand. "Those pratts would have been no match for the pair of us." I was astounded at Bill's confidence in me. He was tough but I was far from sure about myself. I was just thankful that the shove hadn't come to a push!

Thereafter the ex-boy R.S.M. and C.S.M. appeared to me to go about the camp with just a little less swagger than previously. That was an incident that could have ended in a fight but happily for me didn't. Out and out fights in the Army were in my experience few and far between. I believe that this was due in the main to the fact that I was in R.E.M.E. and that the majority of personnel in the Corps, and National Servicemen in particular, were thinking people and didn't see fighting as the way to settle a dispute. There were exceptions to this way of thinking however and two of the regimental policemen were two such exceptions.

The happening I am about to relate came hard on the heels of the N.A.A.F.I. strike. There was the general feeling that one of the two policemen agreed with the action that we had taken, and with the outcome of relaxation of some of the discipline that we had been enduring. The other, we believed, considered that we should have been ground into the dust, and instead of discipline being relaxed it should have been tightened up. Whatever the true reasons for the dispute between the two policeman we were all of the opinion that one of them was a reasonable chap in his attitude towards us, whereas the other was a right bastard. So when it was announced that the two of them were to sort out their differences by a fight on the "Bridge" of the barrack block at 19:00hrs that evening there was a rush to get a good view of the proceedings.

The spot chosen was at the intersection of three corridors so was reasonably spacious, it also had the advantage that stairs rose from the area on one side forming a miniature grandstand. A further advantage was that the chosen spot was far away from prying eyes, consequently the fighters were most unlikely to be disturbed once the fight started. By the time I arrived it was only with difficulty that I found a vantage spot due to the fact that there were already some fifty or sixty persons crammed into the area, and the combatants had yet to arrive. The crowd was beginning to become restless believing that we had all been victims of a hoax, when a cheer went up along the corridor and the two policemen appeared, forcing their way through the crowd. A number of people took control and moved the crowd back to form an area for the two fighters to perform in. The two, who were dressed in their khaki trousers and shirts and wearing plimsolls on their feet, faced each other in the "ring". One of them threw the first punch and they were away in earnest both flailing like windmills with no quarter given. I had never witnessed such a vicious fight in all my life. Soon blood was flowing freely from both of them, and in no time at all the two of them, not to mention the floor, were smothered in blood.

It soon become evident that the crowd was delighted that two of the unpopular Regimental Policemen were knocking Hamlet out of each other and the cheering was indiscriminate. Gradually however the Policeman who we considered to be the more reasonable of the two started getting on top, so we ceased to be indiscriminate and cheered him instead. After all he wasn't a bad chap compared with the one that was getting the worst of it. And it was probably a wise move anyhow to cheer the person who appeared to be coming out on top. I think it's called Insurance!

After the good guy had knocked the bad guy down two or three times and was standing over him with blood pouring from his nose imploring him to get up so that he could knock him down again, the bad guy on the ground said that he'd had enough. A cheer went up from the assembled crowd. The two battered hulks made their way through the crowd back to their respective rooms. Some enterprising person produced a mop to clean the floor of the incriminating blood, and the rest of us dispersed in a state of excitement over that which we had seen. The fight was talked about for weeks after.

The amusing aftermath of the fight was the sight of two very battered policemen standing sentry outside the guard room for some time to come. How they explained their condition to the Provost Sergeant we never discovered. But then the Provost Sergeant was so thick he probably didn't even notice that they were so battered.

HONITON

No maid to do this each day.

"The Digs" - Honiton.

"The Mob" 26 BTN.
Would be officers!!

Join the army!!

The Prison Arborfield.
Spring 1955

No. 10 Platoon - for better or worse.

The Old Hut 11
D.M.E.S. Insp 31.8.54

'D' coy contingent - "Thargent Thuff" on the left.

'D' & 23040258, pre Skinner.

Are we unhappy in the army? Yes!

The rugger pitch Arborfield

The boys at W.O.S.B. No.108 passed.

Michael's car plus passengers. Thames, Reading on
one of our boating afternoons.

Henley on a June evening.

Stick orderlies!!

The nigging!

Gen; McMuddle of the
White Watch.

10 Pltn's dinner? Smart eh?

More "nigging" but
we weren't guilty.

PLYMOUTH

Entrance to Royal Citadel

The RoyalCitadel

The Emergency fuel stock

Finandoes Hidaway? - No, Mine Bill & John's.

Royal Parade, Plymouth.

The Barbican from the Citadel.

Cannons, Royal Citadel.

Battery of 9.3"s at Lentley

Bill & I, "Room mates"

'D' & I, Douglas I.O.M. Xmas 1954

CHAPTER 12

LIFE AT ABORFIELD

The next morning I skipped muster parade and reported sick as instructed. The M.O. without even examining me pronounced me fit for duty and dismissed me forthwith.

I got lost until N.A.A.F.I. break, after which I found out where I could join my new course AA48, I introduced myself to the lecturer and settled down at the back of the class to listen to the lecture to see if I understood the subject any better second time round. I thought this to be extremely unlikely!

What I did understand however whilst in conversation with other course members was the fact that AA48, to my great dismay had been placed on recess duty over Christmas. This meant that I now faced the prospect of spending the holiday in camp with leave being taken over New Year instead. Fine for those who lived north of the border, but not so good for me who lived south of it.

I immediately sought out the C.S.M. to see if the situation could be altered in my instance.

"Excuse me Sir; may I have a word with you?"

"Go ahead Skinner".

"Because I have been sick on leave I've been back coursed to AA48, and I find that they are on recess duty over Christmas Sir."

"Yes Skinner".

"In view of the fact that I have only joined the course today Sir, does that apply to me?"

"Of course it does Skinner," replied the C.S.M." Why shouldn't it if you are now on that course?

"But Sir, I was going to the Isle of Man for Christmas to see my Wife's parents."

"I'm sorry Skinner but these unfortunate things happen to soldiers," he said with a twinkle in his eye.

"But Sir I keep telling you I'm not a soldier, *I'm merely a civilian in uniform*, but you won't take any notice of me".

He gave me a wry smile in reply "Think of the advantages of being here at Christmas, Skinner. You might even have me serving you your Christmas dinner, and after that you will be able to spend

New Year in the Isle of Man.

"Yes Sir".

I left the Company office with that downtrodden feeling. A couple of days later I was once again in the Company office discussing with Captain Slater, the Company Administration Officer, travelling time for my New Year's leave to the Isle of Man when he very surprisingly informed me that in view of the fact that I had only just joined AA48, I wouldn't be required to do recess duty at Christmas after all, and that I could still go on leave as if I was on my previous course. To say that I was surprised would be an understatement, I just couldn't believe it. Neither I nor anyone else seemed to get on with this particular Captain, as he always seemed to have the knack of sorting out which policies would upset the men most, then going out of his way to pursue those policies. He was the most unpopular officer in the Company and yet here he was telling me I could go on Christmas leave when I had thought all was lost, and saying it with a smile on his benefactorial face to boot when he told me. I hurried out of Company office on cloud nine.

The days up to Christmas passed with agonising slowness. Each day I expected to be called back to the Company office to be informed that Captain Slater had changed his mind, such was his reputation. Thankfully no such message came.

On the run up to Christmas we had a series of pantomimes and concerts, where fun was poked at most people in authority from the CO. downwards without seemingly any fear of retribution. I often wondered however if notes were not made in some people's little black books somewhere, for future reference.

After the pantomimes and concerts we then had a grand pre-Christmas clean up of the barrack block in particular and the camp in general. At last at 14:00hrs on 22nd December we found ourselves drawn up outside Company office ready to receive our leave passes.

Pay books and passes were then distributed to the assembled congregation, whereupon a large number of people realised that their leave hadn't been entered up in their playbooks, which of course was to their great advantage. These people felt that they had been given a Christmas bonus in more ways than one.

Captain Slater came out of Company office to address us.

"Everyone got their leave passes?"

"Yes Sir", we yelled in unison.

"All leave correctly entered up in your pay books?" he queried...

"Yes Sir" from those who could see that it was

"Right", he said, I'm coming round to inspect all pay books, if I find any pay book without the leave entered up, that person will not go on leave, understood? Right, now one last time, has anyone not had his leave entered up?

About thirty people owned up to the fact that they hadn't, and made their way very grudgingly towards the front and Captain Slater.

"Ah", he exclaimed with broad grin on his face. "Just as I thought. Right into the Company office and get the clerk to enter it up, and tell him that I'll want to know what went wrong with his system when I see him. Right, all pay books ready for my inspection."

He then proceeded to scrutinise each pay book most carefully, knowing full well that we were all bursting to get away from the camp and be on our way home. This procedure held us up for nearly half an hour. Eventually however he pronounced himself satisfied, he then wished us a merry Christmas and gave us the order to dismiss. This order was complied with in double quick time, by the parade evacuating the camp in every type of conveyance possible, bus, taxi, motor bike, a few private cars, and even bicycles. In less time than it takes to tell, "B" Company had totally disappeared on Christmas leave.

Doreen and I spent the seven days in the Isle of Man at her parent's home. The most memorable part of the leave was arriving in Liverpool in the early hours of the 24th December to find a gale blowing in the Mersey River and the steamer rocking up and down at alarming angles whilst still tied up to the jetty. The Captain not unnaturally decided not to sail until the wind abated. Doreen and I coincidentally met up with a couple who both knew us from our respective schooldays, with whom we passed the day going to the cinema in the town, and generally trying to pass the time of day awaiting a decision to be made by the Captain over when the steamer would sail for the Isle of Man.

Eventually we settled down to sleep on the boat, but were woken up in the night by the violent movement of the boat. We were on our way. It was the roughest journey I have ever undertaken to the island. After the rough boat journey we had a pleasant enough seven days leave on the island, even if the New Year appeared to hold more sway than Christmas over there. Unfortunately the time flew by and the leave was over almost before I realised it had started. All too soon I found myself back at Arborfield wondering once again why time spent on leave went so quickly compared with time spent in camp.

I arrived back at camp to find that all my course compatriots were by this time on their New Year's leave, I found myself on fatigues for the next seven days until their return. Aided and abetted by another soldier called Neil, very little was achieved by us that week, much to the displeasure of the C.S.M. for whom we were working. Taking the lead from Neil we skived off every job we were given, or at the best took about ten times longer carrying out a job than was reasonable. The C.S.M. often lost his temper with us that week over the small amount of work we got through but never took the matter further than that. On reflection I am not very proud of the manner in which I spent that week, as the C.S.M. was a very fair minded man and we must have tried his patience to the utmost. But then in our defence he was still the Army after all. Incidentally I met Neil some 12 months later at the Plymouth N.A.A.F.I. Club one evening, and he appeared to me to have taken his skiving too far, he was awaiting his discharge from the Army on medical grounds, to me he appeared to be completely round the bend. I think he had taken things a little too far! Either that or he was an extremely good actor!

Nevertheless my actions that week did not prevent me from going to see Captain Slater to request that I be excused muster parade on January 1st to enable Doreen and I to spend the night together on 31st December to celebrate our first wedding anniversary. Consent was given without demure. I then hurried down into Wokingham and booked a room for the night at a local hotel, where we stayed after having been to the cinema first.

1955 had arrived and with it the realisation that I could now look forward to the prospect of being demobbed next year, which didn't seem half as bad as the situation a few days earlier when the prospect had been the year after next. Little things like this meant a lot in the Army, even so it was going to be a long slog to June 1956.

I settled down to a new year at Arborfield, where the week days seemed to drag by with agonising slowness in spite of all the duties heaped upon us, and weekend home leave seemed to be over before it had even begun.

The duties were now becoming very onerous indeed. Guard Duties, Wokingham Town Patrol, Reading Town Patrol, Arborfield Road Patrol, Internal Security Platoon, Fire Piquet, Heath Fire Piquet; and general fatigues when the mood took those in authority.

Although I wasn't keen on any of these duties the one I detested most was Fire Piquet. You were usually on it for five to seven days and apart from being shown where the fire pump was housed and being told to assemble there in case of fire, this duty had very had very little to do with fighting fires at all. Each evening you were on duty, after having your name checked off at the fire point to ascertain you were in camp, you would then be directed to the cookhouse where you would be required to spend two to three hours cleaning pots and pans, and peeling potatoes, alongside people on "jankers" who were there for punishment!

As well as the increase in duties the R.S.M. became more and more demanding regarding his requirements for the morning muster parade. It now took on the Appearance of the trooping of the colour in the Brigade of Guards, or so I considered. The R.S.M. was no longer content to refer to platoons by numbers, he dreamt up names for them, from, to him, the glorious past. Because our platoon commander was Captain McKinder we were referred to on parade as "McKinder's Light Horse, other platoons had similar unlikely names. This only reinforced my thoughts on the matter that everyone in the Army was playing a game with us.

In particular the inspection of our working dress muster parade became more and more stringent especially if we were inspected by the R.S.M. His speciality was picking up people for having "twisted bootlaces". At first I couldn't understand what he was talking about. I then realised that he was referring to a twist in our square leather bootlaces as they passed over the tongue of the boot. One morning he was so incensed because a soldier, one of the permanent staff, had two "twisted bootlaces", that after asking the miscreant if he thought he was in the Chinese Army, yelled across the square to the guard room for the Regimental Police to come immediately and arrest the offender and place him in the cells, which they did. Apparently the R.S.M. considered that a twisted bootlace meant a twisted mind. I think he was right, we had the twisted bootlaces, but he had the twisted mind!

And if we weren't picked up for twisted bootlaces then it was the fact that our boots were not as shiny as they might have been due to the fact that they had been dubbined for nearly three months at Honiton. We just didn't seem to be able to win as far as the R.S.M. was concerned

That winter things went from bad to worse as far as so called discipline was concerned, this prompted the start of the famous or "infamous" hate sessions.

We would be sitting in our room of an evening when someone would come in to inform us that there would be a "hate session" on the bridge in five minutes time. The bridge being a particular part of the barrack block where it passed over the top of the dining room. We would all go along to the bridge, there were few dissenters, Pile into the adjacent rooms, and push open the windows. When sufficient numbers of people were hanging out of the windows, we would commence chanting.

"What do we all hate? We hate the Army. What do we all hate? We hate the bloody Army. Hate, hate, hate."

This chanting would go on, with certain impromptu variations, for some five minutes or so, until either we became bored or we heard the clatter of hobnailed boots coming from the direction of the guard room, as some of the guard was sent out to investigate the uproar.

These hate sessions became a regular feature of No.5 Training Battalion, occurring twice and some-times three times a week. I was reliably informed that on a still night our chanting could be heard two or three miles away across the fields at Barkham. Whether or not the locals ever inquired as to what was going on I don't know.

Very often the chanting was timed to coincide with the inspection of the guard by the Orderly Officer at guard mounting. I was on guard on one such occasion when the chanting started up.

"What on earth's that racket Sergeant?, Inquired the very young Second Lieutenant, Orderly Officer, who was in the process of inspecting us at the time.

"Oh it's the men having one of their hate sessions Sir. I shouldn't take any notice of it if I were you Sir", replied the mature Staff Sergeant Guard commander

The Subaltern looked startled. "Surely we should do something to stop it Staff?"

"It will soon stop Sir, after the lads have had their little game, you see if it doesn't.

An agitated Orderly Officer continued to inspect his guard.

Outside the chanting reached a crescendo, as presumably more people joined the chanters in the barrack block.

The Officer was just about to show one of the guard he was inspecting a minute strand of cotton he had found on the back of his B.D. blouse when he stopped his inspection. He looked at the Sergeant with a very worried look on his face.

"I really do think we should do something about this chanting Sergeant".

"Very well Sir, In that case may I suggest that you and I go up to the block to see what we can do. With all due respect I don't think there's any point in taking any of the guard along with us". With the hidden inference, I thought, that the Sergeant felt we might join the in the chanting! Five or ten minutes later after the chanting had stopped, a satisfied Subaltern accompanied by the Sergeant returned to the guardroom just in time for the chanting to recommence!

"I have recently read in the official R.E.M.E. history book, *"Hazebrouck Barracks and the origins of Electronic Engineering"* that as well as the chanting sessions the word "hate "was to be found everywhere, in drawers, under filing cabinets and ashtrays, and under the lids of stoves, behind pictures and cupboard doors, and on the last sheets of rolls of toilet paper. Even bulbs in flower beds were planted in the shape of the word". In my own experience I never came across any of these particular occurrences, only the chanting sessions in which I willingly took part."

Hate sessions or not the rigid discipline continued, and apart from the rare occasions when a sortie would be made from the guard room by an over- zealous and inexperienced Orderly Officer, very little direct action was taken to stop these hate sessions. It gradually became apparent to us however that discipline in the camp was being increased, whether or not this was an attempt to persuade us to stop these sessions I don't know. Regimental Police were now placed at strategic points around the camp and would place course representatives on a charge if they were not marching their class members between lecture rooms. Even when we were already marching we would be bawled at to swing our arms higher.

Course representatives incidentally, were meant to be elected by the course and were responsible for course discipline. It was a job to be avoided, as the position held many brickbats and as far as I could see held no advantages whatsoever. Very often no one was willing to be elected to this post and the position often had to be filled by direction of the C.S.M. or other persons in authority.

We then began to find that the Provost Sergeant, or one of his staff standing outside the N.A.A.F.I. which was some half a mile from any public thoroughfare, intent on charging anyone he considered improperly dressed, whether inside or outside working hours. Improperly dressed could mean as little as having a button undone.

The Regimental Police resorted to working at night, they would stand in the dark watching soldiers playing cards in their barrack room and, as soon as money changed hands, would burst into the room and charge the players for gambling.

Muster parades became an ordeal in the extreme, something to be avoided at all costs if at all possible. You always faced the prospect of being charged for some very minor offence, such as a twisted bootlace even when parading in a working dress of denims. It became dangerous to go more than seven days without a haircut, in fact it was the question of a haircut that caused me to find myself on my first charge.

I had had a regulation Army haircut by the camp barber just

10 days prior to the morning in question.

The R.S.M. was inspecting "McKinder's Light Horse" when he suddenly asked the soldier he was standing behind, "Am I hurting you soldier?"

"No Sir", replied the mystified soldier.

"Well I should be I'm standing on your hair, Take that man's name Sergeant.

The R.S.M. then took it upon himself to have some ten members of the platoon, including myself, to be charged for having long hair.

Persons on a charge had to parade "outside on the veranda" at Company office at 10:30hrs i.e. N.A.A.F.I. break. So not only did you have the ignominy of being on a charge you also missed the morning NA.A.F.I. break!

The ten of us paraded as required, ordered to remove our belts and berets, two unsuspecting passers-by were then roped in to act as escorts, and were placed at either end of the file of prisoners. The C.S.M. then gave the order for "prisoners and escort, right turn, quick march. Left right, left right, Halt, right turn, where we found ourselves facing Major Toombes, the Company Commander.

The C.S.M. read out the charge sheet, whereby it was confirmed that all ten of us had been on muster parade that morning with long hair.

"Thank you Sergeant Major," said the Company Commander. He then ran through all our names asking us in turn if we had anything to say for ourselves. None of us did.

He then stared us fully in the face, and with hair hanging over his shirt collar informed us that he would not tolerate long hair in his Company, and awarded us all two days "jankers" each. It was at this stage that I realised why all prisoners are ordered to take their belts and berets off before being charged! I would willingly have thrown mine at him the two faced so and so.

"Prisoners and escort, right turn, quick march, left right, left right. Halt." Thus called out the C.S.M. from the Company Commander's office. A few moments later the C.S.M. joined us.

"The Company Commander has graciously decided to reduce all of your sentences from two days to one day's C.B, to commence immediately" he informed us. "You will all parade at the guard room at 13:00hrs to be inspected by the Provost Sergeant. At 18:00hrs by the Orderly Officer, and at 20:00hrs by the Guard Commander."

"At 20:00hrs you will parade in best BD. boots and battle order , including your rifle, at all other times you will parade in working dress. You will be required to work in the cookhouse from 18:00hrs until 21:00hrs. Any questions?" There were none.

"Right, as soon as I dismiss you go straight to the regimental barber and get haircuts, otherwise you will find yourselves in further trouble. Dismiss."

Having missed N.A.A.F.I. break I hurried back to our classes. It was no good us all going to the barber at the same time. I'd see him at lunchtime before the 13:00hrs inspection.

I took that one day's C.B. very hard indeed. I resented intently being told that my ten day old haircut was not short enough for my Company Commander who clearly hadn't seen a barber for months. Once again I got the distinct impression that it was a case of someone playing a game with us.

The three inspections and three hours in the cookhouse were not however a game, they were serious. And here was I now with a criminal record, albeit only an Army one!

After the incident of the haircut, I, with Michael French a very good room- mate of mine, decided to go into the haircutting business. Because there appeared to be a market for it, and a captive one at that! We charged three pence a time I seem to recall and guaranteed it would pass muster parade the next morning. What we meant by that remark was, if it didn't pass muster parade we would refund the money or give another haircut free of charge. Not much consolation to someone languishing on a charge due to our haircutting, but then who could really give a guarantee that a haircut would pass muster parade? I had even known people to be put on a charge who had had a *Regimental* haircut the day before being put on a charge for requiring a haircut! The situation was stupid, and I think that the R.S.M knew it, but he insisted on playing his game with us, and he knew that we couldn't answer him back!

We were determined that our clients would pass muster

parade however and went to work with a will. We took off all hair below the top of the ears, but worked on the old adage, that everything under the beret was yours to keep".

Although we took the task seriously, well more or less, the bystanders in the barrack room did not. Roars of laughter would often greet our efforts which was more than slightly off-putting to our clients. Nevertheless we gradually became renowned for our haircuts. Which in our case meant that trade gradually dropped off, until it was non-existent. People preferring to be put on a charge rather than have their hair subjected to our butchery, or so they said. So much for our haircutting venture!

As the conditions in the camp became more and more oppressive, I took every opportunity that I could to leave these unpleasant conditions behind me. One such opportunity presented it each Wednesday afternoon, recreational training afternoon. Now that the weather had become warmer, instead of declaring to the C.S.M. on the sports parade that I was going to play basketball that afternoon, and then go into the gym by the front entrance and immediately out by the rear exit, and return back to the barrack room and bed, to sleep for the rest of the afternoon, I had now joined a running "club". I ran around the local countryside with a group of fellows for relaxation. We ran a very modest three miles or so and usually ended up in a small Café in the woods at a local beauty spot called for some unknown reason, "California". There we usually discussed such subjects as what we had done before being conscripted, and what we intended to do when our two year "sentence" finished.

This particular afternoon however the conversation centred on the Draconian measures that we were being forced to endure back at the barracks; we considered whether or not there was anything we could do to express our feelings over the situation without bringing swift retribution down upon our heads.

We decided that strikes in the classroom were out of the question, that would be deemed mutiny, or so we assumed, refusal to turn up at one of the three meals during the day could also bring punishment as apparently they were termed C.O.'s parades, and in any case we would go hungry, there appeared little we could do in the way of a worthwhile demonstration. Then we had a brainwave. What if we decided to boycott the N.A.A.F.I. one morning at N.A.A.F.I. break? If all those piles of sandwiches and sausage rolls and gallons of tea and coffee remained unsold, even for one morning, surely authority would sit up and take notice? So that is what the three of us decided upon, a N.A.A.F.I. strike. As far as we could see nobody could touch us for that.

In view of the fact that if anyone got wind of our plan, and took some form of evasive action to nullify the effectiveness of such a plan, we decided that the strike should be held the very next morning. We went back to camp to spread the news. As a protest against the prevailing conditions in the camp tomorrow morning there would be a N.A.A.F.I. strike, nobody was to use the N.A.A.F.I.

That evening I became very alarmed indeed as person after person came to our room to enquire whether or not it was correct that I was organising a N.A.A.F.I. strike for the following morning. I had visions of being hung drawn and quartered on the drill square in front of the Battalion. I strongly denied that I had anything to do with the strike, but did confirm that I understood that there was indeed to be one in the morning

To ensure that none of us would miss our refreshments next morning we purchased them from the N.A.A.F.I. that night.

The next morning, the 3rd March, a feeling of expectancy could be detected about the camp. Our message had clearly reached the ears of many people but would they react in the manner asked of them? Came N.A.A.F.I. break, instead of the classes of men being marched into the arms of the waiting Regimental Policemen at the N.A.A.F.I, almost without exception the columns of men wheeled in the opposite direction and made their way towards the barrack block. Once there we watched events from our first floor vantage point, as we drank our coffee and ate our buns.

Sergeant Gill the Provost Sergeant clearly mystified by the absence of customers in the N.A.A.F.I., decided to seek out and consult with the R.S.M. over the phenomena of the empty N.A.A.F.I Building. The R.S.M. and the Sergeant then marched back to the N.A.A.F.I to inspect the situation. The pair reminiscent of the "Grand Old Duke of York" then marched back to "A" Company Office and persuaded "A" Company's C.S.M. to join them. This illustrious trio then entered "B" Company's Office with the obvious intention of persuading C.S.M. Swan to join them, but when they emerged there was still only three of them. Our C.S.M. was not with them. I would like to think that he had a secret sympathy for our cause and didn't see that our boycott was anything to get excited about, but then on the other hand perhaps it was just that he wasn't in his office at that particular moment.

By the time this illustrious group had walked back to the N.A.A.F.I. it was time for us to go back to our classes, N.A.A.F.I. break was over.

We had no sooner started our lecture however, when the Company runner entered the classroom to inform us that all course representatives were required to meet in the camp cinema immediately. We all looked at each other in a questioning manner.

I found out later that on arrival at the camp cinema the course representatives found the Adjutant and the R.S.M. awaiting them.

The Adjutant started the proceedings.

"The R.S.M. has informed me that there has been a boycott of the N.A.A.F.I. this morning."

We found out later that the boycott was in the region of 90% successful.

"I wish to know if there is something wrong with the N.A.A.F.I. or were you trying to make some sort of point over something else?

Silence.

"Come on, come on, speak up somebody," demanded the Adjutant.

A very competent voice spoke up from the back of the cinema.

"It has nothing to do with the N.A.A.F.I. Sir, it was over the conditions that we are having to endure in the camp generally."

"Well in which case then I consider that your actions were extremely childish. There are proper channels for you to pursue concerning complaints."

"We've tried that Sir and got nowhere," said another voice.

"Well you'll get nowhere this way I can assure you," replied the Adjutant.

"I think we have already Sir." a voice called out.

"What!" exclaimed the Adjutant

"Well at least we are all here discussing the subject, which can't be bad, Sir," said yet another voice.

"Well I think that it's bloody stupid," replied the Adjutant.

"Before we go any further Sir, may we speak as man to man and not as Private to Adjutant, otherwise we won't really get anywhere Sir," called out another voice from the back of the cinema.

At this stage of the proceedings the R.S.M. leant over to the Adjutant and spoke quietly in his ear.

After a moment or two of this whispered conversation, the. Adjutant faced the meeting and spoke to it.

"I am going to depart now and leave the R.S.M. to speak to you," With that a slightly red-faced Adjutant got up and left the meeting.

The R.S.M. watched him depart and once he had closed the door, removed his hat and belt and placed them on a nearby table, and then stretched out in his chair.

"Right now lads what's this all about?" he queried.

"Man to man Sir?"

"Man to man." he assured us! In a tone that suggested he was genuinely interested.

"Well Sir we are absolutely fed up with the manner that we are being bullied about the camp by Sergeant Gill and his band of thugs called Regimental Police."

The R.S.M. gave a choking cough, then quickly recovered his composure.

"What exactly do you mean?" he asked in an interested manner.

The meeting in measured tone then gave the R.S.M. chapter and verse on what had been going on in the camp and he listened very intently. This took some 10 minutes or so with nearly everyone at the meeting having their say.

At the end of the dissertation he sat back in his chair and viewed the meeting with a grave look on his face. The meeting waited for the bomb blast. It didn't come. Instead much to our surprise, he answered in a very understanding manner.

"Lads believe me I didn't realise that all what you have just told me was going on. Clearly there must be discipline in the Battalion, you realise that. It would appear however that the Regimental Police have been going a little bit over the top by what you have just told me. You have my word that these activities will cease as from now. That being the case may I assume that there won't be any more N.A.A.F.I. strikes? He said with smile on his lips.

"Yes Sir you may", agreed the meeting.

"Good, and in future if you have any problems remember the door to my office is always open. We don't want any more episodes like this do we?

I think it went through everybody's mind that it would be a brave man indeed that took up that offer. The meeting ended; everyone dispersed and went back to their classes.

The R.S.M. was indeed as good as his word. The Regimental Police forthwith took a back seat, conditions whilst still tough became a little more bearable.

From our point of view we W.O.S.B. "checkouts" felt that as well as having won a round in our battle against mindless authority we had shown that we were still a force to be reckoned with. What we had done once we could, if necessary, do again. It is just possible that mindless authority also now realised this fact.

A fortnight later I attended my long awaited. second attempt at W.O.S.B. It was doomed right from the beginning both as far as my performance was concerned and indeed as far as the interviewing panel was concerned. My performance because I had lost any enthusiasm for the Army that I might have had when I attended W.O.S.B. the previous year, and the panel's because they didn't appear to have a clue over what they were supposed to be doing. They weren't even sure that they should be interviewing me in view of the fact that I had informed them that should I be successful I would be looking for a commission in the Royal Engineers not R.E.M.E. All in all I didn't think that the panel had been briefed very well as to what their purpose was. Anyhow the outcome was that the panel decided that I wasn't going to be given a second crack at a commission in any Corps or Regiment and failed me. I would like to think that the members of the panel were still smarting over our success in organising the N.A.A.F.I. strike and that was the reason that they failed me but in my heart of hearts I don't think that that was the reason at all. What enthusiasm I had for the Army when I attended W.O.S.B. last year had now left me and with the best will in the world I couldn't possibly be commissioned now; I had become a reactionary or so I thought.

In spite of this failure however, or perhaps because of it, I was detailed much to my annoyance, to drill with a squad of men early each morning to represent R.E.M.E. on the Queen's Birthday Parade at Aldershot on June 9th. A few mistakes, mainly accidental, made on rehearsals, soon got me relegated to the reserve benches which was much more to my liking

Came the morning of the parade however and the first choice squad of men was just about to board the lorry for Aldershot, when the C.S.M. suddenly spotted that one of the squad had a copper buckled rifle sling when all the others had brass ones.

"Greenway, fall out there. We can't have you going on the Queen's Birthday parade with a copper rifle sling, when everyone else has a brass one, can we?

Not if you say so Sir". Replied a very relieved Greenway.

"Ah, exclaimed the C.S.M. looking around at the various reserves, Skinner just the man, change places with Greenaway. I'm sure that you will jump at the honour of meeting her Majesty".

"Greenaway can borrow my rifle sling Sir," I said making as if to take mine off my rifle." I wouldn't wish him to be disappointed over a little thing like a rifle sling."

"No my mind's made up. The honour's yours Skinner, up on the lorry you go", he retorted with a smile on his face.

We arrived at Aldershot in the pouring rain, marched to the parade ground which turned out to be a huge field in Royal Avenue and took up our appointed position where we got soaking wet.

I had often heard people talk about seniority in the British Army, and that such and such Regiment was to the right of the line. I never really bothered to understand what they were talking about as it didn't really interest me. This parade forcefully explained it all.

Regiments line up from the right on such parades in order of seniority determined by the date of their formation. There were only two Corps to the left of our contingent, the Catering Corps and the W.R.A.C's!

The W.R.A.C's exercising their prerogative as women, were late on parade and held up the whole proceedings, much to the annoyance of the parade R.S.M.

Needless to say Her Majesty wasn't within a hundred miles of the parade and we were inspected instead by the G.O.C. Aldershot Command on horseback with an escort of Military Police lancers.

Each contingent had a mounted officer at their front. It is unfortunate that ours, not apparently being a competent horseman, had his horse pointing the wrong way at the time the G.O.C. was passing and looked ridiculous trying to turn 180 degrees in his saddle in order to face the G.O.C. when saluting him. You could almost hear the amusement from our contingent.

Eventually the inspection was complete and we started to march off the parade in the pouring rain past the saluting base with the parade band playing bravely alongside. Unfortunately just as we were drawing level with this band, the Parachute Regiment's band marching up the road at the back of the saluting dais started playing in a totally different time to the one at the saluting base. The result was a complete shambles as half of us marched to the time of one band and half to the time of the other. I don't believe that the G.O.C. could have been very impressed with our performance.

We arrived back at Arborfield, wet, hungry, and dejected, to find that whilst we had been on the parade at Aldershot the rest of the Battalion had been given the day off. The camp was virtually deserted. So much for the prestige of being a member of the R.E.M.E. contingent on the Queen's Birthday Parade. If there was some honour attached to it somewhere, I never felt it!

CHAPTER 14

SOLDIERING ON AT ARBORFIELD

With the coming of the better weather, I set aside my prejudices about wearing my civilian clothes in the Army's time and brought my clothes back to Arborfield. This meant that I could now wear comfortable clothes both inside and outside camp when not on duty. This had the great advantage that when out of camp no one could mark me down as being in the Army, I was to all intents and purpose a civilian. In effect I was free from military discipline for that time, I could pass by Military Policemen, Officers and other forms of authority with impunity. For instance one our little pranks would be for Michael to drive into camp in his 1932 Baby Austin, after returning from one of our drinking sprees in the surrounding countryside, with us all sporting our blazers, flannels, and corduroy caps. Having established that it was an obvious "Rookie" sentry on gate duty he would back up and confront the sentry face-to-face.

"Don't you recognise me soldier?" Michael would demand.

The usual response was for the sentry to immediately throw up a salute, at the same time apologising profusely for not recognising such an illustrious personage.

With a non-committal response of, "Hmm. Alright," Michael would then drive into camp.

At other times when he was really pissed, he would say, "Watch this lads," and drive up to the gate hooting his horn and in response to the sentry whipping up the barrier and at the same time trying to give us a smart salute, would give a regal wave to the poor unfortunate as we swept by into camp. I was certain that sooner or later we would be called upon to account for these pranks but as Michael said, "I'm doing nothing wrong, I'm not impersonating an officer, it's all in the sentry's mind".

I suppose he was right, I doubted however that the Army would view it that way. The edict to have to produce ID cards on entry to the camp stopped this little jape of ours of course.

Michael incidentally was Michael French, a roommate that I had teamed up with who was the very proud owner of an old 1932

Austin Seven. In company with a couple of other room- mates we would tour, in the evenings, the Thameside pubs of Henley, Sonning, and other such fashionable watering places.

Often we would be joined by John, in his much more modern 1947 Morris 10, and his pals most of whom were Public schoolboys. In contrast to Michael and me they used to dress in old ragged clothes and looked really scruffy. When I would query their mode of dress with them, their stock reply was, looking me up and down as they said it,

"If you've got the money old bean, you don't have to dress as if you have, but haven't."

Without a doubt they certainly had, presumably from their parents. However they were a good crowd and didn't care a hang about the Army authority or any other authority for that matter, an attitude that I admired.

For example we walked into a salubrious Henley waterside hotel one evening and when it became obvious that the evening dress attired waiters were clearly ignoring the group of us, a loud refined voice rang out across the lounge,

"I say waiter, eight halves of ale over here please." Whilst I curled up in my chair the waiter totally embarrassed by the outcry served us immediately. In view of the inordinate length of time we had waited to be served, most of the group, as a protest they said, walked off with the beautiful pottery tankards that their beer had been served in. I on the other hand, drinking cider, only had a common and garden glass as my spoils of war.

Next morning they brought these tankards down to breakfast from which to drink their tea. The orderly officer remarking on their magnificence, got the reply,

"Well it needs something to brighten up this bloody place sir."

The very young Orderly Officer who was clearly newly commissioned then changed the subject to the matter in hand and asked us if we had any complaints, about the food that is.

"You don't really want to know do you Sir?" drawled one of our number.

"Er, yes of course I do," mumbled an uncomfortable Orderly Officer.

"Well the food's bloody awful Sir, we complain but nothing is ever done about it."

"What exactly is wrong with it?"

"Everything."

"You have to be more specific than that!"

"What can be more specific than saying that all the food is bloody awful Sir?"

"Well, you have to tell me exactly what is awful about it."

"Taste that Sir," said John offering up his tankard of tea for the officer to sample.

"Nice tea that."

"But that's the problem, it's supposed to be coffee Sir," protested John.

"And very nice coffee too," replied the Subaltern, knowing full well that we were never served coffee, and proceeded on his way to the next table with a broad grin on his face.

The group baited every new Orderly Officer in a similar manner, and if he happened to be wearing his "Blues", which after all did resemble a bus conductor's attire to a certain extent, except for the sword of course, would send him on his way with loudly whispered, "Any more fares please, pass down the bus there, hold very tight please," And other such remarks. If the Orderly Officer heard them he certainly pretended not to. We all vowed that if we were ever an Orderly Officer we would never stand for such impudence!

Sometimes we would combine a drinking spree with a swim in the river first, and on Wednesday afternoons, for recreational training we would take a trip to the nearby river Thames either by car or bicycle and spend a very pleasant afternoon swimming and lazing by the river, then arrive back in camp in time for tea.

At other times we would make our way into Reading, present ourselves at the Working Men's Rowing Club, and for a few coppers each, take out a coxed racing four and spend a pleasant afternoon on the river instead of in it.

When on the recreational training parade outside Company Office and the various sports were being detailed off and we called out, "Rowing Sir," for the first time, the C.S.M. frowned,

"Rowing," he queried, "Where do you go rowing?"

"Reading Sir, Working Men's Club."

"Work, you don't know the meaning of the word. How did you manage to fool them?"

"Oh we have to pay sir."

"I should think so too for lying like that. Go on, away you go, I'll look out for you in the next Olympics."

One afternoon however when we called out, "Rowing Sir," and the C.S.M. was just about to send us on our way when Captain Slater emerge from the Company Office.

"Hold on a moment Sergeant Major," he ordered. "Ah! Skinner, just the man. As the MO appears to have excused you of all duties at the present time, I am therefore excusing you from going rowing this afternoon, I have a little job for you to do for me today," he informed me with a strong touch of sarcasm in his voice .

"Right rowing men double away smartly, Skinner stand fast," sang out the C.S.M.

Eventually with all the sportsmen having departed, I was left standing with a load of rookies who were clearly destined for fatigues that afternoon.

After consulting with Captain Slater, the C.S.M. stepped forward, "Skinner, upon you has fallen the honour," he said with a smile on his face, "Of marching these men over to the stores, presenting them to C.Q.M.S. Green, with Captain Slater's compliments and informing him that you and your men are his fatigue party for the afternoon. Away you go."

"Sir! Right you men," I commanded, "Form column of threes. Squad, squad shun, left turn, by the left quick march. Smarten up there," I ordered, "Swing those arms". And with that I marched the squad of men off to the stores under a blazing hot sun, with the C.S.M. looking on benignly.

I arrived at the stores, presented the squad of men to C.Q.M.S. Green, with Captain Slater's compliments, and then stood well back to watch developments.

Whilst the C.Q.M.S. was explaining to the squad what he wanted doing, I slipped behind a wall of the building out of sight. Hearing no outcry over my disappearance I marched swiftly away from the stores, gathered up my rowing gear from the barrack room, "loaned" a bicycle, and cycled out of camp, just at the same time as the C.S.M. was walking out. As we were both in plain sight of each other I couldn't ignore him

"Good afternoon Sir", I called out as I whizzed by on my bicycle

"Good afternoon Skinner," he replied shaking his head with a broad grin on his face.

There were no recriminations from the C.S.M. over this incident, such was the nature of the man. Unfortunately I was involved in a further incident almost immediately after this one, which again drew the name of Skinner to the attention of the C.S.M. Not a sensible thing to do. Reveille, had at about this time just been altered from 06:00 hrs. to 06:30 hrs. which was quite a concession for us, we mistakenly took this as a sign of an overall relaxation of discipline and many of us didn't readily rise at even the new later time. Consequently I was lying in bed some five or ten minutes after reveille when I heard hobnailed boots resounding down the concrete floored corridor leading to our room. In a flash I flung back my bedclothes and swung my feet onto the floor just as the C.S.M. and Captain Slater burst into the room.

"Just as I thought we've caught them red handed in bed Sergeant Major, "called out Captain Slater gleefully. "Take their names Sergeant Major. There's Brown, Smith, Green, Jones, and what's your name soldier?" he asked another poor unfortunate caught in bed. "Greenlove Sir," answered a reluctant Greenlove.

After collecting the names of all those soldiers he had caught in bed and directing them to be on the verandah at 10:30hrs, a joyful and laughing Captain Slater prepared to leave the room, with yours truly thanking his lucky stars that he had heard the marauding pair on their approach.

"Oh and take Skinner's name as well Sergeant Major, he only just beat me to it."

And with that the pair disappeared out of the room.

"Bloody hell," I said, "And I wasn't even in bed."

"No but I was," called out a voice as a locker door swung closed to reveal a recumbent Michael still lying in bed, undetected by the simple expedient of opening his locker door and hiding behind it whilst the name taking was going on.

At 10:30hrs the familiar ritual of prisoner and escort was enacted and once again I found myself along with eight others in front of the Company Commander, on a charge of being in bed after reveille.

"You've all heard the charge have any of you anything to say for yourself?" he commanded.

"Brown?"

"No Sir."

"Smith?"

"No Sir."

"Skinner?"

"Yes Sir" I wasn't in bed," and was about to elaborate when the Company Commander cut me short.

"Sergeant Major march the prisoner outside."

"Sir! Prisoner about turn, quick march," and I was led out of the room and instructed to wait in the outer office.

After about five minutes the other prisoners were marched out of the Company Commander's office and dismissed. They had clearly been let off with a warning. Why hadn't I kept my mouth shut?

I was then sandwiched between the self-same two escorts and marched back into the Company Commander's office for a second time.

"Read out the charge again Captain Slater if you please," instructed Major Toombes.

"Sir, on the 22nd September 1955 in the company of Sergeant Major Swan I entered barrack room 28 at 06:40 hrs. and found a number of soldiers still in bed including 23040258 Private Skinner. I warned them all that they would be charged for being in bed after Reveille."

"Skinner?"

"Captain Slater did not find me in bed Sir, I was sitting on my bed with my feet firmly on the ground,"

"True Sir but as far as I am concerned that is being in bed," replied Captain Slater.

"I don't agree that sitting on my bed is the same as being in bed Sir."

"Hm. How long had you been sitting on your bed?"

"About five minutes Sir."

"Why?"

"I didn't feel very well Sir."

"What was wrong with you?"

"I felt kind of dizzy sir."

"Dizzy! Nonsense, why don't you admit to being in bed and take your punishment like a man?"

"Because I wasn't in bed and I don't see why I should take punishment for something I am not guilty of, Sir."

"Admit the charge and take your punishment like a man," he repeated.

I'm in deep trouble here I thought and began to wish that I had pleaded guilty like all the others, they'd been let off anyway.

The Major was addressing me once again.

"The case is proved. I'm disappointed that you haven't had the guts to take your punishment like a man as the others have."

God, what's coming next I thought?

He stared to his front momentarily, as if making up his mind over my punishment.

"You're admonished." he said suddenly. March the prisoner out Sergeant Major."

I couldn't believe my ears, or my luck.

"Sir. Prisoner and escort right turn, quick march."

In the outer office the C.S.M. looked me squarely in the eyes.

"Don't get caught in bed again Skinner, you might not be so lucky next time. Away you go,"

Lucky or not I wasn't so forgiving over the incident and considered that I must counter attack immediately, to coin a military phrase. I thought the matter over very carefully and the next Wednesday I reported sick. Went through the usual ritual of parading outside Company Office with my small pack and landed the job of marching the group of "dying" soldiers down to the MI room.

By the time the MO put in an appearance there was a very large crowd of soldiers waiting to see him. He walked in through the door, called out his usual, "Morning lads," then stood stock still, slightly abashed at the very large number of troops waiting to see him. Then the penny dropped.

"C.O.'S parade this morning lads?" he queried.

"Yes sir," we all replied cheerily.

"Ah I thought so!" he said as he retired to his consulting room with a smile on his face. After waiting about an hour and a half it was my turn to see the MO.

"Right Skinner what's the problem?" asked the MO.

"It's my ankle sir, it's still giving me quite a lot of pain, I keep on going over on it."

"Boot off let me have a look at it."

He examined the ankle, it was clearly quite swollen.

"I think we'll send you back to Cambridge hospital for them to have another look at it. You'll be informed on orders when you have to go there. Meanwhile I'll put you on light duties," he said as he wrote a chit for me.

Sure enough a few days later it went up on orders for me to attend the hospital to see a specialist over my problematical ankle.

I was waiting at the bus stop outside the camp for a bus to take me to the hospital at Aldershot, when a well dressed female driving a large Buick saloon, pulled up and asked if she could give me a lift. I was slightly taken aback but accepted the offer and settled down to the journey. It transpired that she was the wife of a Colonel in some regiment or other in Aldershot. At first I thought that she was trying to show how progressive she was by giving a lift to a "squaddie", but I soon found out that she was a very pleasant person indeed. How different she was to our Brigadier's wife, who when being driven in her husband's official car, would order her driver to pull up to take the names of soldiers who hadn't saluted the pennant on the car. The fact that the pennant as far as I recall shouldn't have been flying with only her in the car didn't seem to count when these unfortunates were pulled up before their Company Commander and charged with conduct prejudicial to military discipline etc., etc.

My Good Samaritan took me right to the doors of the hospital, and wished me all the best as she dropped me off. I, in turn thanked her very much for the lift.

My ankle was examined once again by the specialists, who whilst agreeing that it had been damaged decreed that there was no remedial action that would be useful. They did however decide to downgrade me, which as far as I could see did me no good whatsoever. I returned to camp after seven days in hospital, this time by bus!

A couple of days later I had to report sick due to my hospitalisation and found myself once again sitting before my M.O. He had the hospital report in front of him.

"Right Skinner, having read the hospital report I'm going to excuse you all duties and parades for a month. Okay?

That'll please Captain Slater I thought. Most people would have immediately replied in the affirmative, and gratefully accepted the chit being proffered by the MO and rushed out of the room before he changed his mind. I was playing for bigger stakes than that though.

"No Sir, I'm not happy with that."

"Pardon," said the MO as he looked up from the chit that he was already signing.

"I'm not happy Sir, with only being excused duties and parades for a month. That is the same as me going to my civilian doctor, and whilst acknowledging that I have a problem, him not being prepared to do anything about it."

"What do you mean?"

"Excused all duties and parades is merely giving me the equivalent of a civilian life for a few days. It is not doing anything to put my ankle right Sir," I said indignantly.

"Well what would you suggest I do?" he queried, half sarcastically.

"I suggest that I am given shoe order sir."

"But boots support your ankle, surely Skinner."

"Oh yes Sir they do, that's the problem."

"Problem, how come?"

"Every time I wear shoes I go over on my ankle, due as you quite rightly point out sir, boots support my ankle."

"I'm not with you Skinner."

"I consider that if I wore shoes all the time my ankle would strengthen up. Whilst I wear boots my ankle is supported and will not strengthen up. It will not get better and I am certainly not going to wear boots when I get back into civilian life Sir."

The MO sat looking at me for a few moments whilst he

digested my diagnosis.

"Alright, I'll excuse you all parades and prescribe you one pair of shoes for a period of three months. We'll see how you are at the end of that period. In the meantime you will hold on to your boots," he said pointedly, as he handed me a very valuable chit indeed.

I left the MI centre feeling that I had just completed my best day's work since I had joined the Army.

A few weeks after my success regarding shoe order one of our room members decided to report sick. When the Orderly Sergeant woke us up at reveille he asked the usual question, "Anyone reporting sick this morning?"

"Yes, I am Sergeant," croaked Roger from his corner bed.

"Right, name and number, said the Sergeant, reaching for his notebook.

"283 Ford, Sergeant."

"Right, Parade outside Company office at 8:00 hrs. to report sick."

"I'm too sick to do that Sergeant. I can't get out of bed," groaned Roger.

"You know the procedure. To report sick you have to parade outside Company office at 8:00hrs, there's no alternative". And with those last words the Sergeant turned on his heels and marched out of the barrack room.

"What's the problem?" asked a sympathetic roommate.

"Nothing really. I'm just going to prove that you can go sick without parading outside Company office. If Skinner can get shoe order, then I am bloody sure I can go sick without parading outside Company office."

"You'll never get away with it".

"We'll see."

We went to breakfast.

When we came back Roger was still in bed. We got ready for muster parade. The Orderly Sergeant came back to see Roger, finding him still in bed, he ordered him to get up if he still intended to report sick. Roger in turn said he was too ill to do that. The Sergeant said that if he wanted to report sick he'd have to get up.

Roger groaned, and buried his head under his bed clothes.

We all went out of the room onto muster parade, and were so occupied with twisted bootlaces, haircuts and the like, that I for one forgot all about Roger.

Halfway through muster parade however an ambulance drove round the square and pulled up at our barrack block, and two medics went inside. After a few minutes they came out again carrying John on a stretcher, they popped him in the ambulance and drove off. He'd proved his point, but what was going to happen to him now? We fully expected him to be returned back to us during the day, probably facing a charge.

That evening, as he hadn't returned, a bunch of us went over to the sick bay to see him. We found him sitting up in bed in the lap of luxury.

We looked around guardedly, saw that there was no one within earshot and asked," What did they find wrong with you?"

"It's a bit of a mystery really", he confided with a wink of the eye. They can't find anything wrong yet, so they're keeping me in for a few days for observation."

"But there isn't anything wrong, is there?" we asked.

"Not that I am aware of, "said Roger, "But it's better in here than in camp so let them do their observing for a few days."

Roger returned to us after four days, they never did find out what the mysterious illness was that hit him so suddenly.

On his release from sick bay he was ordered to report sick and was given the inevitable seven days light duties. This luckily precluded him from taking part in the current round of physical exercise tests, which we had to undertake periodically. Basically I think that these tests were only carried out to see if we were still alive and kicking.

The first real test that we had to do was to carry a person 100 yards on our backs. Naturally to carry out this task we found the smallest person we could and carried them quite easily the required 100 yards. It wasn't until we had done this that the P.T.I. who was supervising the test instructed us, with a grin on his face to change positions with our partners. Our small partners were then expected to carry us back the 100 yards we had just carried them. Unless they happened to be miniature Samson this was an impossible task for them.

"I forgot to tell you", the P.T.I. informed us with a grin on his face, "The best idea is for you to select a partner the same size as yourself as you have to carry each other in turn over the hundred yards".

When we did this. Somehow or other, eventually we all managed to struggle over the hundred yard course in the stipulated time.

The next test was to run a mile in about six minutes. The P.T.I. decreed that three times round the square was a mile as far as he was concerned, so away we went, all starting at once. As soon as I saw that the P.T.I. wasn't keeping a close check on the number of laps we were running I decide to run only two laps by hiding in a little brick building I had spotted halfway round the square for one lap.

Next time round the square I dived into the building as I drew level with it. I was amazed to find that there was hardly any room for me. It was crammed with people with the same idea as me. How on earth our P.T.I hadn't missed all these people I just don't know. It's just as well that some people ran the whole three laps because the brick building would not have held us all! In any case I think that the P.T.I. would have noticed if no one had completed a particular lap. Needless to say we all passed that particular test.

For our next test we had to go into the gym and climb up a rope, a thing I had never been able to do and still can't do. The P.T.I. demonstrated by swarming up the rope, once up at the ceiling level he took the rope off the ceiling hook, and then put it back on again, and swarmed back down the rope to ground level.

"Right that's what I want you to do, with the exception of taking the rope off the hook, you don't have to do that," he explained. "Away you go."

Naturally he had thrown down the gauntlet and a number of people climbed the rope and took it off the hook and put it back on again. Anything the P.T.I. could do they also could do. This is of course what the P.T.I. expected. How some people didn't break their necks I just don't know.

At the end of this activity, I was still standing there looking at the rope, I just couldn't climb it.

"Up you go then said the P.T.I.

"I'm sorry Corporal I can't climb it."

He swarmed up the rope again just for me.

"There you are, away you go."

"I'm sorry Corporal I can't climb a rope."

He swarmed up the rope again, with by this time the whole class looking on.

There you are, away you go."

"I can't do it Corporal."

"But I've just shown you how to do it."

"With all due respect Corporal you have just shown me how you climb the rope, you haven't instructed me on how I am to climb the rope."

He swarmed up it once again. "There that's the way to do it."

"Corporal you have shown me how you do it, you haven't shown me how I am to do it," I again explained.

The conversation went on like this for some time with the Corporal becoming more and more agitated, much to the amusement of the rest of the class. Then to change the subject, I suppose, he noticed the wedding ring I was wearing.

"You're wearing a ring. Rings are not allowed in the gym," he informed me. Get it off immediately he ordered.

"It won't come off Corporal. It's tight on my finger." I explained.

"Go into the washroom and use soap to get it off."

I left to comply with his order without much hope of success.

I returned to the gym a few minutes later with the ring still firmly on my finger.

"I'm sorry Corporal I can't get it off."

"I'll give you two minutes in which to get it off, after which I will cut it off," he informed me.

I'd had enough of this bombastic little runt and thought the time had come to stand up to him.

I said quietly. "That is my wedding ring Corporal, neither you nor anybody else is going to touch it. Do I make myself clear?

Coming only up to my shoulder, and looking me fully in the chest, he then uttered these immortal words, "Are you trying to make me look small?"

The whole class, who had been following the proceedings with great interest, burst out laughing. For the moment the Corporal didn't know where to put his face.

"Quiet," he yelled.

He then composed himself.

"Right there's some sticking plaster in my room, put that over the ring and make sure that in future whenever you come into the gym you have sticking plaster over it. We don't want any accidents. You could easily cut someone with that ring."

"Yes Corporal, I'll go and do that Corporal, I hurried away to find the sticking plaster.

The outcome of all this was that I failed my physical exercise tests and my pay book was annotated accordingly. Mark you this didn't excuse me from having to take part in the many strenuous jobs that were floating around the camp at any one time. Such as starting the generators first thing in the mornings.

In our training we used quite an amount of electricity of various voltages. This electricity was in the main supplied by diesel generators. Our first task each morning was to get the generators started, which could be quite difficult on a cold and frosty morning, it sometimes took the whole of the first session of study. It was not uncommon to come across say ten men swinging on ropes attached to starting handles with other men poking lighted oily rags around the air intakes, all striving to get the reluctant generators started.

This extremely hard exercise did have one big advantage however, it made the classrooms feel warmer than they really were with their diminutive coke stoves, when we eventually got in them. Perhaps this was the reason why we were given all this exercise first thing in the morning, energy conservation. The more exercise we got, the warmer we got, and a smaller amount of coke was needed for the stoves.

We also had plenty of exercise on Friday nights as well! Friday night was known as "Amami" Night, "Amami" was a well advertised shampoo of the time. C.S.M. Swan along with others no doubt, decided to call our interior cleaning by that name. It seemed appropriate to our lords and masters, and it did have a certain ring to it.

At dead on 18:00hrs the C.S.M. could be heard calling out along the corridors of the block, "Amami" night, come on let's be having you. The sooner we get started the sooner we get finished."

We would then have an hour of cleaning before us, both in the room and in the block. Although there was no roll call taken I can't recall that anyone skived off, we all got stuck in to the irksome task, all the walls, ceilings, and floors out in the corridors were washed down. The baths, washbasins, and toilets were then thoroughly cleaned along with the washrooms themselves. Once all that had been done we would then clean our rooms, polish the floors, clean the windows and carry out the endless dusting. And finally if there was to be a room inspection on the following Saturday morning, as there usually was, we would then have to "bull" up our personal kit and effects.

All this work would be carried out under the close supervision of the C.S.M. and his senior N.C.O.s. Come to think of it must have been as big a nuisance to them having to spend their Friday nights supervising us as it was to us having to execute these irksome tasks.

It was during one of these Amami clean ups that I had the only opportunity whilst in the Army, that I recall, of using my building knowledge. In spite of there being an "OUT OF ORDER DO NOT USE" notice on the door of our first floor toilets, there was a huge puddle of urine stretching across the floor, clearly emulating from the urinal itself.

An officer was called. He took one look at the situation, and immediately declared the cause of the problem.

"The dirty tykes on this floor can't be bothered to go to a toilet on one of the other floors, they're just coming in here and peeing on the floor. It's disgusting and filthy Sergeant Major" he said to "Swanee" our Sergeant Major.

I heard this conversation and was incensed by the accusation. I had already told Ernie, the general duties "wallah" the cause of the problem earlier in the day, when the trouble first appeared, but apparently he hadn't taken any notice of what I had told him. Personally the man I think was so thick he just didn't understand what I was telling him, but then that was probably why he was a general duties man!

"With all due respect Sir that isn't what has been happening". I said with indignation as I addressed the officer

"Of course it is, plain as a pike staff," he replied.

"It isn't Sir, and I take exception to being called a dirty tyke.

"The urinal is blocked and you've been told not to use it. But you haven't taken any notice of the instruction, and some of you have been peeing on the floor", he replied with great conviction.

"We have taken notice Sir, and we haven't peed over the floor. As I said this afternoon, to the person concerned, the notice should have been put on the toilets upstairs as well as this floor Sir. The blockage is between this floor and the ground floor, we're not using the urinal on this floor, but they are on the floor above, and it's that use that is flooding this floor."

"Nonsense what do you know about it? What's your name soldier?" he demanded.

"Skinner Sir, and I do happen to know a bit about the subject. If you get the chap here to pour a bucket of water down the urinal upstairs you'll see what I mean."

"I think you're wrong, but alright have it your way,

"Jones go and pour a bucket of water down the upstairs urinal", he said to the general duties "wallah".

I stood well back, whilst the young officer, who was only too willing to prove me wrong stood at the very edge of the puddle staring intently at the urinal.

I heard the water coming down the drain pipe. It surged out of the urinal straight over the Officer's shoes, much to my delight. The Officer looked at his shoes as he shook them dry, and then at me.

"I think you're right you know," he said with great surprise

"Did you say your name was Skinner? Right. How do we get over the problem then Skinner? I explained in detail, how to remedy the situation, then returned to help the chaps finish off the block cleaning.

Sometimes there was a good programme on at the "Gaff, (cinema) we would hurry through our work and complete it under the allotted hour so that we could get there in good time. It wouldn't do us any good though, the C.S.M. would tell us to go back and do the job again, correctly this time. We could never win.

We couldn't even win as far as our catering was concerned, as I found out.

Somehow or other I was appointed to the catering committee. I can't recall how, but I remember attending my first and only meeting. At this meeting amongst other things, the Catering Officer was explaining the rations and the amounts allowed per soldier. We got around to talking about butter and we were informed that we were allotted something like 2ozs per man per week. When I asked the question what happened to it then, I was told that it was used for cooking, that was the reason given for only having margarine to put on our bread. That I just didn't believe, and said so. My statement didn't go down very well. That was probably one of the reasons I only lasted the one meeting on the catering committee.

Then we got around to talking about the disposal of pigs' swill of which there appeared to be plenty judging by the number of people who found the food inedible. Apparently we sold all the uneaten food as pigs' swill to the Brigadier who kept pigs. All the money raised from these sales went into a fund that brought so called "luxuries" over and above the normal ration for the lads, which seemed to me to be a good scheme of things. When however the accounts for the fund were presented to the committee they showed a substantial loss over the current year. I couldn't understand how a loss could be made on the sale of pigs' swill and queried the accounts.

Ah yes", explained an apparently embarrassed Catering Officer, "One consignment of swill had some broken glass in it and killed three of the Brigadiers pigs, so we had to pay him compensation".

"That doesn't seem right Sir", I opined.

"Normal practice I can assure you", replied the Catering Officer

"So the men are having to pay the Brigadier this compensation Sir".

"Oh no not really", retorted an embarrassed Catering Officer.

"But they are Sir. It's coming out of the men's fund Sir."

It's already been paid out. Therefore it's all in the past. Let's forget about it and pass onto the next item".

So much for the catering committee and the problems it was apparently set up to sort out. On the face of it was democracy in action; in fact it appeared to me to be so much window dressing.

Another subject that I felt fell within this heading was the amount of religious instruction we received in the Army. In theory we were supposed to have a padre's hour once a week, or so we understood. What we received was in fact twenty minutes to half an hour whenever the time could be spared, which was usually on a regimental training morning.

The sessions would be held in the N.A.A.F.I. and be conducted by the local vicar, who was jokingly referred to as the "Bishop of Barkham". Barkham being the adjacent parish, where the "Bishop" presided over the local parishioners. When we had our first padre's hour, and I heard that it was to be taken by a Bishop I was very impressed indeed. I should have realised that it was just another leg pull by the lads.

We duly went to the N.A.A.F.I., stacked our rifles in the lobby and then went in to receive some religious instruction. Some took the opportunity to sleep whilst others amongst our number saw it as an opportunity to bait the vicar.

"How do you view the fact padre, that we have just stacked our rifles outside and then come in here to talk about God?"

"God can be worshipped in all types of circumstances my boy. Because you have just left your rifles outside does not mean that you have evil intent within you," the Padre replied.

"But we're all here being trained to kill. In effect we are professional killers padre."

"I'm sure that there is good in each and every one of you, and that is what we are here to discuss. The good things in life not the bad things. Let us think of all things good."

He'd clearly heard all these arguments before, and he had all the answers. We'd got to do better than this if we were to ruffle his feathers

"Do you think that the atom bomb is a threat to mankind padre? Asked one of our number.

"No I am sure that it isn't, not if used, sorry, handled, correctly", replied the vicar

"Do you think that the atom bomb should be banned padre? Another asked.

"That's a difficult question to answer my boy. There is no simple answer to that question".

"Do you agree to us having the bomb padre?" asked another soldier.

"Can you see any circumstances under which we would be justified in using it padre?" questioned another.

"As I have said it depends upon the circumstances my boy."

"What do you think God would have thought of us having the atom bomb padre", queried a further soldier.

"I don't think that he could have foreseen such an event." countered the Padre.

"Not God padre, surely he knows everything Sir?"

"Er".

"Who do you think has the greater power, God or the bomb?"

"That's a difficult question to answer my boy".

"You've got to have an opinion padre."

"Er,"

Surely God can overcome the bomb?"

"Er, well---"

"Come on padre give us an answer." called out a number of people all at once.

Silence for a few moments. We'd got him on the run I thought, then in exasperation he blurted out.

"As far as I am concerned I want to be on the side with the biggest and best atom bomb. It stands to reason doesn't it? The country with the biggest and best bomb will win any future war."

So much for religious instruction for us professional killers!

But there was one event in the Army that I attended religiously and with some enthusiasm, that was pay parade. This took place every Thursday at 16:30hrs in one of the classrooms. Although the actual pay out usually took place in the classroom, we had to wait outside in all types of weather until called. As we all had to be there at the same time and as we were almost always paid in alphabetical order, I usually had a long wait. On the few occasions I turned up late to take account of the long wait, I would find that they had decided to pay out that day in reverse order, starting with the Z's I would then have to have a good excuse ready for not having been there when my name was called if I was to receive any money that week. The actual process of receiving any money involved in you marching up to an old trestle table draped in a grey Army blanket, when your name and last four numbers were called out. Your pay book and your money would be passed to you by the paying officer. You checked the money against the entry in your playbook and called out." Pay and playbook correct Sir". Salute and leave the playbook on the table to be passed back to the Pay Clerk. Quite a performance to receive 10/- (50p) one week and 12\- (60) the next, which is what I was receiving for the first six months in the Army. After that time it did begin to rise, very slowly, until when I left the Army I was receiving a regular soldiers pay of approximately £8:00p per week including my marriage allowance

Whilst we were carrying out all our duties, our studies, our recreational training (and going sick) we still had to cope in addition with regimental training.

At first this took place on Saturday mornings, then it was changed to Wednesday mornings. It usually started with a CO's parade, or some form of drill parade, when the R.S.M. would put the whole battalion through some fancy drill manoeuvres on the square.

This would be followed by revision of certain parts of basic training, when very often, we who were just fresh out of basic training knew far more of the subject than those instructing us.

I remember one morning when we were having revision on how to aim the rifle. I being totally bored with what was going on around me, was lying contentedly on my back on the grass dozing in the warm sunshine with my beret over my eyes to cut down its glare, Suddenly there was a kick of my boot.

"Wake up soldier", an authoritative voice commanded.

I moved my beret from over my eyes to reveal the R.S.M. and Adjutant looking down at me. Heavens I thought lightning does strike twice in the same place and at the same time!

"Name?" the R.S.M. demanded.

"258 Skinner Sir", I replied scrambling hastily to my feet.

"You know it all, so you're bored, is that the case Skinner?" suggested the Adjutant in mocking tone.

"No Sir", I replied.

"Well what's wrong with that man's aiming position?" He pointed to a soldier receiving instruction.

I gave him chapter and verse on what was wrong.

"And that man over there?" I did the same again.

"What is this called," he said pointing to an obscure part of the rifle. I told him.

"And this and that?" I answered the questions with military precision. I had still been enthusiastic over the Army when I had learnt about these matters at Honiton.

"H'M", well keep awake you might learn something new." I breathed a sigh of relief, and lay down on the grass again, pulled my beret over my eyes and continued my dozing. The Sergeant instructor being as bored as me no doubt, hadn't even looked up whilst the Adjutant was speaking to me.

These Regimental mornings usually ended up with some form of inspection in the barrack room. We would be required to parade in battle order, full service marching order, or just in best boots and best battle dress, depending upon the inspecting Officer's fancy. Whatever it was that was required all equipment would be expected to be in pristine condition. Charges would be waiting for those individuals whose equipment wasn't up to scratch.

Occasionally instead of a programme of parades we would spend the morning on an area of ground near the camp known for some obscure reason as Ducks Nest Farm. There we would execute platoon and company manoeuvres amongst the trees and bushes. Great fun on a nice dry warm day, not so funny on a wet morning when uniform and equipment could get caked in mud if you weren't careful. All had to be cleaned immediately on return to camp, before being able to go home for the weekend. If you knew what was good for you that is.

Needless to say I was very careful not to get muddy as I wanted to get off home at the earliest opportunity. Therefore when ordered to fling myself to the ground by a "nig" Second Lieutenant, I would hunt around for a nice dry patch of grass before complying with his order, on the rare occasion when my actions were spotted by an over-zealous Second Lieutenant, I would explain my behaviour away by informing him that I had a damaged ankle and had to be extremely careful with it. It never failed.

At other times we would be tested on our so called "skill at arms", seeing what we knew about our Lee-Enfield rifles, Sten guns and Bren guns. Then every six months or so we would be taken in lorries over to Ash ranges at Aldershot for the day, to see if we could remember how to actually fire our own rifles. If the weather was nice these days on the range could be absolutely marvellous as far as I was concerned. Things would be quite free and easy away from camp, the mobile Church Army canteen would visit us a couple of times during the day for refreshments, and I could indulge in the only thing I really enjoyed in the Army, shooting. I was proud of the fact that I attained classification as a first class shot, but not pleased by the fact that as a National Serviceman I was not allowed to display the appropriate badge. I was sorry that these range courses occurred so infrequently.

Some of the lads hated these range courses, especially if they couldn't shoot I remember being on one range course, when the Sergeant instructor, seeing that so few of us had hit the target at a hundred yards, ordered us to fix bayonets and charge the target. He considered that was the only way some of us were going to hit the target. Needless to say he countermanded the order long before we reached the target area. Eventually, as I have mentioned before, Regimental training was changed to Wednesday mornings, this was very welcome as this had two advantages as far as I was concerned. One was the fact, that if we had a morning without muster parades, then it tended to be a morning with little or no consequence to bother us. If we then added to this factor the afternoon of recreational training we had to all intents and purposes a day off in the middle of the week. Great!

The other advantage of this arrangement was the fact that we now had technical training on a Saturday morning in place of the regimental training which meant that leaving camp on a Friday for an unofficial long weekend became an easier possibility as it was relatively easy to skive off lectures due to the lax nature of the roll call system in the classrooms.

Skiving off when there was a Corps weekend however was a different matter, authority sensing that people would try and slope off home, held frequent roll calls throughout the weekend, which was ironical really, as a Corps weekend was organised with the intention, or so we were told, of giving us fellows a good time. To make sure that we didn't miss this good time we were all confined to barracks for the weekend!

On the Saturday afternoon we were expected to spectate at one of the sports events that were taking place. If we weren't gripped for fatigues that is, and on the Sunday we were expected to take part in such jollifications as treasure hunts and quizzes. As a further boost to our moral and our general titillation contingents of W.R.A.C.s and W.R.E.N.s were shipped in from surrounding camps

On one such Corps weekend I reluctantly dragged myself off my bed to see what the famed treasure hunt was all about to find that we had to form groups of six, three males, and three females. After three of the most gruesome females I had ever seen decided to attach themselves to our group, I called it a day and went back to bed for the rest of the afternoon and read a book.

It appears however that the CO's driver became attached to one of the W.R.E.N's and made a date to meet her the following week. With the intention of impressing her no doubt, he took her out in the CO's Humber Hawk saloon. He stopped in the woods to do some necking, but when he came to drive off he found that the car was stuck in the mud. Leaving the Wren in the car he went back to camp to "borrow" the duty truck to pull the car out of the mud. Unfortunately the duty truck became stuck in the mud also. Not to be outdone he went back to camp once more to get the Matador recovery vehicle. Amazingly enough this vehicle also became stuck in the mud.

He then decided to fix the Matador's winching cable to trees in an attempt to winch the Matador free, which after uprooting a tree or two he succeeded in doing. He then winched out the Humber Hawk and took the W.R.E.N. back to her unit. After that he returned to the woods to recover the duty truck. He then returned to the woods to recover the Matador. After returning all three vehicles to the camp, one at a time, and having washed them all down, it was dawn and time to get ready for another day He breathed a sigh of relief, he'd just made it, there was now no sign of his previous escapade.

When he went on duty however there was a message awaiting him, the C.O. wanted to see him immediately. Apparently the Commanding Officer of the W.R.E.N's camp had phoned up to complain that one of her W.R.E.N's had got into camp well after the midnight curfew and on being pressed had given the name of his driver as the person she had been out with. The driver found himself in front of his CO.

"Thompson I've had a phone call from the CO of the W.R.E.N's camp. She is complaining that one of her W.R.E.N.s got in well after midnight curfew and on being pressed she gave your name as the person she had been out with. If it's true that you took this W.R.E.N. out last night, why on earth didn't you get the girl back to camp on time? If you make a habit of keeping this girl out late she'll find herself in trouble, in more ways than one no doubt, just watch your step. As far as I am concerned that's the end of the matter".

"Thompson sighed a sigh of relief".

"Except for one thing ", the CO added. The W.R.E.N. said you took her out in a large Army car, I wonder whose car that could be, care to tell me?"

Thereafter, so the story goes. Thompson bared his soul to the CO and told him the whole story of the night's escapade. He found himself as duty driver for a week, a very light sentence, I thought, for what he'd done, but then he was in the exalted position of being the CO's driver.

.......As I have mentioned the Army had this misplaced idea that the way to bolster moral and to engender a feeling of Esprit de Corps was to organise weekend events for the battalion. As far as the regular soldier was concerned living in a garrison with his wife and family, who probably got bored out of their minds at weekends for lack of something to do, these events were possibly very popular. But for the majority of National Servicemen whose main object in life, in my own experience, was to get home at weekends, such events were, to put it mildly, not welcomed.

I recall taking part in a heat of a tug-of war competition on a Saturday morning, whereby the winners would represent the Company in the battalion sports the next day. Both teams were composed of National Servicemen intent on going home for the weekend and had no intention whatsoever of winning the heat. With the C.S.M. as umpire, both teams did their utmost to lose. I have never seen anything so funny in my life, even the C.S.M. had to control himself from laughing out loud.

Eventually the other team were declared the winners, much to their disgust, and to them was bestowed the "honour" of representing the Company on the 'morrow.

As the C.S.M. put it. "It had been a close thing, as to who lost!

Whilst all these delights and distractions were going on I was putting in some serious study over my course work, only on weekdays of course. In this period it was even known for me to work in the evening. I was determined to prove that I could cope with the work if I had wanted to. Prove to myself as well as the Army.

Eventually the time arrived for me to take my final exams on the number 10 predictor, the first being the theory paper, followed a couple of days later by the practical exam. As far as the theory paper was concerned I had guessed the right questions and learnt the answers parrot fashion. When it came to the practical exam I didn't know exactly what the faults were so much as where the instructor had wedged his matchsticks and cigarette packets to simulate the various malfunction...

Perhaps with hindsight I'm doing myself an injustice and that my third and fifth places in the two exams were well earnt.

After these exams we had the obligatory course dinner in Wokingham and I prepared to leave Arborfield after spending a period of thirteen months on a seven month course!

At the conclusion of a course the usual procedure was for the course representative to collect the course postings from Captain Slater and the course be given twelve hours in which to sort out the postings between ourselves. If agreement was not reached within that time then Captain Slater would then deal with the matter himself direct.

In the case of our course, Captain Slater required me, not the course representative to collect the postings from him.

"Ah Skinner, here are the postings for AA52, usual conditions, twelve hours in which to sort them out amongst yourselves. Oh and this is your posting Skinner, under no circumstances whatsoever are you allowed to exchange with anyone else. Understood?

"Yes Sir, thank you Sir".

"It's a pleasure Skinner I can assure you. Away you go".

From his attitude I go the distinct impression that somehow or other I had upset the Captain whilst I had been at Aborfield and that this posting whatever it was, was his punishment for me. I saluted, about turned and marched away. Once out of his sight I took a look at my posting. The Coast Artillery School, Plymouth. Oh well you can't win them all I thought but then had I won any of them? On reflection I probably had and that is what had induced Captain Slater to take the action he had over my posting.

For the record the postings for the course were:- 5 Arborfield, 2 Cyprus, 1 Gibraltar, 2 BOAR, 2 North of England , 1 Bicester, 1 Plymouth.

A couple of days later I said my goodbyes to the many pals I had made at Arborfield and prepared to leave for Plymouth.

Michael and I had always said that when we left Arborfield we would purloin a sign we had seen sitting in a local field and put it on the roof of the Company office overlooking the square but we never did, more's the pity.

It proclaimed to the world, "BEWARE OF THE BULL." I regret never having done that deed. I'm sure that it would have pleased the R.S.M. no end!!

CHAPTER 15

IN WHICH I LEAVE ABORFIELD AND ARRIVE AT THE COAST ARTILLERY SCHOOL PLYMOUTH.

On Wednesday 24th October I eventually left No.5.Training Battalion at Arborfield for the last time, I had been there thirteen months on what was officially a seven month course, the reasons for my extended period on course were twofold. One was my total indifference to the course I was on, and come to that my total indifference to the Army as a whole and the other was that whilst at Arborfield I was able to get home each weekend that I wasn't on duty. As I walked past the guardroom in Full Service Marching Order, carrying everything that I possessed in the Army and feeling like the proverbial Christmas tree, I gave a smart two fingered salute to the Provost Sergeant, after first ascertaining that he was standing with his back to me! With typical Army efficiency there was no transport to take me to Wokingham railway station so I had to suffer the indignity of boarding the local bus to the station which with all the paraphernalia I had with me was a feat of genius in itself. I caught a train to Waterloo station, had a long telephone conversation with Doreen when I arrived there, then crossed London to Paddington station whence I caught a train to Plymouth. On that four to five hour journey I had plenty of time in which to speculate and worry over what I would find when I got to my posting at Plymouth. Surely but surely it couldn't be as bad, or even worse, than the conditions I had had to endure at Arborfield? Then my thoughts turned to the distance I was travelling; with 240 miles between Plymouth and home, how often I wondered would I be able to make it back to Enfield? Not every weekend that was for certain. The only plus side about this present move that I could possibly see was the fact that I now only had a further seven months of my National Service to complete so however bad the Plymouth posting might turn out to be I would only have to bear it for half the time that I had been at Arborfield.

It was not until I was nearing the end of my journey that I got into conversation with a person in my compartment who I assumed was a civilian but turned out to be a Sergeant in R.E.M.E.

that I received some comfort over my particular situation. When I explained that I was on my way to my first posting and that I was feeling very apprehensive over being attached to the Coast Artillery School in Plymouth, he was extremely reassuring and told me that he considered that attachment to another Regiment was probably the best posting a R.E.M.E. man could get. I was about to ask him to expand on the subject when at that moment we suddenly emerged from a tunnel on the outskirts of Plymouth and there in full view across the river was a huge edifice of a fort. I inquired from my R.E.M.E. Sergeant if that was the Royal Citadel.

"Oh no", he said, "that's R.A.F. Mountbatten, the Royal Citadel is on this side of the river opposite Mountbatten, you can't see it from the train. In many respects", he continued, "I think it more impressive than Mountbatten". In the mood I was in at that moment I wasn't bothered whether or not the Royal Citadel was more impressive than Mountbatten, just whether or not it would be an acceptable posting to me. By acceptable I meant cushy of course. The train drew into Plymouth North Station and I prepared to disembark with all my equipment. As friendly as the R.E.M.E. Sergeant had been to me on the train, he left me to carry out this operation myself which was quite an undertaking, during which I became very agitated that the train might depart, with me on the platform and half my equipment still on the train. I need not have worried however, I was to find out later that trains appeared to stop in Plymouth station an inordinately long time before proceeding further. I don't think that this was to let people like me off the train. I believe that it was connected with the fact that there was only a single track across the Saltash bridge over the river Tamar on the western outskirts of Plymouth and the delay was waiting for a time slot to enable the train to pass over the bridge. Once on the platform with all my equipment safely spread around me I looked for the R.T.O. office, spotted it, gathered up my possessions and after a couple of false starts by way of dropping equipment made my very unsteady way towards it. Full Service Marching Order was fine for moving around once you had it all securely fitted to your person but if you just tried to gather it all up along with any personal holdall to move say twenty five yards the result was usually disastrous as I was reminded to my cost. Once in the R.T.O. office I explained my situation and inquired over transport to take me to the Royal Citadel. "There's your transport soldier", I was told by the officer in charge, as he pointed out of the window to a row of taxis standing outside the station. "You must be joking", I retorted, "I can't afford a taxi, I'm only a National Serviceman, I don't get the same rate of pay as pay as a regular soldier even if I do deserve it. How about phoning up the Royal Citadel and asking them to come to and collect me?" Adding "Sir", as an afterthought. "Now you must be joking" he said. "I know for a fact that they won't send transport along to collect a single R.E.M.E. craftsman however important you may think you are!

"Right I'll catch a bus, no way am I going by taxi". And with that I stormed out of the R.T.O's. office.

It wasn't until I was outside the office however, that I realized that I didn't have a clue where to catch the bus I required. Nevertheless I gathered my equipment around me once more and struggled through the station to the road outside where I was immediately accosted by a number of taxi drivers plying for custom, who I told in no uncertain terms that I had no need of their services, unless they were free Well you never know your luck!

I was standing on the pavement, presumably looking totally perplexed with all my equipment around me, thinking that I may have to spend some of my precious money on a taxi after all when much to my surprise a brewer's dray pulled up and a kindly driver enquired where was I going. When I explained the Royal Citadel but I hadn't a clue how to get there, he replied "That's okay, I'm going that way myself, jump up on the back". I just couldn't believe my luck and threw my equipment onto the lorry and jumped up after it, banged the top of the cab with my hand and we were away rumbling through the streets of Plymouth. The city was obviously in the process of being rebuilt after the many ferocious air raids it sustained during the second world war. The wide well-laid out avenues of new shops contrasted greatly with the many cleared bomb sites that still remained even in the heart of the town centre

It was then that I espied this forbidding looking fortress on a hill overlooking the town centre towards which the driver was even now making his way. It went through my mind that this must be the Royal Citadel. The driver pulled up outside the main entrance which was a huge stone gateway that gave access to this very impressive looking medieval castle. The only thing it seemed to be lacking at first glance was a drawbridge, though at the top of a hill I suppose it was pretty unlikely that there had ever been one.

"Here we are son, the Royal Citadel", a cheery voice called out from the cab. I jumped down from the lorry, pulled my equipment off the lorry into a small mountain around me and thanked the driver very much for the lift.

"No problem son it was a pleasure, hope you get on okay lad, cheerio", and off he drove down the hill.

I had just started to organize my possessions into a logistical arrangement that would allow me to walk into the fortress entrance with some form of dignity when I was confronted with a terrible vision. It was of a P.T.I. complete in navy and red striped jumper jogging up the hill from round a corner of the Citadel, urging on, of all things a group of R.E.M.E. personnel decked out in battle order, to cover the last twenty five yards of ground to the stone gateway. I stood there aghast. Had I come all the way from Arborfield for this! This, that looked remarkably like basic training, something that even at Arborfield I somehow had managed to avoid. As each person reached the gateway they stopped and almost without exception collapsed on the roadway. However instead of the usual cursing and swearing that one expects from a P.T.I. I heard a cheery. "That's fine lads, you all did it within the time, good". It was then that I realised that one of the group of R.E.M.E. personnel was Bill Witt a person who I had been on course with at Arborfield in the early days before I was back-coursed umpteen times. He immediately saw me and came over, after he had suitably recovered from his exertions.

"Bugger me so you're the new E.C.E. Welcome to the Royal Citadel", he said breezily. He must have seen the look of horror that was still on my face. "Oh don't take any notice of this, we've just completed the six monthly physical jerks assessment and that was our mile run. The P.T.I. seems to think that once round the Citadel is a mile so we're not arguing".

"Right so how's Arborfield these days?" he inquired.

"Bloody awful", I replied.

"Oh you'll like it here, nice and easy", then with a serious note. "Mark you we've got G.O.C's inspection next month and you know what to expect for that, but once that's over it will be down- hill all the way. Come on then he said, "Let's get you settled in. "Right you lot", he called out to the others, who by this time were recovering from their exertions and were wearily getting themselves to their feet. "This is Ray Skinner, the replacement E.C.E, I knew the bugger at Arborfield". He looked at me, "I won't introduce everyone to you now you'll get to know them soon enough". For the umpteenth time that day I loaded myself up like the proverbial Christmas tree and prepared to enter the Royal Citadel.

"Book in at the guard room, otherwise they'll get upset", advised Bill grinning at the guard commander, "And, then I'll show you where the Battery Office is". Battery Office I noted not Company Office. I could see that from now on I would have to get used to the fact that I was now in a unit of the Royal Artillery.

I booked in at the guard room amidst some good humoured banter and then reported to the Battery Office where my details were noted down and I was given directions to my accommodation. The main concern of the battery clerk however was to make arrangements for me to have a kit check. The fact that I had only just had a kit check at Arborfield yesterday didn't seem to cut any ice with him. He insisted that now I had joined another unit I must have another kit check. I never did really understand the reason for this fetish in the Army for kit checks. I had a sneaking feeling that it was because it was one of the few things that the Army could do with any efficiency, because, Lord knows, in my opinion the Army could do very few things efficiently. On reflection perhaps they could and it was only my twisted mind as a National Serviceman that thought they couldn't. I arrived at my accommodation to find that I had been directed to a bunkhouse, (it wasn't superior enough in my book to be called a barrack room), that appeared to be full of attached personnel, situated in one of the back waters of the Royal Citadel. Even at 16:00hrs the room was swarming with personnel seemingly with little or nothing to do. It was noticeable that none of them belonged to R.E.M.E. On inquiring from the inhabitants which of the spare beds I should take, I was given the answer of "Dunno" with total indifference. I chose the bed nearest to me and let my equipment fall off my person onto the bed in question and then sat down on it myself to take stock of my surroundings. I was in a first floor dormitory of an old run down stone building that took about fifteen beds. Compared with the bulled-up appearance of the Arborfield barrack room it was dingy, run down, and not as clean as it might have been. I used to complain of the bull at Arborfield but here I was confronted with the opposite end of the scale. All in all I began to think that I had fallen out of the proverbial frying pan into the proverbial fire. I then remembered that the clerk in the battery office had warned me to get down to the stores before 16:30hrs to draw my bedding otherwise I would be sleeping on a bare mattress for the night. Leaving my equipment on the bed and wondering whether or not it would all be there when I came back, I made my way to the battery store. Having collected my bedding I returned to the bunk house to make up my bed for the night where I found all my equipment exactly where I left it. Maybe the rest of the fellows in the room weren't the desperadoes they looked at first sight! Once I had made my bed and put my gear in some form of order that would enable me to squeeze into bed later on, I picked up my mug, knife, fork and spoon and made my way along to the cookhouse, or dining room as the commissioned ranks tended to call it. I collected my meal, which looked quite appetising and prepared to find a table, when I heard a yell of, "Over here". I saw that the voice came from Bill calling me over to a table that was inhabited exclusively by R.E.M.E. personnel, most of whom I noted I had already seen collapsing outside on the road when I had first arrived.

"I suppose they have put you in one of the attached personnel barrack rooms, have they?" asked Bill.

"Yes they have and it's bloody awful", I replied, "Where do you live"? Everyone around the table laughed.

"One thing's for sure", said Bill, "We certainly don't live in the barrack rooms. We've all found ourselves various places around the Citadel which half the time no one in authority knows anything about and I think I can say that we are all quite comfortable, but don't worry, after we have seen the "Old Man" tomorrow you'll be out of that jolly old barrack room and in with us, in with me in fact. Just put up with the barrack room for tonight but don't unpack, I'll come and collect you in the morning and show you where you'll really be living, but let the Royal Artillery have their way for tonight before we show them who really is in charge of R.E.M.E. personnel accommodation around here".

"And who is that?" I inquired.

"Us", said Bill, and once again everyone around the table laughed. I was beginning to warm to these people. When I had finished tea and said cheerio to my R.E.M.E. compatriots I returned to the bunkhouse.

On arrival I perceived that a large number of the lads had changed into civvies and were preparing for trip into town for the evening. This struck me as a good idea. I'd do the same and change out of uniform and go for a walk outside the Citadel to see what was what. It was as I was changing into flannels and blazer that one of the chaps called out to me in a not unfriendly manner. "'Ere mate I think we should warn you that the guard room won't let you out in civvies if you ain't been in six months and got your permanent pass". I smiled,

Thanks," I said, "I'll remember that" and carried on changing. It then occurred to me that some people got posted to the Royal Citadel within the first six months of their being in the Army and that the person who had been speaking to me was only trying to warn me of the pitfalls that I might fall into.

"I have got my permanent pass", I called out, "but thanks for letting me know".

"'Ow long you been in then?" he queried.

"Just over sixteen months", I replied. It was amusing to see look of surprise on his face and the way his jaw dropped at this news.

"How long have you been in then? I questioned.

"Oh nearly eight months now", he said in a vacant sounding voice. I gave him a sympathetic "get some in look" but resisted the temptation of adding "nig nog" or any other derogatory remark, after all it appeared that for better or for worse from now on we were all one team on the same permanent staff. How wrong I was going to find this line of reasoning in the weeks ahead. Right from my first days at the Royal Citadel it was clear to me that the R.E.M.E. personnel acted as if they were of team of their own, a superior team of their own at that! Amazingly enough this frame of mind was actually fostered by the R.A. technical Senior N.C.O's attitude towards us; with some of it bordering on reverence! I was staggered. For instance the first time an R.A. W.O.1. approached me and in apologetic terms asked if I had possibly got the time to repair a certain piece of equipment for him, or if not, could I give him some advice on how to repair it himself. I think it was this incident that changed my attitude towards the Army, albeit only in a small way. Here was somebody, superior, in rank at least, who was actually asking for my advice. But I'm jumping ahead. Giving my possessions a last cursory glance before I left the room, I made my way up past the square towards the main gate and strolled out of the Citadel into the evening air. I found that the Royal Citadel was situated on a promontory at the eastern end of Plymouth Hoe looking down Plymouth Sound towards the sea, and in the other direction across the Cattewater to the fortress that I recognized as Mountbatten. The

fortress I had seen from the train a couple of hours or so ago.

The sound was an inlet that stretched some three miles inland from the sea and had a breakwater constructed across it at the seaward end and an island known as Drake's Island near the landward end. On a headland to the south east of the mouth of the sound were apparently, two Army establishments, Wembury, and Lentley, that I would get to know quite well in the next few months. The Hoe itself was surmounted by a broad tarmac promenade that gave good views in all directions. Towards the sea, grassy slopes swept down to a rocky shoreline where the sea usually pounded away incessantly. I was intrigued to find that there was a lighthouse constructed on the Hoe and walked over to investigate. It had a plaque on it which explained that it wasn't in fact a working lighthouse but the remains of Smeaton's Tower, a lighthouse that had originally been erected on the Eddystone Rocks some ten miles out to sea from Plymouth. I was to find that on a clear day the remaining stump of Smeaton's Tower could still be seen out at sea standing on the Eddystone Rocks along with the new lighthouse, which had been built, I believe, in the 1800s. I climbed back to the top of the Hoe and then walked down the landward side and was surprised to find that within five minutes walking I was on the edge of Plymouth town centre, a very pleasant looking centre indeed. I did some window shopping only, as by this time all the shops were closed. Through the gathering dusk I made my way back to the Royal Citadel, where I decided to call in at the N.A.A.F.I., for a glass of orange. Unlike the Arborfield NA.A.F.I, I was to find the place almost deserted. It wasn't until I was introduced to the magnificent Plymouth N.A.A.F.I. Centre not ten minutes' walk from the Citadel that I realised the reason for this emptiness. The only people that regularly used the Citadel N.A.A.F.I. was the one and only forty odd member basic training unit that was situated within its walls, members of whom were usually confined to barracks, or only allowed out under the strictest supervision. Even allowing for these restrictions those people probably had the easiest basic training conditions in the whole of the British Army, though I doubt that they recognised this fact at the time. I retired to the bunkhouse and elected for an early night and in spite of all the noise that was going on around me I was soon fast asleep.

CHAPTER 16

IN WHICH I HITCH HIKE 250 MILES FOR A WEEKEND AT HOME.

On my first morning at the Royal Citadel I was disturbed very early by various personnel going to their early morning duties, for as quiet as they tried to be there was no way that they could dress and leave the barrack room without making any noise. Gradually everyone else in the room raised themselves from their slumbers and eventually got up to prepare themselves for whatever duties they had that day. It would appear that I was now out of the atmosphere whereby the Orderly Sergeant came round and knocked Hamlet out of the fire bucket with a truncheon to wake everybody up and then for good measure pulled the bedclothes off selected personnel. Seemingly we had now entered a more civilised era, whereby people knew their duties for the day and within reason were allowed to rise in their own time in order to carry out those duties. Although I didn't know what I had to do that day and therefore the time required to do it in I nevertheless decided to get up with the rest of them. It was at this stage that I realised that there was some merit in getting up earlier than the majority of people, in as much that ablutions had to be carried out in a very primitive out-house adjacent to the bunkhouse and that the hot water ran out at a very early stage. Latecomers therefore had to wash and shave in cold water, or in my case just wash in cold water because I was still able to shave the night before and pass muster parade the following morning. This process saving me valuable minutes in the mornings. I then proceeded to the cookhouse for breakfast. On arrival I noticed that all the R.E.M.E. personnel were conspicuous by their absence and it wasn't until I had almost finished that I espied Bill coming into the building.

"Good Lord", he said, "You're up bright and early, couldn't you sleep?"

"Well I thought I'd better get up earlyish I didn't know what time muster parade was".

"Muster parade!" he sputtered, and then laughed out aloud. "You've got to be joking haven't you? We don't have muster parade or any other parade for that matter, Oh no sorry there's pay parade on a Thursday, better not miss that as poor as the pay is. So long as we are down at the workshop between 08.30hrs and 09.00hrs each morning everyone is happy. I told you this is a good place to be. The only real problem is the fact that you can't get breakfast after about 08.00hrs which means that if you want breakfast you have to get up earlier than you would otherwise need do. But there you are that's life I suppose".

If what Bill was telling me was true then this was indeed a good place to be. I bet that if Captain Slater had realised that it was going to be like this he would never have sent me here. I was always convinced that Slater, in view of my attitude towards the Army, sent me to Plymouth because it was the farthest posting from home available for him to give me without sending me abroad, which with only eight months service to do even he thought would be frowned upon by higher authority. Or was I doing him an injustice, and that he knew all the time what it was like at Plymouth and he felt that I deserved a reasonable posting in which to spend what remained of my National Service?

I was pulled out of my day dreaming by Bill speaking to me again. "If you're going back to the barrack room now I'll meet you outside the wash house at half past eight and I'll then take you down to the workshops to meet the old man, and he added looking at my uniform, "I think I'd wear my denims not my battledress if I were you. As soon as we have time we'll chop your denims in for overalls, you don't have to wear a belt with overalls, less bull, and in any case the R.A.'s don't like us wearing overalls, not military enough for them, so we do it just to annoy them and of course to be different." "Right I'll see you at eight thirty then".

I made my way back to the barrack room and whiled away my time until it was time to meet Bill.

Dead on 0830hrs, I was as instructed, standing outside the wash room when Bill emerged from an adjacent building that had all the appearances of a storeroom even down to the fact that its windows were whitewashed over.

"You're not going to tell me that's where you live?" I queried.

"That's right", he said, with a grin on his face, "Come in and have a quick look round". On entry I found that the accommodation consisted of two rooms. The first room that we entered had an open fireplace with two single beds placed either side of it, with a door leading out the back to a small courtyard that backed onto the Citadel ramparts. A further door led to an inner sanctum with a further fireplace and two more beds, it was in this room that Bill lived. Out of the two rooms it had to be the more comfortable for the simple fact that it had no external doors and therefore fewer drafts than the other one. If the truth were told the two rooms were just as tatty as the bunkhouse from which I was about to move. The walls were gloss-painted in a drab olive green and cream and the floor was covered in the usual brown battleship linoleum...

The whole place was clean but not by any stretch of the imagination in a state of "bull". I was particularly amused to find that although top kits were placed in their usual position on top of the timber lockers they all had dust covers over them and couldn't be seen. Bill perceived that I was a little taken back by the condition of the two rooms.

"Cheer up", he said, "There's one great thing about this accommodation, nobody knows we live here and consequently there's never any room inspections, it's just down to us to keep it clean for our own sakes. John who has a sleeping out pass keeps his kit in here for the time being until he decides otherwise; you'll be sleeping in with Jack out in the other room. Right that's it let's get down to see the Old Man". We exited from the rooms with Bill carefully locking the door and in so doing said, "Whenever you're the last person to leave the rooms make sure that you lock up after you. We don't want anyone nosing around and finding out that somebody actually lives here, okay?"

The way to the workshops was out through the rear Sally Port gate and down quite a steep grass embankment leading to a public road and in through some gates about a hundred yards along the road. Bill explained to me that there was another way down to the workshops which entailed a circular route up and over the ramparts but he considered that the route that we were now taking was the more convenient of the two. And it was certainly to prove an easy route by which to exit the Citadel when we were making one of our clandestine trips home. The only thing we had to make sure of on such an occasion was that we didn't meet anyone in authority coming up the embankment track on our way out of the Citadel, if we were in civvies that is. If we were in uniform of course it didn't matter, for if challenged, which was most unlikely, we were on our way to the workshops. The workshops turned out to be a really tatty collection of stone and timber buildings in a very poor state of repair, the timber huts generally having been erected within derelict stone buildings. It is no surprise to me that I saw an article in The Government "Construction Journal" of 1992 that a multi-million pound project had just been completed to bring the whole of the Royal Citadel up to modern Army standards for the present occupiers, the 29th. Commando Regiment R.A. I reckon however that the project was forty years too late! I was to find that at the time I am talking about the unit employed quite a number of civilian workers mainly drawn from time-expired Army personnel. Bill took me into the workshop office and introduced me to the W.O.1. who actually ran the workshops which were under the titular head of Major Hounsell who apparently hadn't arrived yet. I was to find out subsequently that the Major, who was an ex-boy soldier, rarely arrived at the workshop much before about 10.30hrs, he always apparently had an urgent meeting to attend prior to coming to the workshop! I was then introduced to Staff Sergeant Brown who with Bill and I comprised the total strength of the Electrician Control Equipment group. It transpired that Staff and Bill were going to Wembury later that day, one of the two satellite units that came under our auspices, where the pair of them had an urgent repair to attend to. When I queried with them what I should do for the day, I was told by Bill, with Staff nodding in agreement, to get my kit out of the barrack room and move into my new accommodation and spend the day in settling in. With that he threw me the keys of our accommodation, and with a parting, "Don't forget to lock up each time you leave the rooms", they disappeared to catch the 09:00hrs lorry to Wembury. As instructed I made my way up to the Citadel, this time by taking the route over the ramparts, collected my kit and moved into the new accommodation and spent the rest of the day settling in, which in reality meant skiving for the rest of the day, an occupation in which I was now very well versed since joining the Army.

Having moved in I sat on my bed and reflected on the situation in which I now found myself. As far as I could see it was going to be pretty fair here. If one had to be in the Army, and I had to, I don't think I could ask for a better posting. That evening after tea, having first changed into my civvies, I decided to go into Plymouth, make my way to the Technical College which I had established was out there somewhere, and see what it had to offer in the way of technical courses that I could benefit by attending. I found the College without too much difficulty and signed on to study for two endorsements to my Higher National Certificate on Tuesday and Wednesday evenings. At least that would keep me busy on two nights a week. In view of the fact that I was in the forces, I was informed there was no fee to pay for the course of study which was very pleasing to hear. I returned to the Citadel with the feeling that for the first time in nearly eighteen months I had achieved something worthwhile.

Next morning we got up at about 07:30hrs and had breakfast, it was then that I found out that John the chap with the sleeping out pass made a habit of coming into the Citadel in his civilian clothes and changed into his uniform before going on duty. It appeared that he lived at his girlfriend's parents' house and didn't feel inclined to keep all his Army equipment there. Perhaps it was also at the back of his mind that if he fell out with his girlfriend he wouldn't be homeless so to speak! Once again we made our way down to the workshop area in general but this time to the E.C.E.'s workshop in particular which boasted a complete timber hut all to itself, where Staff was already busying himself with some paperwork.

"Morning Staff", said Bill, "This is Ray Skinner the replacement E.C.E. I introduced you to him briefly yesterday morning before we went to Wembury, remember?"

"I remember, Morning all, The Old Man wants the schedules for these searchlight conversions completed as soon as possible. I've completed most of the work but I'd be obliged if you and Ray could just check through the work I've done so far while I'm completing the last sheet".

"Yes sure", replied Bill, adding, "I'd like to get off as soon as we've completed them if that's okay with you Staff?"

"That's all right by me", replied Staff. We got busy and between us had them completed by N.A.A.F.I, break, then Staff handed them into the workshop office. N.A.A.F.I. break in the workshop I was soon to find out, consisted of all ranks and the workshop civilian workers sitting around the two pot-bellied stoves in the main workshop building having a chat and a yarn for half an hour or so and drinking tea out of the filthiest cups I have ever seen. I resolved there and then to go out at the earliest opportunity and purchase a cup of my own and keep it for my personal use. After N.A.A.F.I. break on our way back to the E.C.E workshop the "Old Man" Major Hounsell, called us over and handed the schedules back to us with the comment, "Staff, I distinctly remember asking for these schedules to be compiled using Whitworth bolts, you have used B.S.W .bolts, will you please alter the schedules immediately as I am in a hurry for them." And with that he disappeared into his office. I looked at Bill and Staff in wonderment, even I realised that B.S.W. stood for British Standard Whitworth.

"What do we do about that Staff," queried Bill.

"I'll just put them back into the office, by then he's sure to have realized his error.

With that Staff took the schedules back into the office and handed them to the workshop W.O.1. When he returned Bill informed him that he was off now if that was okay, and with Staff's assent disappeared off home, with the parting remark that he would see us Monday morning. Once we had returned to the privacy of the workshop I enquired from Staff if Bill had been granted a 48 hour leave pass for the weekend, even if he had been I couldn't quite see why he was leaving at 1130 hrs., after all at Arborfield we used to have to parade for our 48hr passes and then they weren't issued until 17:00hrs on Friday night.

"No", said Staff, "But there's not much going on until Monday morning so he may as well go home for the weekend". I couldn't believe my ears. "We E.C.E.s tend to look after each other in all ways that we can", he said rather reassuringly. "Bear in mind that if anyone enquires after Bill, you don't tell them he's gone home, you just say that you haven't seen him lately, which is perfectly true you haven't, and then offer to give him any message they wish to leave for him as soon as you see him". Our conversation was interrupted by the Major storming into the workshop in an obvious state of anger. "Staff these schedules are still showing B.S.W. bolts and not Whitworth as I have asked for, what is your explanation?" he demanded. "You do know the difference between the two I take it?" I coughed and Staff blinked and the Major stared at the pair of us and stood there clearly awaiting an answer. With admirable restraint Staff, no doubt influenced by the fact that he was a Staff Sergeant addressing a Major, replied, "B.S.W. stands for British Standard Whitworth Sir."

"What! Er, yes of course it does," and with a nervous twitch Major Hounsell turned on his heels and disappeared very quickly out through the door taking the schedules with him.

"We appear to have a C.O. with a great grasp of all matters technical," I observed.

Staff smiled, and winked his eye.

For the rest of the afternoon I was thinking about the weekend leave that Bill had apparently given himself and wishing that I was in his shoes, then at about 1600hrs I plucked up courage to have a word with Staff.

"Staff", I queried, "Would it be possible for me to go home this weekend as well as Bill?"

"It's all right by me if you want to, we don't do anything on a Saturday morning worth talking of. The only thing is you realize that I can't give you permission to go home, but I will do all I can to cover for you should the occasion arise. In the very unlikelihood of you being caught out, then of course this conversation didn't take place. But there's no train up to London at this time of night so how will you get home?" asked Staff.

"Hitchhike", I said quite confidently.

"Well I think if I were you I should hurry off and get some tea first before starting out". Suggested the Staff Sergeant, which is precisely what I did.

I then left the Citadel at about 17:15hrs caught a bus to the outskirts of Plymouth where I quickly got a lift over the next ten miles, landing me on the edge of Dartmoor. By this time it was dark but it didn't even enter my head that I must be mad tramping over the moors, in the dark, in winter with over two hundred miles in front of me trying to pick up a lift just to get home for a few hours. Such was the average National Serviceman's enthusiasm for the Army! His initiative however was boundless when the mood took him, or at any rate when it took me. It was at this stage that I had a small slice of luck. A large, old, furniture lorry pulled up in response to my "thumbing". When I informed the driver that I wanted London he bade me to jump in, and I immediately found myself in company with a Royal Marine on the same errand as mine. On getting into conversation with the driver I was pleased to find that he was headed for London and then delighted to find that he was headed for Turnpike Lane which was only about five miles from home. I then settled down to what I thought would be a reasonably comfortable journey of about five hours duration. Unfortunately however the lorry was quite old and was far from draught proof and the cold winter air blew into the cab in icy blasts from seemingly all directions. Although this was extremely uncomfortable and was one of the main reasons for the Marine and I for not falling asleep it was also probably our salvation, for after a couple of hours of driving we noticed that the lorry kept slewing across the road. On looking at the driver through the gloom we realised that he was apparently so tired that he kept nodding off to sleep causing the lorry to swerve across the road each time he did so. Consequently we kept up a constant conversation with him in an attempt to keep him awake and thus stop this dangerous process. In the course of conversation it transpired that he had been driving eighteen hours without a break. We eventually persuaded him to pull in at the side of the road and have a sleep. He asked us to make sure that he only had a ten minute nap but he was soon so soundly asleep that we left him for over an hour before waking him up. The sleep seemed to do the trick and we didn't experience any more untoward deviation of lorry's direction for the rest of the journey. The Marine was dropped off somewhere in West London and at about 5:00 hrs. I found myself at Turnpike Lane. I thanked the driver very much for the lift bade him farewell and then proceeded to walk the last five miles home to Enfield. It is surprising to realise in these modern days that the reason I couldn't get a lift to Enfield was not because people were frightened to pick someone up at that time of morning but merely the fact that there was no traffic around. When I eventually arrived at our flat in Wellington Road I was wondering how I could wake Doreen to let me in without waking anyone else in the house because I didn't keep a key with me in the Army. Eventually I hit upon the idea of getting the clothes prop from the garden and tapping gently on the window of the bedroom where I assumed Doreen would be sleeping. I assumed correctly and after first ascertaining who it was tapping on her bedroom window at six o'clock in the morning she came down and let me in. It was amusing to see the look of astonishment on her face and even more amusing when she said "I might have known it would be you".

We spent an idyllic week-end together cramming into the two days twice as many activities as any ordinary couple could have done, such was the pleasure of getting home and away from the Army. Every minute as far as I was concerned had to be savoured to the full. It was on occasions like this that I swore that one day I would make someone pay for these two futile years that made me so happy for such a simple act as being able to be home for the weekend and having to make a round trip of five hundred miles to achieve it. To date no one has been made to pay for those two lost years. In some small way however the writing of this book has helped me feel a little less bitter about those far-off times. Before I realised what was happening it was time for me to think about my return journey. Bill had mentioned something about a train that left Paddington station at half past midnight on a Monday morning arriving in Plymouth at 5.00am, but when I phoned Paddington station no one knew anything about such a train, or so they said. It appeared that I had missed the last train that could have got me back to Plymouth on time. It wasn't until I mentioned that I was in the forces and that I simply had to get back to Plymouth early Monday morning and that I had heard something about a paper train or such like that left for Plymouth at about half past midnight that the person at the other end of the phone admitted to the existence of such a train. He hastily added however that it wasn't a scheduled timetable train and that although it was possible for service personnel to travel on it, it would only have a couple of passenger coaches attached and that the journey could be very uncomfortable. I found that although that train never appeared on any timetable it always left and arrived on time and only took a quarter of an hour longer to get to Plymouth than the crack "Cornish Riviera" express. After bidding fond farewell to Doreen I set off for Wood Green tube station only to find that I had missed the last tube train to central London. I certainly wasn't going to be caught out on my first illegal trip home from Plymouth, so I immediately stepped into the road outside the station and had no trouble at all in thumbing a lift into central London. I arrived at Paddington station, purchased my ticket and then set about finding the platform from which this train that wasn't on any timetable ran from. At first no one would admit to the train's existence and I began to get a little bothered once again. At that time of morning however there weren't too many trains leaving Paddington and it was relatively easy for me to track down the train in question. I found a compartment with one spare seat in it and gratefully settled down to an extremely uncomfortable four and a quarter hour journey squeezed between two large matelots. In future journeys on this train I would find that the trick was to get to Paddington station some half an hour before the train departed, find an empty compartment in a carriage that was preferably sandwiched between two luggage vans to prevent access to it from the rest of the train, take the light bulbs out, draw the blinds and settle down on one of the seats as a bed. By all means allowing one other person into the compartment to take possession of the seat opposite, that way the pair of you had an unofficial sleeper and had a good chance of getting some sleep on the journey. For a train that wasn't on any timetable the tickets were always scrupulously checked by ticket inspectors just before departure. Some inspectors were very good to us and clipped the tickets and left us in the dark with a pleasant "Have a good sleep lads", or some such remark, others would insist that the bulbs were replaced immediately and that all the blinds were raised. Some would even go as far as to call out along the corridor that, "There is plenty of room in this compartment," with disastrous results for us. I can only assume that the former had been in the forces and the latter hadn't. If however you were lucky enough to be in your unofficial sleeper you had to make sure that you woke up at Plymouth, especially if you had the compartment to yourself which I had on a number of occasions, and didn't travel on to Cornwall. Mark you it was my experience there was so much noise on arrival at Plymouth station that only the dead wouldn't have been woken. Alighting from the train I was then confronted with a twenty minute walk through the streets of Plymouth back to the Royal Citadel. As I started to climb the hill up to the Citadel I overhauled Bill who, it had transpired, had caught the same train as I had. It was fortunate that I had come across Bill because I wasn't quite sure how to re-enter the Citadel in view of the fact that I had been home without a pass and in consequence hadn't booked out. Knowing Bill was in the same position as me I decided to take the lead from him. He rang the bell at the huge heavily iron-studded entrance gate, and stood back and waited. There was slight delay and then the noise of boots were heard traversing the ground between the guardroom and the gate. The vision grill in the door opened and the guard peered through it to scrutinize us. Bill and I showed our identity cards and the small picket gate was immediately opened to let us enter. As we walked past the guard room the guard commander was standing in the doorway silhouetted by the light inside. I suddenly felt hot around the collar when he called out, "don't forget to sign in lads".

Bill with a nonchalant air said, "We're R.E.M.E Sergeant".

"Oh, right", replied the Sergeant, and we continued on past the brightly lit guard room and on into the safety of the inky darkness towards our accommodation.

"How come", I inquired of Bill, "That by saying we're R.E.M.E. they don't insist on us signing in?"

"No idea", said Bill, "But it always works".

"What would we do if they insisted on us signing in", I persisted, "And then found that we hadn't signed out anyway?" I was only trying to allow for any future eventualities.

"In that case we'd say that we hadn't signed out because we're R.E.M.E. Oh I don't' know, I shouldn't worry about it, it won't crop up. If it does then improvise. Use your initiative." By this time we had reached our accommodation, we crept quietly inside without waking anyone up and slipped into bed still partially clothed and settled down to two or three hours sleep.

We eventually got up at about 0830hrs and made our way breakfastless down to the workshop area where we met Staff who with a smile on his face asked us if we had both had a good weekend. We replied that we had! It was then that Bill and Staff filled me in as to what our joint responsibilities were as E.C.E.s at the Coast Artillery School and the type of work I would be engaged upon. We were apparently responsible for all the control equipment on the searchlights, guns and ancillary equipment, and anything else that anyone might ask us to look at. And no there were no Number 10 predictors here, the piece of equipment that I had been specifically trained on for the past thirteen months! I would come across plenty of equipment that I hadn't been trained on, but not to worry between us we would cope. I got the distinct impression that on a point of honour we did our utmost to repair anything thrown at us. If we couldn't repair it there was no one else in the Citadel that could either. The trick, according to Bill, was to put on an authoritative air as if you knew all about the equipment that was put before you and if all else failed pass a hefty current through it and declare it B.L.R.'d".

"B.L.R.'d?" I queried.

"Yep!" said Bill, "Beyond Local Repair", and then it's sent back to a main workshop for repair, it's all quite simple really". I couldn't work out whether he was joking or not, but in the weeks and months ahead I was to realise that Bill was an extremely competent person, well after all he had got a B.Sc. Engineering, and we very rarely had to resort to the necessity of "B.L.R.ing" anything. It was clear to me that Staff really respected Bill's knowledge (and qualifications) and this appeared to be one of the deciding factors as to why we worked as a close-knit team. We did our utmost for Staff and in return he really looked after our interests in every way possible, which considering that he was a regular soldier was, with hindsight, rather surprising. Even I tried to sharpen up my knowledge of electrical equipment in an endeavour not to let the team down, to such an extent that in just a few weeks after my arrival Staff and Bill were sending me out to attend to repairs on my own confident that I wouldn't let them down. In this period I changed from "Skinner the Skiver" to "Skinner the Bullshitter", confident in the knowledge that if

I didn't know very much about the equipment I was trying to repair. I could be certain that the Royal Artillery personnel around me knew absolutely nothing whatsoever about it. In all instances therefore I had the edge on them. This newly found confident air of mine was really put to the test one night when I was the duty E.C.E. on an officer's course night shoot out at Wembury. But I'm racing ahead. My time at Plymouth started to pass by in as a pleasant time as one could expect in the Army. We didn't have to get up very early in the morning, there were never any room inspections or leastwise none that we participated in, and there were certainly no muster parades. Work within the Royal Citadel was carried out without undue pressure and if we felt like a change we could take a trip out to either of the two satellite sites at Wembury or Lentley situated some six miles away on Plymouth Sound. Wembury housed the sharp end hardware of the school, the actual coast artillery itself. A battery of three 9.2" calibre guns of 1901 vintage, and a battery of two 6" calibre guns of the even earlier vintage of 1895. The 6" guns were often fired as part of the course, but the 9.2" guns never. Rumour had it that on the rare occasions when they had been fired in the past, the surrounding properties had all lost the glass from their windows, due to the tremendous blast effect, and had to be replaced at the Army's expense. Consequently now whenever they had a course on the 9.2's the personnel went through all the drill of preparing the gun to fire but in point of fact only actually fired a two pounder gun situated on top of the larger gun's barrel, which when fired sounded rather like a damp squib going off. On reflection I suppose this was one of the first of the many post-war Army cut backs, and there have been cut backs ever since. Lentney on the other hand housed a radar unit that was used in conjunction with the guns at Wembury and boasted its own resident R.E.M.E. garrison of radar mechanics. Although things appeared to be very relaxed at that unit it was out in the wilds and difficult to get to the fleshpots of Plymouth.

Another point was the fact that they were commanded by a full Lieutenant, a recently commissioned W.O.1, who tended to be a trifle unpredictable, or so I heard.

On balance I believe that we were better off being in the

Citadel, as in a manner of speaking we had the best of both worlds, being billeted in the Royal Citadel but being able to visit Wembury and Lentley when necessity or the mood took us. Weekend home leave wasn't too bad either only being restricted, more or less, by whether or not the weather was good enough to attempt to hitch-hike home or if I felt in a position to spend nearly two weeks of my pay on the train journey home. When either of us felt a little more adventurous we would award ourselves a long weekend and leave for home Thursday morning. In these cases however the pair of us very rarely went home at the same time, the idea being that the one left behind could cover for the other and cause less need for Staff to cover for the pair of us. In the meantime, unencumbered as we were with evening duties, I was busy working away at the Plymouth Technical College studying for my endorsements to my Higher National certificate, and usually relying very heavily upon Bill to help me with my homework. Yes, life wasn't too bad; if you had to be in the Army, and we had to be, there were worst postings than the Coast Artillery School in the Royal Citadel at Plymouth, though I would never admit to it within earshot of anyone in authority.

CHAPTER 17

IN WHICH WE DECIDE
WE'RE NOT GOING TO BE COLD

I have previously mentioned the door in our billet that led out to a small courtyard at the rear. In this courtyard we used to keep our weekly fuel allowance for our two open fires, in practice however the fuel allowance was so inadequate that we only usually lit one fire and that was the one in the inner sanctum. The fuel allowance for these two fires as I recall was a small galvanized tub of coal per week along with a similar allowance of logs. This allowance, or ration, was supposed to be collected on a Saturday morning but it was so unusual for us to be anywhere near Plymouth on a Saturday that we arranged with the Stores Quarter Master to allow us to pick up our fuel on a Friday or even on a Thursday, due to the fact that we were far too busy on a Saturday morning carrying out urgent maintenance work! You can fool some of the people some of the time was our motto. We found no need to fool all of the people all of the time to gain our ends.

When we were ready to pick up our fuel allowance, Bill and I, in company with our other roommate, would take a trolley up to the fuel compound, fill up the tubs just as high as we possibly could and then proceed to wheel the trolley out of the compound very carefully indeed, doing our utmost not to spill any of the coal.

Some Quarter Masters would laugh at our initiative and agree that if we could get the trolley out of the compound without dropping any of the fuel then it was ours, if any fell off we had to give the extra fuel back.

Some would even go as far as chalking a line on the ground to denote the point that we had to reach before the fuel was ours, and then have bets amongst themselves as to whether or not we would make it. Other Quarter Masters would be nowhere near as sporting and would ask. "What the hell are you playing at?" and give the tubs a hefty kick spilling the extra fuel onto the floor, then order us to put all the fuel above the top of the tub back on the fuel piles, at the same time stating that regulations only allowed us that amount of fuel and no more, not tubs piled up like

"Bleeding Everest". Needless to say this fuel allowance didn't go very far even though we were down to only one fire, in view of the fact that that winter was a particularly cold one in Plymouth we were also cold. Even when we were allowed to draw more than our official ration by the Quarter Master it only lasted us three or four nights a week, we were cold for the rest of the time. As the winter grew harder and we grew forever colder we realised that we simply had to do something about the fuel situation. It was then that we cast an envious eye on the huge pile of coke that was situated in a compound hard against the rampart walls. This coke compound was guarded at ground level by a very substantial stone wall surmounted by barbed wire accessed by a pair of very strong oak gates. There seemed to be very little prospect of forcing these gates or climbing the stone wall but we felt that the pile of coke must be able to be exploited in some way or other to our advantage. At this point Bill and I decided to hold a council of war with our R.E.M.E. compatriots housed as they were in their various hideaways around the Citadel all suffering from the cold as we were. We put it to them that the coke store looked promising and what did they think about trying to "win" some of it. Sandy, a dour Scotsman thought long and hard then alerted us, in detail, to all the possible consequences of carrying out such an operation. In spite of Sandy echoing most of our own misgivings, we all agreed that the scheme was worth looking into. So that weekend, when there weren't too many people around, we decided to have a very serious look at the prospects of "winning" some of this coke.

Four of us took a Sunday afternoon stroll around the ramparts. In a serious attempt to look totally innocent in our intentions, I took my camera along with me and made a great play of taking photographs of Plymouth from our high vantage point. All the time I was taking photographs however we were all taking sidelong glances at the coke store and its massive defences and generally summing up the prospects of getting hold of some of this valuable, to us, fuel. It was when we were all huddled together in a group looking out over Plymouth and the others taking an over-zealous interest in the photograph that I was attempting to take, that Bill with his back to the coke store asked if we had all noticed the electric supply cable to the workshop area which came up over the ramparts ran down over the top of the coke before disappearing down the side of the wall that enclosed the stock of coke. Bill continued, as we all still looked out over Plymouth, that provided we could make the cable secure enough someone could climb down from the ramparts by holding onto this electric cable, fill up some sacks from the top of the pile and then come back up again. Whilst still apparently taking a great interest in my photography, each of the group in turn took a furtive look at the coke store to the rear of us to confirm what Bill was talking about. We all agreed that such an operation had strong possibilities. Having taken all the photographs that I required, we then strode nonchalantly back to our billets passing the coke store on the way. As we did so we noticed that the electric cable was fixed none too securely to two poles on top of the ramparts to enable persons to walk underneath unimpeded by the cable. We returned to our hideaway to discuss our future plans regarding the coke, we all realised the seriousness of that which we were contemplating but we had all had enough of being cold. I think it was Sandy, our serious minded Scotsman who first spoke.

"You all realise", he said quietly, "that if we get caught we'll be put away it won't just be CB we'll get".

"Surely not", said I.

"Bloody well will be", said John.

I looked around the group of seven very serious faces who even at that very moment were cold and fed up with being cold.

"You've seen the problem, it will be virtually impossible for Ray and I to do it on our own, if it's to be done safely, it needs a team", Bill informed the meeting. "Whatever coke we get we'll share equally, who's in and who's out?"

After a very few moments contemplation we all agreed that we were all in, even though I don't think any of us looked with relish upon a visit to Colchester Military Prison. But in doing so we all considered that it was essential that we work out a good plan to eliminate any possibility of us being caught whilst carrying out this clandestine operation. We therefore prepared a plan whereby first and foremost, in accordance with good Army practice, we guarded our flanks by posting a person at each end of the ramparts to give us warning of any approaching danger. Should anyone come from one end of the ramparts we would withdraw via the other end, should we be approached from both ends at once, we would withdraw down into the workshop area down the little used timber staircase leading from the ramparts down to the workshops. In normal circumstances however no one, to our knowledge, walked along the ramparts at night, the time we anticipated carrying out our operation. The area in question would be in total darkness and should anyone in authority hear something they felt that they should investigate it was most unlikely that they would do so from both directions at once. It required brains to think of doing that and we confidently considered that we had a monopoly in that field, such was our confidence of success! We all agreed that there was no time like the present so we would go for the coke that night at about 21:00 hrs., a time when we stood little possibility of meeting people whilst carrying out our operation and at a time when any noise made would not be treated with any great suspicion as it would be, at say, 02:00hrs. Before we made the actual assault on the coke we had to secure the cable that was to be climbed down. This of course we couldn't do in daylight without raising suspicion so we decided that this job would have to be carried out immediately prior to the assault being made. It would mean a slight delay, whilst this operation was carried out, but we didn't see that as a problem. At 08:55hrs seven slightly apprehensive people met at the foot of the ramparts in dark overalls and plimsolls. We posted our guards and quietly climbed the slope up to the top of the ramparts. We then proceeded to where the cable crossed the ramparts and ran down to the top of the coke pile, and secured the cable with a hefty fastening of insulation tape. It was our intention to let two people down on to the coke to enable the operation of the coke purloining to be carried out as quickly as possible. Unfortunately however we hadn't allowed for the noise that would be generated by persons moving around on top of the coke. As we lowered Bill down and his feet touched the coke, to us the noise that was made was earth shattering and we prepared to beat a hasty retreat. After waiting a few moments however we realised that our actions did not appear to have generated any unwanted interest and that our guards had not warned us of any impending danger, so we proceeded with the task in hand at top speed with only the one person on the coke instead of the two as we had anticipated. Bill worked so fast however that he and the precious bags of coke were up with us within a couple of minutes. We withdrew our guards, split up and made a silent retreat back to our respective billets. On arrival at ours we deposited our share of the spoils in the small courtyard out the back of the billet and locked the door happy in the knowledge that we had put one over on the Army, leastwise that's the way I saw it. Never for one moment did I see it as an act of stealing which of course it was.

We repeated the operation several times that winter the only problem we encountered was that as the mound of fuel diminished, both by our efforts and legitimate usage, was that the climb down onto the coke became longer and a little more difficult to achieve but our gang of desperadoes was equal to the task. Gradually we built up a large store of coke in our courtyard, away from all prying eyes. Long after our last coke purloining escapade however this large pile of purloined coke was nearly our undoing, but for the time being it was our saviour and never again did we go cold that winter. It was always a source of mystery to visitors, who were not in the know, as to how we managed to make our fuel ration last so well! We never let them into the secret. In spite of our fuel bonanza we still played our little game each time we picked up our weekly fuel allowance, we felt not to do so, could have given rise to suspicion in the minds of at least some of the Quarter Masters. Mark you the use of coke on our fire did have its little problems mainly in the ignition department. Coke was very difficult to get burning with sticks and paper in the conventional manner, so we welded up a mild steel plate in the workshop, that covered the fireplace except for a small gap at the bottom to induce a draught under the fire grate. This worked so well that we set the chimney on fire at least twice that winter much to our embarrassment. As well as keeping us warm the fire was used on many an evening to cook our late night supper of fried anything and beans and of course for the endless pots of tea that we brewed up. Needless to say we soon acquired by fair means or foul a comprehensive collection of cooking utensils which we used to good advantage. In fact we started to get quite a reputation for our culinary skills and hospitality during the dark nights of that winter, especially on a Saturday night when we often had a card school going. Our pay was so low however that we usually played for matchsticks because we just couldn't afford to lose any money. In the absence of any duties other than the very occasional night shoot, on Tuesday and Wednesday evenings we had a change of cuisine for supper, on those evenings I went to classes at the local Technical College and almost without exception on my way home I would bring in chips for the pair of us from a "chippie" that was very close to the Citadel. "Home" being a relative expression of course. The evening classes were somewhere for me to retreat to for a couple of hours a night, two nights a week, and had the advantage of getting me out of the Army environment and mixing with people allied to my civilian occupation. It is worth relating however that only myself and one other member of the course, who it transpired was in the Navy, took the course seriously and attended regularly. The others who all appeared to know each other attended very infrequently and when they did were quite disruptive, much to our annoyance. "Navy" and I got a little fed up with their attitude and took the clique aside one night and suggested that if they weren't interested in the subjects then they should stay away. They all then confided in us that they hadn't any real interest in the course and were only attending it as an official way to put off doing their National Service. At this stage "Navy" and I revealed our colours so to speak and informed them that although we couldn't care less whether or not they attended regularly but if they insisted on being disruptive when they did attend they'd have to suffer the consequences as "Navy" put it. Such was obviously the reputation of the Navy in Plymouth in those days that we never had any further problems from the clique. I never did ask "Navy" what the consequences were likely to be but I got the distinct impression that they'd be pretty dire! Whilst attendance at the college broke the week up quite nicely and alleviated the boredom of the winter evenings it did little to alleviate the boredom of the weekends, a large portion of which was by necessity spent in the billet. Due to the fact that happily we had no bulling or duties to carry out time weighed very heavily on our hands with only an old radio of mine, that was forever breaking down, for entertainment. Consequently we rose quite late, and on Sundays in particular, in fact just about in time to go to lunch. We would then while away the afternoon waiting for Hancock's Half Hour to come on the radio before going to tea. Then in the evening we would probably go into town to the N.A.A.F.I. club to spend some of my 22/-d Army pay; I'd had a rise in the pay that I was receiving each week at the time. One day three of us did decide to be particularly energetic, got up early, caught a bus to Yelverton,

and then trekked over Dartmoor to Princetown, a distance of about ten miles. We took with us all the accoutrements for cooking a lunch on the moors. Taking our time in the superb weather we had a thoroughly enjoyable time, until we reached Princetown! After having a cup of tea in a Café we found open, we enquired where we caught the bus back to Yelverton, to be told there were no buses on a Sunday, so at about three 'o clock in the afternoon we then had to walk the ten miles back to Yelverton. After that experience we tended to stay in bed on a Sunday once again. On another Sunday we were all detailed to attend Church Parade. As it was a Church of England church and I was a declared Methodist, I informed the Battery Office that I felt that I was unable to take part in the service due to my religious beliefs. Surprisingly, I was told that would be alright, the B.S.M. quite understood my reasons for not wishing to go into a Church of England service, he had come across this problem in the past, but before I had a chance to congratulate myself on my successful ruse, he then added that in the circumstances it was quite in order for me to wait outside the church for the duration of the service. It was then that I reluctantly decided that I would rather sit in the church for an hour or so rather than stand outside it!

Our workshop W.O.1. for ever having the welfare of his men foremost in his mind and no doubt hearing about our weekend boredom, did dream up an activity to combat it. He decided to have what he called regimental training on Saturday mornings. This apart from anything else started with a roll call, which immediately made going home early for an unofficial long weekend very difficult indeed. I eventually I got over the problem by going home on the Saturday lunchtime express train and not coming back until Monday evening.

This regimental training caused us to draw our Sten Guns

out of the armoury in order to carry out various forms of fire-arms practice, but thankfully no arms drill as such, for as far as we could gather there was none known for Sten guns. The Regimental Training soon became a fiasco, the senior N.C.O.s who were trying to instruct us, being technical N.C.O.s, were very much out of touch with drill instructor's techniques and soon realised much to their embarrassment that we knew far more about the subject than they did. For once discretion proved to be the better part of valour and the training was stopped. We put our Sten Guns back in the armoury. We no longer had a role call and once again we either slept in on a Saturday morning or were already home on unofficial long weekends, in between the official 48 hour leaves that we were granted every four weeks, which on most occasions we extended to at least 72 hours anyhow without any consequences that I recall. As well as the official 48 hour leaves, and the unofficial ones which I gave myself, I could look forward to receiving between seven to fourteen days leave at Christmas, Easter and Whitsun before I left the Army in June of 1956. I went home at every opportunity I possibly could, just to be with Doreen and get away from the Army environment. If this in the Army's eyes made me a bad soldier then so be it. In my defence however I would say that when the occasion arose and I felt the situation justified it, which wasn't very often, I considered that I could easily hold my own with most regular soldiers at drill, shooting and technical expertise, and I totally eclipsed them at skiving!

The most attractive feature of being posted to the Royal Citadel was the almost total absence of parades for us R.E.M.E. personnel, and when there was an occasional parade it was the easiest thing in the world for us to be excused from it by virtue of urgent work that had to be carried out. Amazingly enough repair of equipment used on the courses, took priority over parades, under no circumstances whatsoever were courses to be delayed on account of defunct equipment, especially when that course consisted of overseas personnel in Britain for training. This attitude suited Staff, Bill and I very well indeed. Provided we kept all the equipment under our care in good working order we were left to our own devices and were readily excused non-important parades and duties. The important parades and duties we excused ourselves from anyway. We didn't feel inclined to have anything to do with them if we could help it! Regular room inspections were however a feature of the Royal Citadel, when we got wind of such an inspection we would get up earlier than usual that day, lock the door of our establishment and disappear down to the workshop, with an "out of sight out of mind type of attitude". This procedure was helped by the fact that although our room was adjacent to barrack rooms to be inspected it was in such a dilapidated building that no one in authority realised that we lived there and therefore did not query the fact that the door of this "storeroom" was always locked whenever they carried out an inspection of the living accommodation. One day however our best laid plans nearly backfired. I seem to recall that it was one of those Monday mornings when Bill and I were particularly tired having just returned to the Citadel on the night train and not got to bed until about 0:500hrs after one of our long weekends at home. We explained to the other two lads in the rooms who were up early to catch the lorry out to Lentley that we were going to lie in that morning so would they make sure that they locked the door after them when they left. Bill and I then went to sleep again. We were suddenly woken up by the noise of the door handle of the room being vigorously rattled and a voice, that was immediately recognised as that of the adjutant calling out. "I can't open this door, Mr Gilbey, it's locked" Bill and I looked at each other in shocked horror. Bill putting a finger to his lips. A guardian angel came to our aid in the form of the Battery Sergeant Major.

"That's all right sir, nobody lives in there that's only a store room".

"Right you are Sergeant Major".

We sighed a sigh of relief as we heard footsteps recede into the distance Now wide awake with any thought of further sleep deserting us, we hurriedly dressed, for we couldn't be certain that the illustrious pair wouldn't be back. We did a quick reconnaissance through the key hole, saw that the coast was clear and beat a hasty retreat down to the workshop in a slight sweat. It transpired that we had been extremely careless and had not read battery orders before we had departed for our clandestine weekend leave or we would have noticed that there was to be a room inspection that Monday morning. We resolved to be more careful in future. We didn't want any more close calls like the one we had just experienced.

CHAPTER 18

IN WHICH THE ELITE ARE PUT ON GUARD

I have previously mentioned that situated within a five or ten minute walk of the Royal Citadel was the Plymouth N.A.A.F.I. Club. This was a newish building of four or so stories high with recreational facilities on the first two floors and bedroom accommodation on the other floors where officers and their ladies, N.C.O.s and their wives, and other ranks and their women could stay! The recreational facilities took the form of quite a nice dance hall where a live band played once or twice a week, a bar where there was often a skiffle group, complete with tea chest double base playing, a billiard room with half a dozen tables, a table tennis room, a television theatre with a large screen set, black and white only of course in those days, and a music room containing a radiogram which was only allowed to be used under the strictest of supervision. This supervision usually taking on the guise of a folded arm middle-aged W.V.S. volunteer, in uniform, sitting in the corner waiting to manipulate the records, which could be your own that you had brought along, or ones selected from the resident collection. The resident collection I might add left a lot to be desired and it was advisable to bring your own if you didn't wish to be bored to tears. Oh yes and there was a caféteria which sold snacks and meals of all types, at it must be said, very reasonable prices. Bill, I, and the others used the N.A.A.F.I. club on numerous occasions, usually to watch something special on television such as a football match or similar entertainment, and to play table tennis or the occasional game of snooker. In the latter case the loser buying the drinks usually a 6d (2.5p) pint of orange. Being family men neither of us participated in the dancing although we did occasionally go into the dance hall to listen to the bands, some of whom were very good indeed especially when you realise that they were all composed of service personnel.

We used to operate a little racket for entering the dance hall, although the entry fee was very modest it was a point of honour to try and gain entry free of charge. No tickets were issued for entry but raffle-style tickets were issued as pass-outs, the trick was to get a pass-out ticket late on in the evening and not go back into the dance and retain the pass-out ticket. The plan being to obtain a collection of pass-out tickets of all available colours. When visiting the N.A.A.F.I. Club on the next occasion one would find out what colour pass-out tickets were being used that evening and gain entry to the dance by the simple expedient of offering up a pass-out ticket of the correct colour gained at a previous dance.

Unfortunately the organisers of the dances eventually grew wise to this wheeze and after one of our number had been thrown out by the scruff of his neck one evening for trying to gain entry on an old pass-out ticket, we realised that the doorman was now scrutinizing the serial number of the pass-out tickets as well as their colour. Unfortunately things were never the same again! Not unnaturally there were never enough service females to satisfy the demand for dancing partners at these dances so female civilians were allowed into the NA.A.F.I. Club provided they were signed in by a serviceman. Sometimes therefore when entering the Club you could be confronted by a female asking to be signed in to enable them to attend the dance, or so they said! One evening when I was visiting the N.A.A.F.I. Club on my own I was confronted by such a female. Being good natured, and possibly an idiot to boot, I took up her request and signed her in. In theory I was aware that you were meant to stay with the person that you signed in like any other club. In practice however the females were signed in and then usually forgotten about for the rest of the evening. Consequently after signing in this particular female I left her to her own devices and went off to play table tennis and thought no more about her. Later on in the evening I was walking through the main concourse of the club when I noticed the female in question coming down the staircase from, I realised later, the general direction of the residential sleeping accommodation. A W.V.S. worker standing by her office door pointed an accusing finger at her and in a very commanding voice demanded to know how she had got into the club. At that precise moment the female on the stairs spotted me walking through the hallway swept a hand towards me and said

"He signed me in".

Taken by surprise I wondered what all the fuss was about.

The W.V.S. worker in a very authoritative tone now pointed

to me and said,

"You in my office over there", then confronting the female on the staircase said,

"And you out, now", she said pointing to the girl, who after a token protest scuttled out through the entrance doors. I was standing in the office totally mystified over what had just happened, when the W.V.S. lady entered the office carefully closed the door behind her and then confronted me.

"Did you sign her in?" she asked.

"Well yes I did, what's all the fuss about? I had no idea I was doing anything wrong, people do it all the time. She wanted to go to the dance".

"And I suppose you are going to tell me that you had no idea that that young lady", she spat out the words, young lady, "Is one of the most notorious prostitutes around these parts? " And", she continued, "I also suppose you are also going to tell me that you didn't know that if you signed a female, or anyone else for that matter into this club you were expected to stay with them all the time they are on the premises?"

"But surely that rule isn't strictly enforced for females coming into the dance?"

She nearly exploded. "Dance, dance, you don't really think that she came in here for a dance do you?"

"Well, yes that's what she told me", I said defensively.

"Well you can take it from me that she didn't" The W.V.S. lady continued, "She's a well known prostitute and came in here to drum up some trade and to pick up some clients for when the club closes no doubt".

I was totally embarrassed, I apologised to my stern inquisitor for my naivety and promised that I would bear in mind what she had told me and would never sign females into the club ever again. Completely flummoxed I hurried out of her office as fast as I could, all thoughts of further table tennis having deserted me, at the same time resolving in future to brush up upon my prostitute identification ability. As an "old married man" I was a trifle naive on the subject, mainly I suppose because I had no need of such services! Over the next few weeks I quickly made great friends with that particular W.V.S. lady, so much so that I became one of the few service personnel allowed to have the key of the music room and to play my records unsupervised. Gradually this trust went even a stage further and I was allowed to take my R.E.M.E. compatriots up to the room and hold musical evenings of my own. After a while, as we got to know each other better, we often had a laugh over the incident of the prostitute. That particular incident had however taught me a lesson and thereafter I resisted the temptation of ever signing another female into the N.A.A.F.I. club. Whenever any of my compatriots did, I was always trying to decide whether or not they were signing in prostitutes, but I was hopeless at the task, they all looked like nice young girls to me!

Although the facilities offered by the N.A.A.F.I. Club as a place of entertainment for service personnel were first rate and cheap, it had one large draw- back, it closed at 10:00 pm each night. This factor was particularly frustrating on a Saturday night when one was anticipating staying out a little later than usual, especially if you were in the middle of watching an interesting programme on television. We found the answer to this particular problem however, we would rush out of the club round to a nearby television shop where the proprietor by way of an advertisement would have a set running in his window until midnight. There on the pavement a crowd of us would stand outside the shop watching the end of the programme. This was all right if it was say a football match or something that didn't really require any sound but hopeless if it was a programme that did, and the practice wasn't to be recommended if it was raining or indeed snowing. Other than the N.A.A.F.I. Club the only other source of entertainment readily available to us were the cinemas. Although there were quite a number of these in Plymouth there were so many service personnel in the area, especially sailors off the ships at Devonport, that they were usually very difficult to get into especially on a Saturday night. This being the case I remember an occasion when Bill and I particularly wanted to see a film called "Davey Crocket" starring Fess Parker, we decided that our best chance of getting in to see it was by skiving off work one afternoon and going to the cinema then, which is precisely what we did. Whilst watching the film it hadn't escaped our notice that the film was being received in a very raucous manner with the theme song being taken up by the audience every time it was played and lots of yelling and shouting going on. At the interval when the lights went up, we realised the reason for the raucous behaviour, we were virtually the only two adults in a sea of children. Sitting there amongst them in our uniforms we felt very conspicuous indeed. Not as conspicuous however as on another afternoon a few days later however when the pair of us on agreeing that a haircut was long overdue decided to take a trip to a civilian barber rather than visit the regimental sheep shearer. The civilian barber in question was situated in the Barbican area of Plymouth some quarter of a mile from the workshop, and close by the Pilgrim's Steps from whence the Pilgrim Fathers had sailed to the "New World" in 1620. It wasn't until we had entered the barber's shop and sat down to await our turn that we realised that the person in the chair having a shave and a haircut was in fact our C.O. Major Hounsell, commander of the workshop. Safe in the knowledge that we were all in the wrong place at the wrong time, and rather than stare at each other albeit through the large mirror on the wall in stony silence, Bill gave a spontaneous, "Hello Sir, nice weather we're having for the time of year". He received a nod of agreement in return from the Major. On completing his toiletries Major Hounsell was brushed down by the barber and left the shop without uttering a single word to us.

"Friend of yours?" Enquired the barber with a broad smile on his face.

"We come across him from time to time", replied Bill with an even bigger smile. Next day in the workshop I half expected the pair of us to be called in to the Major's Office and be asked to explain our presence in the barber's shop the previous afternoon. I needn't have worried however, we were never called to account for our visit to the barber. Maybe the Major was too embarrassed over his own indiscretion. As Bill pointed out, "It grew in their bloody time so surely we were entitled to have it cut in their bloody time". An argument that I don't think would have found very much favour with the Army authorities. It was soon after this incident that I was summoned to see the unit's medical officer. I was reminded by him that my three months temporary excused boots order was coming to an end and that he required me to have my ankles examined by a specialist at the Plymouth Naval

Hospital to determine whether or not my shoe order should now be revoked or confirmed. The present situation was that although I still retained two pairs of boots, I had been issued with one pair of shoes along with a tatty little chit, which was worth its weight in gold to me, declaring to the world, and to the Army in particular, that I was excused boots and all parades for a period of three months. It was that three month period that was now about to reviewed. Excused boots in the Army was as far as I was concerned was the equivalent of being sent on a luxury holiday in civilian life. I had no intention of having that privilege being withdrawn from me if I could avoid it. It was one of the few things that had made my life in the Army bearable over the past three months. I arrived at the Naval Hospital on the due date for a 10:00hrs appointment to see the specialist in question, to find that all forty or so patients to be seen that day had all been given the same appointment time of 10:00hrs, naval efficiency at its best! To be scrupulously fair, or so the medical orderly said, the consultant had decided to take every one in alphabetical order, as my initial was "S" I would probably get to see the doctor at about 17:00hrs a wait of some six hours. I was ordered however not to leave the premises in the meantime just in case the batting order was changed. I got into conversation with a naval rating called Ron Smith, who we determined also had an appointment to see the specialist immediately following my one. We then went off to find the Hospital N.A.A.F.I. Club and the pair of us passed a very pleasant day there indeed, alternating between playing table tennis and snooker, and occasionally popping back to the waiting room to see how the appointments were progressing. Other patients less wily than the pair of us spent the whole of their time sitting on the hard wooden chairs patiently waiting their turn to see the consultant. Eventually at about 17:30hrs my name was called and I was ushered into the presence of a very severe looking naval Surgeon Commander. (I only knew his rank by the fact that the medical orderly had informed me so).

"Right Skinner", he said looking at the notes before him, "How is the ankle?"

"Strengthening up quite nicely Sir", I replied.

"What exactly do you mean by that?" he queried.

My story has got to be good I thought.

"Well Sir, when I was wearing boots I found that each time I put on shoes to wear in civilian dress I would invariably turn my ankle over due to the fact, I suppose, that it didn't have the support of the boot. Now that I am wearing shoes all the time I find that I very rarely turn my ankle over at all. That's why I said it appears to be strengthening up quite nicely Sir ".

"Hm, so what you're saying is that if you were returned to boot order, every time you wore your shoes you would possibly turn your ankle over?"

"Yes Sir, that's what I think Sir". He then examined my ankle in a cursory manner.

"Can't have you falling over everywhere when you go back into civvy street can we Skinner?" he said with the vestige of a smile on his face.

"No sir", I agreed.

"Hm", he breathed, looking me full in the face. "Right I'm recommending that your shoe order be confirmed, alright?" he queried.

I nearly fell over, I thought that there had been a good chance that my temporary shoe order was about to be cancelled not confirmed.

"Yes Sir, thank you Sir". You can't say too many Sirs on an occasion like this I thought as I let out a great sigh of relief at the news I was being given.

"That's all you may go, I'll write to your Medical Officer informing him of my decision." I felt like kissing him let alone saluting him, but as I wasn't wearing my beret I did neither and merely retired from the room in a soldier-like but hurried manner before he changed his mind. I couldn't believe my luck, Skinner does it again I thought.

Outside in the waiting room I exchanged au revoirs with my naval compatriot for the day and prepared to depart for the Royal Citadel feeling that it had been a day very well spent indeed. How well I was about to find out the very next day.

The Royal Citadel housed two distinct units which were however closely inter-related. One was the 47th Regiment, Royal Coast Artillery, and the other was the Coast Artillery School. The

47th Regiment, as far as I recall, amongst other things catered for basic training of raw recruits whereas the Coast Artillery School ran a series of courses for experienced soldiers including officers, and whilst the 47th Regiment had its usual quota of attached personnel, the Coast Artillery School had an abundance of them to maintain all the sophisticated equipment required for the courses. It had been, up until now been normal practice for all duties, such as guards, fire pickets, fatigues etc. to be carried out by Royal Artillery personnel especially those engaged on basic training, but with the gradual demise of Coast Artillery in favour of missiles the 47th Regiment now appeared to be only catering for a very small basic training intake, and the Coast Artillery School now only catering for officer courses of mainly overseas personnel, consequently the number of duties having to be carried out by Royal Artillery personnel had therefore become very onerous indeed. The attached personnel were well aware of this fact and in consequence were keeping a very low profile at the present time. Eventually even the Battery Sergeant Major tripped over the fact that there were apparently more attached personnel in the Royal Citadel than there were Royal Artillery personnel. Henceforth it was decreed attached personnel would now carry out their fair share of guard duties alongside their Royal Artillery comrades. This decision of course sent a shiver down our spines.

As a direct consequence of this decree the very next morning I was in the workshop when I received a telephone call from the Battery Sergeant Major informing me that I was on guard that very night. I can only assume that the reason that he telephoned personally is that he knew from experience that it was unlikely that I would take any notice of the battery clerk giving me such a message especially if it hadn't been published in battery orders which it hadn't. He was a trifle put out, to say the least, when I explained that I couldn't do the guard duty as I was officially excused boots (and had a chitty to prove the fact) and as far as I was aware one couldn't go on guard mounting without boots. I was also just about to explain to him, when the phone went down with a crash, that no R.E.M.E. personnel possessed the other guard mounting accessory, e.g. a rifle. Realising the problems involved in owning a rifle, such as having to keep it clean etc., we had all opted instead for the safer alternative of having Sten machine guns issued to us. As all automatic weapons, for some reason best known to the Army, were required to be kept in the armoury they caused us very little problem indeed, there was never any chance of us "losing" them or having their bolts secreted away by an over-enthusiastic Second Lieutenant. Mark you the B.S.M. soon got over this little problem by making a pool of rifles available for R.E.M.E. personnel who were required for guard duty.

I had just congratulated myself on how well I had handled the situation when the 'phone rang again.

"Skinner?"

"Speaking."

"Battery Sergeant Major here".

"Yes Sir".

"You're on fire picket tonight parade on the square at 06:00hrs, understood?"

"Er, yes Sir. Excuse me Sir I can't actually parade on the square though".

"What the hell do you mean you can't parade on the square," he demanded, "You're only excused boots aren't you?"

"Well no Sir, I'm excused boots, and all parades. I'm sorry Sir, but if it's all the same to you Sir I'll wait in the guard room whilst the Orderly Officer inspects the fire picket on the square. All right Sir?" I queried.

Once again the 'phone slammed down at the other end of the line. Hard as I tried I could think of no way that I could get out of the fire piquet so with bad grace resigned myself to the fact that I was on fire piquet.

The evening was quite warm and sunny as I watched with interest the Orderly Officer inspecting the fire piquet on the square from my vantage point sitting on the guard commander's table in the guardroom. Having finished his inspection, the officer of the day, a nig Second Lieutenant by the look of him, came hurtling over to the guard room presumably in search of his missing fire piquet member. On entering the guard room and seeing me sitting on the table he became extremely agitated.

"Are you 258 Skinner?" he demanded in a very loud voice.

"Er yes Sir that's me Sir," I said sliding off the table and standing up.

"Stand to attention when you speak to me", he yelled in near hysteria. "And stand still", pause, then, "Why aren't you wearing a belt?" he demanded.

"I'm R.E.M.E. Sir. We wear overalls and we're not required to wear webbing belts with overalls, Sir". I replied in as soothing voice as possible as I realised that the officer now before me appeared to be on the verge of a nervous breakdown.

"And, well until yesterday I was excused boots for three months Sir as a temporary measure and in consequence I only have one pair of Army issue shoes and at the moment they are at the repairers sir, until they come back I have to wear my plimsolls sir, as I didn't think it appropriate to wear my civilian shoes on duty Sir, especially as they are suede leather and might be thought of as brothel creepers, Sir. But yesterday Sir, I saw Surgeon Commander Green at the naval hospital and he has confirmed my shoe order Sir, and today I have ordered my second pair of shoes from the stores, so this shouldn't occur again Sir.

The Second Lieutenant looked at me intently, apparently speechless, searching in his own mind for something to say. "About turn," he commanded, his voice reaching a crescendo. In my haste to obey his command I inadvertently left about turned, instead of the regulatory right about turn. The result was that the Second Lieutenant nearly went into a dead faint on the spot.

"You did a left about turn", he shouted in accusing disbelief.

"Sorry Sir", I apologised, "I'll do a right about turn".

"Stand still and don't you dare move, you're an absolute disgrace to the Royal Artillery".

"R.E.M.E. Sir". I ventured!

"What?"

"Disgrace to R.E.M.E. Sir", I said pointing to my cap badge, "I'm in R.E.M.E. sir".

There was silence for a few seconds whilst he stared at me intently. Then he erupted.

"Get out of my bloody sight and join the rest of the fire piquet in the cookhouse and don't you let me see you again, ever!" As I stood there contemplating the improbability of him not seeing me again, ever, in the close confines of the Royal Citadel he let out one last explosive, "Move!"

Sensing that it really was time for me to move, as I had clearly overstayed my welcome where I was, I hurried out of the guard room and made my way up to the cookhouse to join the rest of the fire piquet, where having been very quickly versed in the intricacies of fire fighting they were now engaged in the far more important task of "spud bashing". It was always a sense of annoyance to me that being on fire piquet in the Army had very little to do with fire fighting it was merely an excuse to get a squad of men into the cookhouse for two or three hours per night for the purpose of washing up and peeling potatoes, very often working shoulder to shoulder with men on jankers. They would be there for punishment and you would be there on duty. On reflection I suppose there was, in the Army, only a very fine line between punishment and various forms of duty, personally I always felt that I had been put on duty as a punishment anyway. But then perhaps that was all part of my persecution complex. Washing up and potato peeling completed I crawled back to my "pit" with the feeling that the Army had won that round.

CHAPTER 19

IN WHICH BILL GETS PROMOTION
AND I LECTURE THE OFFICERS

As time went by it was decided by Major Hounsell that one of
the craftsman should be "made up" to Lance Corporal and Bill
was singled out for this promotion. He was called before Major
Hounsell to be informed of the honour that was about to be
bestowed upon him. Apparently the conversation went something
like this.

"Witt I am very pleased to inform you that in view of your very
hard work and dedication to your job I have decided to promote
you to Lance-Corporal with immediate effect, "Congratulations",
he said standing up and making as if to shake Bill's hand.

"Hold on a moment", said Bill looking at the proffered hand
with the utmost suspicion. "I'm only prepared to accept the stripe
if I'm paid for it. I'm not prepared to accept if it is case of me
being in a temporarily acting unpaid situation". Major Hounsell
looked slightly abashed and the workshop W.O.1 standing at the
side of him nearly choked on hearing Bill's words.

"Oh, no, no. Yes of course you'll get paid for the stripe
Witt", .assured Major Hounsell.

"Right, fine, I accept", said Bill grasping the Major's hand
and shaking it, and at the same time ruminating on what he would
be able to do with another 3/6d per week.

"This promotion is immediate you say, so I can put my stripe
up right away?" queried Bill...

"Yes right away".

"Does Staff know about this promotion Sir?"

"Yes, yes, indeed he does".

Bill was to find out that Staff had in fact been the main
instigator in him obtaining the promotion. I felt that it was Staff's
way of helping Bill over the expense of the baby that his wife
was about to give birth to. Though Lord knows 3/6d a week
wasn't going to help very much. As far as I was concerned it was
promotion well earnt. Bill really knew his job and his knowledge
of the subject often got Staff and I out of many a difficult

situation. In spite of this fact however I was a trifle alarmed to see Bill immediately go down to the stores draw out his stripes and put them "up". I thought surely the promotion hasn't gone to his head? Then I realised what Bill was about, as far as he was concerned this promotion was one great giggle even if it was a marginally serious giggle and he was going to take advantage of it as far as he possibly could. For a start off he insisted that all Royal Artillery personnel now addressed him as Corporal whether they were senior or junior to him. He took great delight in pointing out the error of people's ways when they addressed him incorrectly. They got a special flea in their ear if they ever addressed him as Bombardier. Bill considered that was a far bigger insult than being mistaken for a craftsman even! The fact that he was now a Corporal did however bring its problems and brought them probably quicker than he anticipated. That evening we went to the cookhouse for tea and as usual we R.E.M.E. personnel sat on our own at a table set apart from the rest of the garrison. We were in the process of pulling the newly promoted Lance Corporal's leg unmercifully when the duty Bombardier obviously thinking that this type of behaviour was likely to undermine authority, informed Bill that he must leave us and sit and eat at one of the tables reserved for junior N.C.O.s. When Bill explained that he preferred to sit where he was the Bombardier became very officious and ordered him to move tables. Bill then suggested that he go away and deal with matters of a more urgent nature rather than bother him. On being told this the Bombardier became even more insistent that Bill changed tables. This was clearly becoming a trial of strength between the R.A. Bombardier and the more junior R.E.M.E. Lance-Corporal. In exasperation Bill whipped off his stripe, which was only held on with elastic, and stuck it in his pocket and informed the Bombardier that he'd decided that he didn't want to be a Corporal anymore and that the Bombardier should bugger off and mind his own bloody business. At this we all laughed, much to the Bombardier's discomfort, but he was so taken back by Bill's attitude that he did just that and "buggered" off. I fear however that if the Bombardier had been a regular soldier instead of a National Serviceman as he obviously was, the outcome might have been very different. Such however was Bill's superior personality, aided and abetted by the rest of us of course, that I cannot recall him ever again being ordered to eat his meals with the Royal Artillery N.C.O.s. The very next morning however there was another incident that really did test Bill's new promotion to the utmost. Staff had asked Bill and me to go out to Wembury to carry out some urgent repairs on a searchlight that was required to be used for a night shoot later that week. Strange to relate although the Royal Artillery had radar they would only use it to ensure that the area of the shoot was clear of shipping, they would never use it for the actual shoot preferring to use, as they put it, the old and trusted method of searchlights. Perhaps in some strange way they thought that the old 1899 vintage guns that they were firing wouldn't like being laid on with radar, and preferred the searchlights! We had picked up the more than adequate dry rations for our fry-up lunch and boarded the lorry for Wembury. This particular morning the B.S.M. was personally supervising the loading of the lorry with a squad of R.A. gunners who were to travel with us on this occasion. As we considered ourselves senior, and superior in all respects to the R.A. personnel, we always sat in the seats immediately adjacent to the tailboard of the lorry so that not only could we watch the scenery go by but at the same time wave back at the many females who seemed to delight in waving at us as the lorry trundled on its merry way through the streets of Plymouth. Due to the fact that this morning the B.S.M. was trying to get as many people on the lorry as possible, he was forever ordering everyone to move down the lorry as more and more people clambered aboard. Bill and I not wishing to spend the journey in the dark interior of the lorry kept standing up to let the Gunners pass by us. In all honesty I suppose our action did slightly slow down the process of loading the lorry but there was no way that Bill and I were going to vacate our pole positions. Apart from anything else it was a tradition that R.E.M.E. personnel occupied these positions and who were we to buck tradition especially when it was to our advantage not to do so. Once again the B.S.M. ordered everyone to pass down the lorry, and once again Bill stood up to let people by and I dutifully followed my superior officer's example. The B.S.M. on seeing this called out, "You two at the back move down the lorry". As I went to comply I heard Bill mutter under his breath "Stay where you are, ignore him". The B.S.M. once again ordered the pair of us to move down the lorry and emphasised his order this time by pointing at Bill and me and saying, "I mean you two". I decided that it really was now the time to move before things got nasty. Bill however resolutely refused to move down the lorry and remained standing, requiring people to pass him by instead. On seeing this, the B.S.M. went red in the face tapped Bill on the leg with his pace stick, and roared. "Hey you, get down off the lorry immediately." Bill having no alternative but to comply with the order, reluctantly climbed down and stood facing the B.S.M.

"When I give you an order to move down the lorry you bloody well jump to it and comply with my order immediately, understand?" shouted the B.S.M., his red face by this time turning a delicate shade of purple. "You don't turn it over in your mind deciding whether or not you agree with it. If I have any more of this impudence your feet won't touch the ground, understand?"

The new R.E.M.E. Lance-Corporal then explained to the B.S.M. in fairly polite terms what he thought of the situation whereby two experienced R.E.M.E. personnel were being bawled out in front of squaddies who were still undergoing their basic training. At this point the B.S.M. reminded Bill who he was speaking to and demanded to be addressed as Sir, at which Bill retorted, "If you expect me to call you Sir, Sir, then I expect similar respect and to be addressed as Corporal, Sir, instead of being referred to as hey you, Sir". He said this whilst pointing to the newly acquired stripe on his sleeve. Bill was in an unrepentant mood all the pent up feeling that was in most of us National Serviceman was clearly coming out, the resentment of being forced into the Army, the resentment of being treated like children, the resentment of being kept away from our homes and in our case our wives also. Bill somehow kept his temper however and said all he had to say in measured tone.

Sitting in the lorry I nearly curled up as I listened disbelievingly to this conversation. I thought that's it, that's the end of Lance-Corporal Witt he's got to lose his stripe for this, and it won't surely end there charges are sure to follow, after all Bill is talking to the Battery Sergeant Major. Bill having finished his dissertation resolutely stood his ground looking the BS.M. full in the face awaiting his next move; which Bill told me afterwards he expected to be pretty drastic indeed. Instead the B.S.M. appeared to be lost for words, he stood there for a few seconds poker faced and without speaking, he then ordered Bill to get out of his sight and onto the bloody lorry as he was holding things up. Without blinking an eyelid Bill climbed up onto the lorry ordered the person sitting in the seat next to the tailgate to move down the lorry and sat down staring resolutely to the front. I had a feeling that Lance-Corporal Witt was going to be no pushover for anyone. As the lorry got under way Bill visibly relaxed, smiled at me and emitted a quiet whistle.

"Crikey, for a moment I thought I was for it there", he observed.

He certainly echoed my sentiments. We arrived at Lentley and were directed to the defunct searchlight, where we spent a couple of hours diagnosing the fault and putting it right. When I say that we diagnosed the fault and carried out the remedial work I mean of course Bill diagnose the fault, I merely looked on in wonderment and handed him the appropriate tools at the appropriate time. I mustn't underrate myself too much however, I was gradually getting the hang of the job but unfortunately I was still extremely slow compared with Bill, but then he'd been an electrical engineer before coming into the Army whereas I'd been a reinforced concrete detailer. Having effected the repairs Bill then proceeded to give me a résumé on how this particular piece of equipment worked as it was the one that was going to be used on the night shoot two nights later when I was going to be Duty E.C.E. (Electrician Control Equipment). A night shoot was usually the culmination of one of the gunnery courses which entailed leaving the Citadel for Lentley at approximately 14:00hrs with the squad of gunners undertaking the course, and checking and preparing the electronic equipment to be used that night, which is the technical way of saying that we tried the switch to see if the searchlight worked. Whilst we were doing this the gunners would be preparing their guns for use. Then there was generally a break for tea by which time it was dark and the firing commenced. The idea of having an E.C.E. on duty was to enable any faults that occurred to be repaired without hindering the shoot unduly. The night shoot over, we would usually return to the Royal Citadel by about 20:30hrs or so. Just late enough to make it useless doing anything else that evening. Due to my inexperience, to date Bill and I had attended the night shoots together, this was rather a waste of resources as it meant that we were on duty twice as many times as we need be. Henceforth therefore we decided that only one of us would attend each night shoot thereby reducing by half the number of duties that each of us had to carry out. One of the reasons we came to this decision was the fact that we very rarely had a fault to attend to anyway, and that we could have sent a cardboard cutout for what necessity to date there had been to have an E.C.E. on duty. However instead of sending a cardboard cutout it was decided to send me. Lips were sealed however as to whether or not this move was considered to be an improvement over a cardboard cutout or not!

I approached my first solo night shoot with great apprehension but once I realised that I was the only electronics "specialist" technician on duty and that the other RA. duty technicians assumed that I knew all there was to know about electronics I began to feel a lot more confident. This confidence was further enhanced when I found that the course instructors both Warrant, and Commissioned officers tended to treat Bill and me as their equals especially when there was a problem; after all we were the "specialists". Whilst on duty we "specialists" had a hut of our own where we passed the time away brewing up our tea, cooking our supper and reading our Hank Janson novels, and awaiting any urgent calls to carry out emergency repairs. The Royal Artillery did hold day shoots as well as night shoots but due to the fact that the searchlights and other electronic gear were not used we were seldom called upon to attend them. As I have said previously, although the R.A. had radar available they would only use it to ensure that the seaward area was free of shipping, they would not shoot with it, they would always shoot at their target with searchlights. I never fully understood the reason for this practice. The target incidentally was the space between two plumes of water produced by two sledges being pulled through the water by a motor launch, with I noticed a very long tow rope!

The distance between the two plumes of water would be adjusted to depict various types of boats. The launches were manned by R.A.S.C. personnel who were billeted in the Royal Citadel, and kept their boats in the Barbican harbour just alongside the Royal Citadel. Except for the very unlikely possibility of being hit by a stray shell when participating in a shoot, they had in my opinion an absolutely wonderful time sailing up and down the coast testing their craft as they felt fit and sunbathing no doubt to boot. It could be a bit rough in winter but idyllic in summer as I was to find out when Bill and I spent a week with them in the spring of 1956 out on Plymouth Sound testing the ancient radio controlled target launches for which we were responsible for the maintenance. It was during this week that I further damaged my ankle by getting it caught between two boats whilst testing the radio controlled launches. As a special treat a course of Egyptian officers were allowed to sit on top of these launches and drive them around under manual control. After a couple of these gentlemen tried to ride off into the sunset on their steeds this treat was discontinued. In view of the fact that we went to war with Egypt over the Suez Canal some five months later (after I was out of the Army, thank goodness). I often wondered whether or not they were trying to abscond with what they thought was one of our secret weapons. Compared with a dugout canoe I suppose they were!

The first night shoot that I attended on my own passed without incident. The fact that everyone that evening appeared to hold me in great esteem raised my confidence no end and made me look forward to my next night shoot duty which started off in a mildly amusing manner. We specialists were in our hut frying our tea of eggs and bacon on the coke stove in the middle of the room when there was a knock on the door. Without stopping our culinary operations we called out "Come in". The door opened and framed in the doorway was a Captain of the Devonshire Regiment with a haversack in his hand. I recognised him as being an officer in command of one of the basic training squads who I observed had obviously never got the knack of marching, for when in front of his squad of troops and gave the order to "Quick march", always swung both arms forward at the same time, until he managed to synchronize his arm movements with that of his legs.

"Mind if I mess in here with you lads?" he asked in an apologetic tone. "I'm not all that keen on the officer's mess out here".

"No sir, come in", I said a trifle taken back that an officer was actually electing to be with us rather than his fellow officers. But then on second thoughts perhaps the man before us had good judgment!

He came in, sat down on a chair and proceeded to empty the contents of his haversack onto the table. Out came tea, sugar, a tin of evaporated milk and a packet of sandwiches. He looked enviously at us cooking our eggs, bacon and fried bread, clearly our cook looked after us a darned sight better than the officer's cook looked after him.

"What I like about messing with you fellows is the way you make your tea, bloody cowboy style, smashing."

"Cowboy style sir?" I queried

"Yes you know tea, milk, sugar all mixed in the same mug, I don't think you can beat it; marvellous."

I considered that tea made that way was absolutely revolting, but in view of the fact that we hadn't a teapot we had no alternative, but to prefer it made that way was beyond my comprehension, still if it made the Captain happy, who was I to argue. He stayed all evening until a phone call informed us that the night shoot was over and that the lorry would depart for the Royal Citadel in fifteen minutes time. Whilst he was with us the Captain talked about every subject under the sun, not only did he treat us as equals but in many ways he treated us as his superiors. It was clear to me that he must have been like a fish out of water in the Officer's mess. I almost felt sorry for him, but only almost. The second night shoot that I attended on my own was a different kettle of fish altogether. Right from the start there were problems with the searchlight and in spite of my best endeavours, which to be honest was limited to me actuating the on off switch in between lifting up covers and "tutting" in what was meant to sound like an intelligent manner, the searchlight refused to function. Eventually I informed the course Major, who had been watching this fault finding procedure of mine with great interest, that I had diagnosed the fault but unfortunately could not affect the repair that evening as I required specialist equipment that was only available in the Citadel workshop. That was indeed if the part could be repaired of which I had doubts about at this stage. I explained that I was extremely sorry and that I could do no more that night. In truth I only had a very vague idea what was wrong and was stalling for time, time to have a word with Bill. In spite of this the Major appeared to be very impressed with my explanation.

"That's alright "Tiff" I can see that you have done all you can, thank you very much". He then stood there deep in thought for a few moments. "The problem is", he confided, "They are all officers on course tonight and I think that it would do them the world of good to stay out here for the evening rather than to get back to the mess early. You say that you have diagnosed the problem but can't effect the repair out here tonight?" That's correct Sir", I replied confidently.

"Hm, I wonder then if you could do me a favour "Tiff". Do you think you could give the course a talk on what has gone wrong with the equipment tonight and how it is to be repaired. Could you do that for me?"

I nearly fell over backwards, I then recovered my composure and still basking in my newly found confidence as an E.C.E. and to a certain degree in a moment of complete weakness, replied.

"Certainly Sir, could you give me ten minutes to make out some notes?" "Of course 'Tiff, see you in the lecture room in about a quarter of an hour then, thank you very much", and with that he departed. Strange to relate, on thinking the matter over I really did think I knew what the problem was and how to overcome it. Fifteen minutes later I found myself in the lecture room standing on a platform in front of twenty or so officers ranking from lieutenant to major all with expectant expressions on their faces. I took a deep breath and reminded myself that however little I knew about the subject there was probably nobody in that room who knew any more about the subject than I did, in fact they probably all knew a jolly sight less, I hoped! I launched into my lecture quite confidently with long explanations backed up with diagrams on the blackboard, I answered all questions in a flamboyant manner, and my audience looked visibly impressed. As my lecture proceeded even I realised that some of my diagnostic reasonings didn't quite hold water. I began to analysis my lecture as I was giving it. I was talking a load of cobblers but judging by the look of rapt attention on the faces of my audience I was the only person in the room who realised it. I carried on bringing in to play every conceivable technical term that I could think of, steering clear of any simple expression that they might understand. By the time I ended with, "And that gentlemen is a brief resume of the fault and how the repair is to be executed", I had room of blank looking faces before me. When it occurred to them that I had finished however they recovered sufficiently from their stupor to give me a round of applause. This was followed by a vote of thanks from the course Major. This wasn't the end of the affair however, next day when I was passing the officers mess in the Royal Citadel a number of the officers singled me out and congratulated me on "my very clear and concise lecture". They were astounded to learn that I was not an electrical engineer in civvy street, and one officer on hearing that I was connected with reinforced concrete offered me job with his brother-in-law's Company. Unfortunately he was under the influence of drink at the time so I didn't take his offer too seriously. I can only assume that he'd been celebrating my superb lecture of the previous night! After I had fully explained the previous night's event to Bill, he looked at me with a pained expression on his face and uttered these immortal words to me. "You told them a load of old cock!" On refection I could not but agree with him. I did my best but in spite of all my training I still didn't understand all aspects of the work that I was called upon to carry out. This fact however did not stop me from having a certain amount of pride in the fact that I was an "X" class tradesman, one of only six or so such trades in the British Army. It was however always a source of disgust to me that as a National Serviceman I was never allowed to "put up" the appropriate "X" class trade flash to advertise my accomplishment. This pride of mine was sorely tried a couple of days later when I made a solo trip to Lentley to carry out some equipment repairs. We were all sitting around together having lunch in one of the huts, when a R.E.M.E. W.O.1. whom I hadn't seen before, decided to start baiting me. "I see we've got a new E.C.E. amongst us, one of the elite who believe that they're God's gift to the R.E.M.E. and think they know everything there is to know about everything" He said looking at me with a smirk on his face. Receiving no comment from me he continued. "Why is it that you blokes always think that you're so bloody superior to the rest of the tradesman in R.E.M.E.? Still receiving no reply and clearly wishing to provoke me further, he carried on with this one sided conversation.

"Do you remember", he said, addressing the others, "That E.C.E. we used to have here called Jones? now no one could have had a more bloody superior attitude than him, he really thought he was the cat's whiskers, knew it all or so he believed, but when it really came to it, knew sweet fuck all. I hope that you're not going to be like him?" he queried, glancing at me again. Everyone in the room sat looking at me, clearly I was expected to say something.

"Well", I replied, "I certainly don't think I know it all, far from it. I am not an electrical engineer in civvy street as most E.C.E.s are, therefore I only know what I've picked up, on course, in the Army. I am in fact a reinforced concrete draughtsman, now that's a subject I know something about."

"Hm, well I think all E.C.E.s are rubbish", he replied, "and when I think of E.C.E.s I will always think of that bloody idiot Jones who thought he knew it all but was in fact bloody useless, like most E.C.E.s".

I had no knowledge whatsoever of this man Jones, maybe he had been useless but I doubted it, clearly what this W.O.1. was really trying to tell me was that he didn't like National Servicemen. Well the feeling was mutual, I didn't like the Army.

"Come on", he taunted "Haven't you got anything to say for yourself?" I was silent for a few moments only.

"Well, I suppose you're entitled to your opinion about E.C.E.s, but when I get out of the Army and think about W.O.1.s, I'll always think of that miserable blighter Warrant Officer Barnaby", and with that I stormed out of the room. I was seething, I wasn't going to stand there and take those insults, supposedly against Jones but really aimed against me. I had no sooner got into the adjacent room however when I was joined by a Sergeant who had been one of the audience in the other room. He was in a high state of excitement.

"You'll get charged for speaking to a Warrant Officer like that; he'll put you on a charge; he'll charge you as sure as eggs are eggs. I wouldn't like to be in your shoes for anything!"

I had always thought that this particular Sergeant was frightened of his own shadow, and this incident seemed to confirm it.

"Why wouldn't you like to be in my shoes?

"Because you're likely to get charged by Warrant Officer Barnaby".

"What makes you think he will charge me?"

"You insulted him".

"What the hell do you think he did to me Sergeant?"

"He's a W.O.1. and can do it, but you can't".

"Well I've done it", I said with a casualness I didn't really feel. Even I realised I'd gone over the top. "Tell me Sergeant have you in fact been sent out here to charge me?" I queried.

"No, I've just come out to warn you that you probably will be charged for insubordination".

"You've been instructed to tell me that?"

"No", replied the Sergeant

"Thank you Sergeant. We'll just have to wait and see what happens won't we? If you'll excuse me I've got work to do". With that I disappeared out of the door towards the searchlight emplacement where I had been working before lunch. On the way I started to prepare in my mind my defence should I in fact be charged. On the face of it what I had done in the eyes of the Army hierarchy was indefensible, why didn't I just keep quiet? Although for some days afterwards I was expecting a summons to Major Hounsell's office, none came and the surprising thing is I got on well with that particular W.O.1. after the incident I have just mentioned. On making enquiries I found that he had been taken prisoner by the Japanese at Singapore in 1940 and apart from having served over four years in a prisoner of war camp and all that went with it, had lost years of promotion prospects. I began to understand why he resented E.C.E.s, the cream of R.E.M.E., especially when most of them were National Servicemen who were only in the Army for a short period of time and generally had no promotion ambitions only an overriding ambition to get out of the Army and get on with their real lives.

There was some light relief for us E.C.E.s a couple of weeks later at Wembury when we had to stand by to carry out any emergency repairs, should it prove necessary, at a demonstration of some elderly 3.7inch anti-aircraft guns to a group of foreign officers. The R.A. personnel were driven about their duties by their N.C.O.s making wild accusations about "Wanking pits" and "Pulling plonkers," etc., etc. I can only assume that such statements were explained to the foreign dignitaries as being technical jargon. Most of those present appeared to be very impressed by the demonstration even if they didn't realise, as we did, that these world war two guns couldn't react quick enough to shoot down aircraft travelling at over some 500 miles an hour. But even I could see the logic in selling your potential enemies inferior equipment. I did however ponder on whether or not any of this equipment did in fact find its way to Egypt and was eventually used against Britain in the Suez War, which was only six months in the future. Still business is business I suppose, and as we are all well aware this type of ugly business still goes on today.

CHAPTER 20

IN WHICH I LEARN TO DRIVE AND GET A JOB

With the closure of the Coast Artillery School, once all the School's equipment

had been cocooned and safely stored away, there was now virtually nothing for us to do. We began to look around to find ways of occupying our time. Needless to say of course we didn't think much of the B.S.M.'s recent solution to the problem, Such as putting us on guards and other duties. No we wanted something more useful than that.

That morning on our way down to the workshop, walking through the Motor Transport yard we found it, in the form of Royal Artillery personnel undergoing driving instruction.

We decided there and then that that was the way ahead for us. We would learn to drive and at least gain something useful out of our two years stay in the Army.

On our arrival at the workshop we immediately went in to see Major Hounsell regarding our idea. We explained to him that with the closure of the Coast Artillery School we now had a certain amount of spare time on our hands. (That was putting it mildly; we hadn't anything whatsoever to do.) And as most of the R.E.M.E. personnel couldn't drive, this spare time could profitably be put to remedying this deficiency. This would have the effect of making all R.E.M.E. personnel mobile. [both in and out of the Army}, and must be to the Army's great advantage!

He didn't hesitate he thought it a wonderful idea, marvellous initiative of the greatest order. There was only one snag; he and his staff were so busy now that the school had closed down! Doing what I have no idea, whilst any driving course had his blessing he would have to leave it to us to organise.

At this distance in time it seems incredible that a craftsman and a Lance-Corporal were able to go to the Royal Artillery's M.T. section and negotiate with the Warrant Officer in charge the terms and conditions of a driving course for eight or so R.E.M.E. O.R.'s. but that is precisely what we did and the following week the driving course commenced.

The eight of us arrived down at the MT yard bright and early on Monday morning and were introduced to Sergeant Ferguson, who was to be our instructor. He showed us over the 30 cwt. platoon truck in which we were to receive our driving tuition. It looked a formidable monster indeed compared with a car. The first day was spent in familiarising ourselves with the vehicle and taking it in turns to drive it around the motor transport yard. The most difficult operation to me was double de-clutching the gear box when changing gears. Our crashing of the gears was usually followed by the gnashing of the Sergeant's teeth, gradually however we became more proficient at the whole operation and came the evening the Sergeant professed himself to be reasonably happy with our day's progress. We went away happy in the knowledge that we could now drive, albeit only at about five miles per hour within the close confines of the MT yard.

When we arrived for our second day's session we were informed by Sergeant Ferguson that we had made such fantastic progress on the previous day that he had decided to take us out onto Dartmoor today where we would begin our tuition in earnest. We all piled into the platoon truck and discretion obviously being the better part of valour, in spite of our fantastic progress the day before, the Sergeant took the wheel and drove us through the busy streets of Plymouth out onto the almost deserted roads of the moor.

After driving for twenty minutes or so we arrived at our destination, a disused airfield. He then proceeded to take one of us at a time and give us tuition on the intricacies of changing gear whilst keeping the truck in a straight line. After a very short time he professed himself reasonably satisfied with our progress, announced that it was N.A.A.F.I. break time, and instructed the driver to head for a cluster of old airfield buildings that we could see on the edge of the aerodrome. When we arrived there we were surprised to find that one of the buildings had been converted into a first floor café with a commanding view over the airfield. As we sat there consuming our tea and buns it became obvious that the Sergeant was a well known visitor to the café, no doubt by virtue of the fact that he often brought his driving courses out to the airfield for their tuition.

It also became obvious to us that the main attraction of the café to the Sergeant was not confined to the refreshments obtainable there, unless of course the waitress came under heading of refreshments. Clearly over a period of time he had struck up a relationship with the said waitress and was now in deep conversation with her.

After half an hour or so we became bored with gazing out over the airfield and were anxious to resume our driving tuition, The Sergeant noticing our restlessness reluctantly said his good-byes to the waitress and bade us all to get to the truck. An instruction that we were only too willing to obey.

After a further hour or so of driving around the airfield roads the Sergeant took over the wheel and drove us back to Royal Citadel in time for our mid-day meal. He then informed us that the truck wasn't available for driving instruction that afternoon but that if we turned up in the morning we would continue our instruction from where we had left off.

The next morning the Sergeant again drove us out to the airfield where under his vigilant eyes we once more took it in turns to drive around the perimeter roads. Dead on 10:30hrs however he declared it time for N.A.AF.I. break, and we headed for the café whereas before the Sergeant got into deep conversation with the waitress. As on the previous occasion, we once again became very restless. This time however rather than break off his liaison with the waitress the Sergeant had a brilliant idea.

"I think," he declared, "That if you lads hadn't got me breathing down your necks you would be a lot more relaxed and pick this driving lark up a darn sight quicker. I suggest that you all go down to the lorry without me, and take turns in driving the lorry around whilst I observe you from up here."

In spite of the fact that none of us thought that much observing would go on, leastways not of our driving, we didn't need a second invitation. We rushed down to the truck all eager to resume our activities. We then set about in a democratic manner to decide the order in which we would take the wheel. It was sheer coincidence that this democratic process resulted in the biggest member of our group taking the wheel first! We then appointed our most experienced driver to be the honorary driving instructor, to sit alongside the appointed pupil driver, and give guidance in what he was to do. I suppose that with hindsight there was a great deal of the blind leading the blind in this action. Still anything for the Sergeant and his piece of crumpet!

With a spinning of wheels and a crunching of gears we roared away from the café with a spirit of adventure in our heart, with the stupendous speed of thirty miles an hour being achieved in no time at all.

I should explain that over the years the aerodrome had become quite overgrown with trees and shrubs so that in places visibility was severely restricted. It was as we were skidding through one of these areas in a four wheel slide, that we narrowly missed a civilian learner driver in a car coming in the opposite direction. We then realized that we were not the only people learning to drive on the airfield that morning. Being at heart sensible people we sobered up immediately, dispensed with our speedway tactics and thereafter drove in a responsible manner. None of us wanted to kill anyone, least of all ourselves in our quest to learn to drive

At the appointed hour we returned to the café to pick up the Sergeant, who was still in deep conversation with his waitress, for our return trip to the Royal Citadel. This time however he didn't take over at the wheel of the truck for the journey back to Plymouth but instead instructed the driver to stay in his seat for the return journey. Sitting in the back of the lorry it was difficult to gauge the driver's reaction on receiving this instruction. I would imagine that it would have been one of momentary shock horror over the thought of having to negotiate all the vehicular obstacles in returning to the Royal Citadel.

The Sergeant wasn't that foolish however, much to the relief of the driver no doubt; when the cattle grid and gate which denoted the end of the moor was reached he instructed the driver to pull over and stop. He then changed seats with him and drove the rest of the way into Plymouth himself.

We soon got used to this procedure on following days and when the Sergeant instructed us to drive away from the airfield we did so in the safe knowledge that before we got to the busy roads the Sergeant would take over the wheel from whoever was driving

So a couple of days later when it was my turn to drive off

the airfield I wasn't at all bothered. This time however when we reached the moorland gate and I wasn't given the order to pull over and stop, I became a trifle agitated. Especially in view of the fact that we were actually meeting other traffic on the road, and I was having to do such things as change gear whist keeping the lorry in a straight line within the confined space of a road! This was nothing like driving on the airfield, but I was gradually getting used to this new challenge, when on turning a bend in the road I espied in the distance a tank transporter complete with tank coming towards me. I began to sweat.

It would have been bad enough to have turned the bend and be immediately confronted with the monster, but to see it approaching from about half a mile away was far worse. I had too long to think about all the consequences of making an error of judgment and hitting the bloody thing, we'd all be ground to a pulp!

I gritted my teeth and concentrated on the Sergeant's instructions. The forthcoming confrontation was made worse by the fact that we were going to meet each other on a bend in the road. The driver of the other vehicle, seeing no doubt the "L" plates on our lorry pulled over to his left, and at the same time slowed right down to walking pace. I just had time to notice a broad grin on his face as we passed each other with about a foot to spare. Amazingly enough this incident far from unnerving me, in some twisted way it gave me new found confidence and I drove the rest of the way back to the Royal Citadel without incident. At the end of my journey I sighed a sigh of relief and expressed the hope that I never, ever had the misfortune to meet a tank transporter ever again on those narrow roads. As he got out of the lorry the Sergeant merely looked me up and down as I expressed my thoughts out loud, smiled and said. "If you were worried you should have done what I did, and closed your eyes." And I thought he'd had confidence in my driving!

That was the last time we went out to the airfield, I concluded that the Sergeant either lost interest in the waitress, or what was more likely, he decided that he must now concentrate on teaching us the rudiments of driving on the roads in and around Plymouth. Unfortunately this decision coincided with the start of many setbacks in our driving course. We would often arrive for the course to find either the Sergeant, or the vehicle were unavailable and sometimes neither.

The situation started to become very frustrating indeed.

Time was marching on and my demobilisation date was beginning to appear on the horizon and we were getting very little concentrated tuition. One bright spot in all this despair however was that in an effort to keep the course running we sometimes now had to resort to the use of a Hillman utility van for our tuition. This van wasn't so far removed from a private car and was much smaller and easier to drive than a lorry. Best of all it didn't require the horrendous, to me, double de-clutching of gears

Nevertheless in spite of all our many setbacks we did feel that we were making progress, of that I was certain.

After a further two or three weeks of spasmodic instruction, when we would drive through the streets of Plymouth and surrounding areas, scaring the living daylights out of the good citizens no doubt and frequenting all the cafés for our N.A.A.F.I. breaks. The Sergeant suddenly informed us that he was going on leave the following week and that the driving course would have to be wound up that week. Our driving tests would have to take place in the next few days. Meanwhile he had to test some R.A. drivers and he thought that it would be good experience for us if we accompanied him on these tests to observe procedure. The idea being that he sat in the front of the vehicle with the driver being tested whilst we sat in the back of the vehicle.

When we arrived at the MT yard that morning we noticed a very worried looking gunner standing beside the vehicle to be used for the test. As Sergeant Ferguson approached he instructed us to get in the rear of the lorry, and the gunner to get into the driving seat.

"Right start up", instructed the Sergeant.

"Before I do Sergeant, could you please run through with me once more where the gears are", pleaded a very timid gunner.

"What," roared the Sergeant, "you mean to tell me you don't know where the bloody gears are after two months instruction?"

"Well I think I know where they are Sergeant, I would just like you to confirm where they are for me." Replied a very timid gunner.

"Get out of this vehicle", the Sergeant's voice roared again," and don't let me see your face in this yard again, ever".

We heard the sound of the cab door opening and shutting and caught a glimpse of the poor unfortunate gunner scampering away.

There was silence for a few moments whilst our erstwhile Sergeant no doubt composed himself.

"Okay lads", he called out, "Let's have one of you round the front here, preferably someone who knows where the gears are", he added in what we hoped was in a jocular vein.

I drew the short straw and made my way round to the driver's seat and under his critical eye drove off as instructed. In no time at all the Sergeant had resumed his usual jocular self.

It was quite incredible how all the Royal Artillery senior ranks, With the exception of the B.S.M. seemed to treat the R.E.M.E. personnel as human beings, well more or less. After about half an hour's driving round the streets of Plymouth, N.A.A.F.I. break time was declared and I was directed to drive to one of our favoured cafés, which I did with reasonable confidence. As I pulled up outside, the Sergeant looked at me with a glint in his eye, smiled and said," I am sure that you will be pleased to know that you have just passed your driving test, your turn to buy the tea I think!"

At first I didn't believe him. Then I realised that he was serious, I thanked him very much and enjoyed the happiest N.A.A.F.I. break I'd ever had in the Army.

On reflection I suppose the Sergeant adopted the attitude that if we weren't aware that we were taking our driving test we were more likely to be relaxed whilst being examined.

That week in spite of a number of hiccups everybody passed their driving tests. We all then eagerly visited the local vehicle licensing department and exchanged our provisional licenses for permanent ones.

Although we were now all qualified drivers to my knowledge none of us were ever called upon to drive Army vehicles. This was due, I suppose, to the fact that with the closure of the Coast Artillery School and Coast Artillery generally there was now absolutely nothing for us to do, let alone anything that entailed driving.

After the very pleasant experience of the driving course extreme boredom set in. We literally had to dream up things for us to do to keep ourselves occupied. I was lucky I was able to devote as much time as I wished to work connected to my course at the local technical college, but even that didn't require five days a week of my attention. To fill in my time I learnt to weld, under Bill's guidance, and made myself some small aquariums for use at home. I also reverted back to one of my schoolboy hobbies, that of model aeroplane modelling, anything to keep myself occupied. Unfortunately however the only paint that I managed to scrounge from the workshop, never seemed to want to dry which was extremely frustrating.

In view of the fact that we didn't seem to be required for work in the Army our thoughts inevitably turned to going home as much as we could. Bill and I found ourselves sloping off home for the weekend as early as Thursday morning. This procedure allowed us to spend a whole day hitch hiking home and still allow us a fair amount of time at home. Usually however when we decided on such a clandestine trip home only one of us would go, the other staying behind to cover for any unforeseen circumstances. On more than one occasion whilst at home I received a telephone call from Bill advising me to return to the Royal Citadel by a certain time because I had suddenly been put on duty, usually as skivvy in the N.A.A.F.I. washing down all the tables and the like, and I recall having to do the same for him.

We worked as a team and never got caught out even when I am sorry to say there was a panic reaction from one of our R.E.M.E. colleagues who was given a message for Bill to report to the Battery Office immediately, Bill being at home at the time. I phoned the office back and explained that he wasn't around at the moment but I would give him the message as soon as I saw him. When Bill returned the following Monday I suggested that he went to the Battery Office and tell them that I had forgotten to give him the message until now. By that time however no one at the office could recall why Bill was required so urgently anyway.

Even those in authority realising that the men were totally

under occupied did not resort entirely to the old standby of more "Bull" I am pleased to say, but instead organised many more sports activities. That is how I came to volunteer for a series of cricket matches.

Although no cricketer myself, the thought of playing on some pleasant sports field away from the restrictive confines of the Royal Citadel for a few hours appealed to me greatly. As the day of our first match approached, however, I was extremely surprised to be told that the match was going to be played on the asphalt parade square. I was convinced that a mistake had been made until I carried out a very close inspection of the square, I found two very small patches of soil twenty two yards apart, which I was informed was for the stumps. Between these two points would be laid the pitch of coconut matting.

My expectations of playing a series of cricket matches in idyllic surroundings away from the Royal Citadel were completely dashed.

The day of the match, which was to be between a team of selected R.E.M.E. personnel and a team of Royal Artillery personnel, dawned bright and sunny. The two captains tossed up and the Royal Artillery were put in to bat. Although our two opening bowlers weren't particularly fast the ball rocketed off the coconut matting with the speed of a cannon ball each time it was thrown down the pitch, it only took a touch of the bat for it to fly off into space for a boundary. It was a toss-up who was in more danger, the batsman having the ball bowled at him, or the fielder having the ball directed in his direction by the batsman, in either case if in doubt you just let the ball go by you. Then we got our first wicket, or so we thought, the ball just touched one of the bails and it fell to the ground. Howzat", we yelled in unison. "Not out", the R.A. Sergeant umpire said, as he replaced the bails with a smile on his face. "The wind blew them off". We were disheartened but immediately brightened up as the very next ball sent a stump flying along with the bails. "No ball," called out the R.A. Sergeant umpire, much to our and the bowler's disgust. The bowler didn't argue however, but quietly measured out his run for a third time, came thundering down the pitch and let go of the ball with the speed of light. This time the ball hit the wicket square on, all three stumps along with the bails were strewn all over the parade square. The bowler looked the umpire full in the face and said, "By Christ that was close Sergeant, I almost got him that time". All in all it was the most dangerous cricket match I have ever played in, I was surprised that no one was seriously injured, in spite of the fact that it was something to do to relieve the boredom I resolved to skive off any future matches on the basis that I wished to leave the Army all in one piece, especially as the date for my leaving the Army was not so very far in the future. I seem to recall that the first match was an honourable draw which didn't necessarily reflect either the number of runs scored or the wickets taken so much as how quickly one could get of the way of the missile disguised as a cricket ball when it headed in your direction. In the course of the match a number of windows were broken which entailed a quick whip round amongst the players to pay for the damage sustained, a second reason for me withdrawing from any future matches! Apart from cricket our other recreation activities were very much home spun so to speak. Within a stone's throw of the Citadel for instance was a putting green where a group of us spent many an early summer evening putting away, with the winner receiving a pint of orange squash at the N.A.A.F.I. club. Amazingly enough beer featured very little in our activities. On other occasions we would fish off the rocks alongside the Citadel all day Sunday and not catch a thing. On reflection maybe the fish did give some attention to our baits but we were so busy asleep sunbathing in the glorious sun that we didn't notice. When we weren't putting or fishing we would sometimes take a trip to the swimming pool that was situated on the rocks right next to the sea at the end of the Hoe. Bill and I would usually make one of these trips on one of our Wednesday recreational training afternoons; rather than be gripped for another one of the dangerous cricket matches. It must be said however that I did very little swimming as the water was so bitterly cold, but the sun bathing was pleasant enough however. It was here one afternoon that I met Bill and Doris, neighbours of my parents in Amberley Road at home. If it sounds as if my last few weeks at the Royal Citadel were idyllic, in a sense I suppose they were. I was being clothed and fed and paid - pittance as it was for doing nothing except when gripped for a duty, and I didn't have so many of those, thanks to my "Excused Boots and Parades" chitty, I could come and go virtually as I pleased. Whenever we left the Citadel to go into Plymouth or elsewhere we naturally dressed in our civilian clothes which through choice were usually flannels and blazers. In this attire we were not readily recognisable as members of Her Majesty's armed forces by the local populace which was probably a good thing as the locals were getting a little tired of the troubles caused by the many armed forces personnel stationed in Plymouth.

Civilian dress also brought with it the added advantage of being totally inconspicuous to the Military Police and Naval Shore Patrols if ever we came across either of these two illustrious bodies of men (or women) carrying out a security check whilst we were out and about in the town. They were very reluctant to approach any one in civilian dress as they had no way of telling whether or not they were indeed service personnel. Basically however the occasion never arose as we R.E.M.E. personnel never went into any pubs and kept well away from the many known trouble spots which by and large were remote from that part of the town where the Royal Citadel was situated. Although I like to think that if it came to a pinch we could have looked after ourselves I don't really believe that we would have been any match for some of the marines and light infantrymen that we came across from time to time. There were some of our number who would refute that statement and would qualify their thinking by relating an event that befell them prior to my arrival.

A large scale scheme had been enacted around Plymouth with all types of service personnel involved including a R.E.M.E. contingent from the Citadel. Plymouth as well as having the Royal Citadel at its centre was ringed by a number of small forts, built originally, I assume, for defence of Plymouth from the landward side. The scheme, which was to last overnight, was for a defending force to garrison these forts, including the normally uninhabited ones, with troops drawn from the Plymouth Command, whilst an attacking force of Royal Marine Commandos attempted to capture the forts. The story as related to me was that the R.E.M.E. contingent from the Citadel, with a Sergeant in charge, was given the task of defending one of these normally uninhabited small forts.

Having secured the fort and made it as impregnable as possible they settled down to what they hoped would be an uneventful night, as it was only a very small fort and they considered that it would probably escape the attention of the attacking force of commandos. Well they prayed that it would! In the early hours of the morning the duty sentry, yes they had taken such precautions, woke up his compatriots with the news that what he thought was a scaling ladder was being put up the outside walls of the fort. Entering into the spirit of things and possibly also not wishing to have their night's sleep disturbed any more than necessary, they rushed up onto the roof and pushed the scaling ladder away from the building thereby unwittingly seriously injuring one of the attacking commandos who happened to be on the ladder at the time. The story continued that the Royal Marines were so incensed by the injury inflicted on one of their number that they then used all their resources to gain entry to the fort and wreak vengeance upon the defenders. Apparently the assault continued on and off all the rest of the night without success to the attackers, such was the resistance of the R.E.M.E. personnel, or so I was told! In view of the fact that most of the R.E.M.E. personnel I came across at Plymouth were by no stretch of the imagination tough I can only assume that they kept the attacking force at bay by their strong sense of self preservation and what would happen to them if ever the commandos succeeded in breaching their defences. Apparently they were saved next morning, not in the form of a relief column but by the fact that the scheme ended and the attacking force returned to their barracks. Nevertheless just to be on the safe side the R.E.M.E. contingent for some two hours after the scheme had officially ended, stayed in their fort and only came out when they were absolutely certain that the attacking force had gone home. I was never involved in such a scheme as the one described and I can't say that I was sorry, they sounded far too dangerous for the good of my health.

It was about this time that I saw an advertisement in a paper for a building construction draughtsman at the British Oxygen Company at Edmonton. I applied for the post, was called for interview and was successful in obtaining the post which was for when I came out of the Army in a couple of month's time.

What was particularly welcome about this incident was the fact that as I had applied for the post from Plymouth, the Company insisted on paying all my expenses for coming up from there to attend the interview, in spite of the fact that my home address was only four miles away. Happily I was successful in obtaining the post of draughtsman at the interview. So here I was only weeks away from demobilisation and a civilian job already under my belt. It was at this stage that I wrote to my old employers informing them that I had decided not to rejoin them after completing my National Service. I seem to recall that they were a little bit upset over this piece of news. I can't say that I can see why, they certainly hadn't paid me any money in the time I'd been in the Army, and hadn't even written to me, even though I had been down to see them some three times whilst on leave from the Army during my National Service,

So here I was a couple of months away from demobilisation and a civilian job already under my belt. I was really looking forward to picking up my civilian occupation from where I had left off nearly two years ago.

I felt reasonably happy with life for a change

CHAPTER 21

NEARLY DISCOVERED THEN HOMEWARD BOUND

The most attractive feature of being posted to the Royal Citadel was the almost total absence of parades for R.E.M.E. personnel and when there was an occasional parade it was the easiest thing in the world for us to be excused from it by virtue of urgent work that had to be carried out. Amazingly enough repair of equipment used on the courses, took priority over parades, under no circumstances were courses to be delayed on account of defunct equipment, especially when that course consisted of overseas personnel in Britain for training. This attitude suited Staff, Bill and I very well indeed. Provided we kept all the equipment under our care in good working order we were virtually left to our own devices and were readily excused non-important parades and duties. The important parades and duties we excused ourselves from anyway. Regular room inspections were however a feature of the Royal Citadel, when we got wind of such an inspection we would get up earlier that day, lock up the room and disappear down to the workshop, with an "out of sight out of mind type of attitude" This procedure was helped by the fact that although our room was adjacent to barrack rooms to be inspected it was in such a dilapidated building that no one in authority realised that we lived there and therefore did not query the fact that the door of this "storeroom" was always locked whenever they carried out an inspection. One morning however our best laid plans nearly backfired. I seem to recall that it was one of those Monday mornings when Bill and I were particularly tired having just returned to Plymouth on the night train and not got to bed until about 05:30hrs after one of our long weekends at home. We explained to the other two lads in the rooms who were up early to catch the lorry out to Lentley that we were going to lie in that morning so would they make sure that they locked up after them when they left. Bill and I then went to sleep again... We were suddenly woken up by the noise of the door handle of the room being vigorously rattled and a voice that was immediately recognised as that of the Adjutant, calling out, "I can't open this door Mr Gilbey, It's locked." Bill and I looked at each other in shocked horror. Bill putting a finger to his lips. A guardian angel came to our aid in the form of the Battery Sergeant Major.

"That's all right sir, nobody lives in there that's only a storeroom".

"Right you are Sergeant Major".

We sighed a sigh of relief as we heard footsteps recede into the distance. Now wide awake, with any thought of further sleep totally deserting us, we hurriedly dressed, for we couldn't be sure that they wouldn't be back. We did a reconnaissance through the key hole, saw the coast was clear and beat a hasty retreat to the workshop in a slight sweat. It transpired that we had been extremely careless and had not read battery orders before we had departed for our clandestine weekend leave or we would have noticed that there was to be a room inspection that Monday morning. We resolved to be more careful in future, we didn't want any more close calls like the one we had just experienced.

CHAPTER 22

IN WHICH WE CHANGE ACCOMMODATION AND ARE RAIDED BY THE "I.R.A." FOR A SECOND TIME

Bill and I were busy beavering away in the workshop one Wednesday morning when we had a telephone call from Sergeant Thompson that we were required urgently back at our billet. Immediately thinking "coke", we made our way very warily back to our one time hideaway which by now "The Powers To Be" had unearthed and we knew were well aware of; Sergeant Thompson who wasn't a bad type was waiting outside.

"Morning Sergeant, "we called out in unison as we approached.

"Good morning, if it is good," he replied with a harassed look on his face. "There's a load of rubbish out the back of your billet and it's got to be cleared up prior to hand over. Let's go and have a look at it," he said looking at the locked door obviously requiring us to unlock it.

"Don't understand you Sergeant but let's go in," said Bill unlocking the door to the billet and bidding the Sergeant to enter; we followed looking at each other with raised eyebrows

"That's where the rubbish is, in the yard through that door, you can see it from the ramparts," he said, pointing to the door which led to the yard where we kept our ill-gotten coke.

"Haven't got a key of that door Sergeant, never been out there," lied Bill.

"I'll see if any of my keys fit." said the Sergeant. After rummaging through his bunch of keys for a few minutes he produced one that fitted and opened the door and walked through it out into the small yard. The moment of truth I thought, Colchester here we come unless we can bluff our way out of this...

"What the hell's all this bloody coke out here?" called out The Sergeant through the doorway.

"Coke, what coke do you mean Sergeant?" We exclaimed in unison

as we joined him out in the yard.

"I mean this bloody coke," he replied accusingly, pointing to our remaining pile of coke that we had covered over with some old sacking to avoid detection from all but very close inspection. The sacking now lay to one side, pulled off by the Sergeant.

"What do you know about this," he said with a very slight smile around his mouth. I gave Bill a quick sideways glance.

"What do we know about this?" said Bill stalling for time. "Not very much, not having a key to the door we've never been out here before. "Then with a flash of inspiration. "But I tell you what Sergeant, if we'd had a key to the door you wouldn't be asking us what this coke was doing here, we'd have burnt it instead of going cold this winter."

The Sergeant looked us straight

in the eyes. "Hm! You're such a scrounging lot of buggers but I'm inclined to believe you, if you'd known this coke was here there's no way you wouldn't have used it."

Thank goodness the truth didn't seem to occur to Sergeant Thompson, which was that we had stolen so much coke over that winter for our fire and had then been caught out by the early warm spring weather and hadn't been able to use it all up. Or did it occur to him but he didn't wish press the point because of the dire consequences that would have been heaped upon us should we have been found guilty of stealing the coke? I'll never know the answer to that one.

"Right I'll have to arrange to get this coke moved, don't use any of it, I've counted every piece and know exactly how much is there. In the meantime get this bloody yard swept out and cleared up. This is part of your billet and now I've given you a key you've no excuses," he said with a broad grin on his face, and with that Sergeant Thompson departed. After his departure we both let out a sigh of relief but still wondered if we really had heard the last of the matter.

"Oh hell," I exclaimed looking at my watch, "We've missed N.A.A.F.I. break. "We can't have that," said Bill, "Let's go along to "Joe's" on the Barbican," which after locking up our billet is precisely what we did.

As it was getting on towards lunchtime we stayed at "Joe's" until it was in fact time to go to lunch. We then slowly made our way up the grass bank back in to the Citadel, after first calling in at our workshop to ascertain that Staff had left it securely locked up, which of course he had. We had hundreds of pounds worth of equipment in that workshop all signed for by one or other of the three of us and we didn't want any of it "walking". Being a Wednesday we could look forward to an afternoon of recreational training, which in my case meant completing my college homework and in Bill's case meant carrying out some more work on his model boat. After lunch Bill and I were busy in our hideaway home with our own form of recreational training having decided not to take any further part in the Army's version of the subject having long since decided that hockey or cricket on the square was far too dangerous an occupation, and it in any case cost us money in paying for broken windows! I was therefore beavering away at my homework and constantly interrupting Bill with his boat building, for he seemed to know far more about my college work than I did, when we heard the door of the outer sanctum open and a voice call out,

"Anybody here?"

"Yep," we replied, "Come in." Much to our surprise the Battery Quarter Master Sergeant accompanied by a Sergeant, unknown to us, entered our room. I think that they were as surprised to find a room in such a mess, with papers and books all over the place, not to mention all the wood shavings on the floor; as we were to find ourselves being visited by such an illustrious pair. Mark you it could have been far worse as it turned out; it could have been the B.S.M. and adjutant again. They gazed around the room in what appeared to be quiet disbelief by what they saw. Heavens we thought lightning does strike twice in the same place, and on the same day at that! Bill gulped, and then found his voice,

"What can we do for you gentlemen." Since he gained his promotion I always let him speak for the pair of us, anyway he got 3/6- a week for doing so but "gentlemen". I thought that was overdoing it a bit, then I looked at the mess that surrounded us and realised the reason for Bill's flattery.

"The place is in a bit of a state isn't it?" queried the Battery Quarter Master Sergeant.

"Ah well yes," replied Bill, "We were out early this morning to attend to some urgent work in the casements so we didn't have much time to tidy up then, and well we're on recreational training this afternoon and we'll clear up this evening so that the place will be spick and span for tomorrow.

"I see," said the B.Q.M.S. in an unconvinced tone. "What's up there?" he queried, pointing to the mounds on top of our lockers covered with a couple of tatty old dust sheets.

"They're our top kits "Q", laid out in the prescribed manner, the only difference being is that we keep dust sheets over them to prevent them getting dirty. These coal fires play havoc with this place. It's terribly difficult to keep anything clean.

"Terribly difficult," I chimed in, thinking it time I contributed at least something to the conversation.

"Q" and the Sergeant continued to look around the room in quiet disbelief. Lightning striking twice in one day was one thing but I think that the pair of us were now wondering how long we could put off the thunderbolt that was surely to come and in the not too distant future? We'd got to be for it this time, but no we weren't. "Q" took his eyes off what must have been to him a room in "shite" order and confronted Bill.

"You're Lance-Corporal Witt aren't you."

"That's correct "Q", said Bill politely. Here it comes I thought!

"Right you're aware that you're vacating this billet and moving up into one of the barrack rooms next week?"

"I knew we were moving but I didn't know it was to be next week Q," replied Bill.

"Well it is, you're moving next Wednesday and I'm holding you responsible for seeing that this billet is clean and tidy and in a fit state to be handed over at that time. Got it?"

"Right, got it "Q"," said Bill.

"Oh and by the way," continued "Q" I understand that you are going to be in charge of the new barrack room so I require you to meet me at barrack room 4 at 11:00hrs Tuesday morning to take on charge the barrack room. Got it?

"Got it again Q," said Bill. With that "Q" and his Sergeant compatriot, who hadn't said a word throughout the meeting, turned on their heels and disappeared through the door.

"Crikey," said Bill "That was a close shave. You didn't have much to say," he said looking at me accusingly.

"I always leave the talking to my superior officer, any way I'm making sure that you earn your 3/6- a week," I said with a grin on my face.

"You bugger, you."

"So we're due for a move to the barrack room next Wednesday eh? That's not very good news, is it?" I said in a disappointed tone

"Ah well we'll see," said Bill getting back to his boat building.

"Yep, I suppose so," I agreed turning my thoughts once again to my homework. It was no use thinking too deeply in the Army, well apart from anything else we weren't paid to think - or so we were always being told!

The following Tuesday at 11.00hrs, Bill accompanied by myself and a small contingent of REME personnel made our way up to barrack room 4 which was situated in one of the stone-built blocks overlooking the square; our days of living in the shadows was over by the looks of things and I didn't like it. On arrival we found the Battery Quarter Master Sergeant standing outside the room awaiting Bill's arrival. He looked a trifle surprised to see the accompanying contingent that was with him, but then immediately dismissed us from his mind and got down to the business in hand.

"Right there's the barrack room Corporal, and here's the inventory," he said thrusting a clipboard under Bill's nose, "Sign here, and that's that."

"Hold on a moment, I think I should check everything before signing," said our Corporal.

"It's all there. I checked it all just before you arrived, me, myself, personally," replied an agitated "Q".

"Sorry "Q" if you want me to sign for it I'm going to check everything first. If you're not going to allow me to check everything then you can have the inventory back," said Bill offering the clipboard back, to the Quarter Master Sergeant.

"Q" was a trifle taken back. "No that's all right of course you can check it but be quick about it as I've got four more barrack rooms to do before dinner." He looked up to see a group of grinning R.E.M.E. personnel faces looking over Bill's shoulder, whose expressions immediately changed to that of serious contemplation a soon as his eyes met theirs. Bill proceeded to work his way through the inventory, calling out as he did so for us to check for the various items entered on it as he came to them. Missing items were marked down accordingly. "Q" became visibly angered by this action, but when Bill called out to us to check windows for broken and cracked glass "Q" veritably exploded. "There's no bloody need for you to do all this, all you have

to do is to sign for the room and take it off my hands, then when you move on someone will sign for it and take it off your hands.

"Yes "Q" and if the person who takes it off my hands does a detailed inspection as I'm doing, all the defects will be recorded and, and the people living in the barrack room at the time will all be charged that amount in barrack room damages. Just the same as if there is an inspection of this room tomorrow and all these defects are discovered and it is found that I have signed for the room without noting any of the defects, my men, (I loved that little touch) will be held responsible and will be charged barrack room damages accordingly. I've seen it happen before "Q" and so have you." Right "Q" there we are I've noted all the defects and signed it accordingly, thanks very much." "Q" snatched the clipboard from Bill's hand in anger and turned to dive out of the room.

"Just a moment "Q" you have to countersign the inventory to show that you agree with it and then you let me have my carbon copy, now please if you will.

"Q" scrawled his signature and thrust Bill's copy into his hand along with the keys of the room. Red in the face he face stormed out of the room, I could not but admire the cool manner in which Bill had dealt with the situation. We had heard lots of tales, whilst we had been in the Army of people signing for something that wasn't there with the understanding that on the 'morrow someone would again sign for it, and take it off their hands and so on and so forth. That was okay until something untoward happened, like it did at Arborfield, and you were suddenly caught with your signature against something that everybody knew didn't exist but pretended that it did. It was rather like the childhood game of passing the parcel only a little more serious.

"Well, it looks as if we're back in the real Army again and

that our days of hiding away are over," said Bill as he closed and locked the door and we all made our way back to our billet for the very last time. In the next few days we very reluctantly moved our kit from our relatively obscure storeroom billet into the barrack room where "The Powers To Be" now thought they had total control over us. We were now part of the real Army once more, as Bill put it; with bulled-up floors, made up bed boxes, room and kit inspections. Our old billets were duly handed over to their next custodians, there was no problem over inventories however as none could be found. We considered that even if they could have been found the signatory would almost certainly had died along with the Duke of Wellington many years previously. I felt that a new and unpleasant period was about to dawn for us at the Royal Citadel and I thanked my lucky stars that I only had a further eight weeks or so of service to do before demobilisation, though in the new present circumstances that was probably going to seem a very long time indeed! The new environment took a lot of getting used to. As well as the downside of bull, there was also the downside of some the non-R.E.M.E. personnel that we had forced upon us in the barrack room. People who came in habitually drunk on Saturday nights, taking great pride in waking you up and boasting of their sexual prowess and how many females they had got through that night. Yes some people enjoyed their National Service, on Saturday nights at any rate. They were lucky that they didn't get my fist in their faces. Then there were the less offensive ones who would wake you up when they came in, to enquire if you were absolutely certain that you didn't want to go for a pee, or perhaps want to sell you a battleship. Bill and I still attempted to skive off when room inspections where scheduled but the Officers soon got fed up with being confronted with rooms without any R.E.M.E. personnel to inspect and things were tightened up. R.E.M.E. personnel were specifically detailed to attend room inspections. Penalty for not being present was death by firing squad, or so it was rumoured. As I didn't want to die in the Army. I for one reluctantly started to attend these inspections, if only to bait the inspecting Officers over the reason I hadn't any boots for them to inspect! These last eight weeks or so were quite an unpleasant experience for me. One night soon after our transfer to the unpleasant barrack room I was woken one night by something or other, to find all our barrack room lights on. Looking around the room and seeing that everyone appeared to be in bed and fast asleep I assumed that not for the first time one of our Royal Artillery colleagues had come in late Brahms and List, and had been totally incapable of switching the lights off. I therefore decided to get up and switch them off and visit the ablutions out on the landing at the same time. There I found all the lights on as they were in the barrack room. I switched them all off as well and then made my way carefully back to bed and gave no more thought to the incident and was soon back in the land of Nod, dreaming of my forthcoming demob no doubt! It seemed that I had no sooner gone back to sleep however when I was rudely awoken by a raucous bombardier charging into the room rattling a cane up and down the radiators bellowing with a large grin on his face, "Wakey wakey rise and shine who's got a bigger tool than mine?", or words to that effect. Amusing as the saying may have been to him it wore a bit thin with us hearing it nearly every morning and didn't even raise a titter from the recumbents lying in their beds. In view of the fact that we were now woken up regularly each morning by the Orderly Sergeant or by some Bombardier who thought he was the Orderly Sergeant, we found that we had so much time to kill each morning before going to the workshop for about 09:00hrs, that out of sheer boredom if nothing else we now went to breakfast. This procedure was totally at odds to our old style of living when we were in our REME store room hideaway when we didn't get up until about 08:15hrs, wander down to the workshops which were situated outside the Citadel walls and having missed breakfast hang about patiently waiting for 10:30hrs to arrive by which time the Barbican's local bakery would have baked our usual breakfast of cream doughnuts topped with chocolate. Whilst having our breakfast that morning in the dining hall, which in all fairness was usually edible, we heard murmurs from the Royal Artillery personnel about "last night's raid", but being R.E.M.E. and not very interested in their problems we didn't take too much notice of what they were talking about. Breakfast over we collected our gear from the barrack room and made our way to the workshops outside the Royal Citadel walls. There we found most of our R.E.M.E. personnel with large grins on their faces avidly listening to a tale that was being told by John who had been on guard the night before. As we had come along halfway through his story telling we asked him if he could start at the beginning again, which he did with relish. To set the scene I would remind you that we were all billeted in the Royal Citadel on Plymouth Hoe that had high ramparts all the way around it and the only way in was via the main gate and the Sally Port door at the rear of the Citadel. At 18:00 hrs. each evening the Sally Port door was closed and secured, the only access to the Citadel after that time being via the main gate where the guard room was situated. At 19:00hrs each night the main gates were closed and secured until 07:00hrs next morning. Anyone requiring access between those hours had to ring a bell when a guard would come from the guard room open the vision grill in the picket gate, check the person's identity and if satisfied let the person in through the picket gate. John now repeated his story. He was on guard duty at the sentry box overlooking the guard room and the main gate, when at about 01:00hrs, after the Orderly Officer had done his rounds and had gone to bed, the main gate bell rang. A Royal Artillery guardsman crossed from the guard room to the gate and opened the vision grill to see who was there. On seeing his Commanding Officer standing there impatient to be let in, without giving the matter further thought, he immediately threw open the picket gate to let him in. He was a trifle surprised however when his C.O. came charging through the gate brandishing a revolver and was even more surprised to find that he was followed by a platoon of Somerset Light Infantry armed with rifles and fixed bayonets. The whole conglomeration rushed into the guard room pushing the unfortunate Royal Artillery guard before them and securing them in the cells. John recognising the C.O. and assuming quite rightly that he had been on a "binge" at the SLI's officer's mess and was Brahms and List, and what he was seeing was the result of some bet or other, decided to move from the limelight of the sentry box, where for the moment he hadn't been noticed, and hid in the shadow behind it and await events. They were not long in coming. The SLI, having tied up the complete guard and locked them in the cells of their own guard room, led by our own C.O.

now brandishing a key and a revolver, rushed over to the armoury immediately opposite the guard room and proceeded to unlock it. At this stage John who was watching the proceedings with interest, was suddenly confronted with a figure who was attempting to rest his rifle from him. For a brief second, (or so he said), it flashed through his mind that in spite of what he had just seen, perhaps this was a genuine I.R.A. raid after all. Entering into the spirit of things he automatically lashed out with the butt of his rifle and caught his attacker full in the chest and knocked him to the ground. A close look at the person on the floor however revealed the fact that he was an officer of the S.L.I. Unabashed at what he had discovered John stood in the "on guard", position above the recumbent figure. Once the S.L.I. officer had recovered from the blow to the chest he managed to wheeze out the fact that John had to consider himself dead and could not take any further part in the proceedings. In spite of being pronounced dead, John was bothered that he would still be charged for losing his rifle if in fact he allowed it be taken away from him, replied. "Yes Sir fine I'm dead Sir, but if you don't mind I'll hang on to my rifle Sir".

The S.L.I. officer probably fearing a further thump in the chest from the butt of John's rifle readily agreed to this arrangement. With the terms of the armistice negotiated, the officer returned to his men who were busily emptying the armoury of all its contents and loading them onto a S.L.I. lorry that had been backed up to the armoury through the now open gates of the Citadel. John with his rifle tightly grasped between his hands, sat in the shadow of the sentry box continued to watch the proceedings from his vantage point in his temporary "dead" condition. With the Lorry loaded the S.L.I, plus our C.O. withdrew from the scene carefully closing the Citadel gates after them. John, having decided that he need no longer consider himself dead was making his way across to the guard room when he realised that there was movement within. He was just wondering whether or not there were still S.L.I. personnel inside when the alarm klaxon started to sound off, and Royal Artillery figures came tumbling out. Apparently they had been tied up none to securely and had managed to set themselves free and sound the alarm. Here the story became slightly confused but the bones of it appeared to be that the Orderly Sergeant was contacted on the telephone and told by the guard commander about what had happened. Apparently he wasn't convinced that the whole thing had been a C.O.'s prank, so on his way to the guard room, presumably deciding that discretion was the better part of valour, he called in at all the barrack rooms on the way, switched on the lights, or so he said, woke everybody up in each barrack room, explained that there had probably been an I.R.A. raid on the armoury, ordered everyone to get dressed and armed, and follow him up to the guard room. A little bit different to the story as I knew it! Apparently he had quite a following of armed men when he started off to the guard room but by the time he got there he only had half a dozen soldiers with him, mainly in their pyjamas. The rest having got fed up with the fun and frolics, and at the same time probably not relishing a possible brush with the I.R.A. without any ammunition for their rifles had gone back to bed. Seeing that there were still some arms in the armoury and seemingly no keys to lock it up with. The Orderly Sergeant placed two "Nig" pyjama clad gunners on guard and retired to the guard room to try and unravel the night's events. After a period of time he returned to the armoury to find the doors wide open and the remaining arms gone. He searched around for his guards and finally found them hiding in the dark behind the armoury. When the Sergeant demanded to know what had happened they explained that a lorry had driven up with Army personnel on board informing them, that they had come to pick up the rest of the weapons and that if they didn't want to get hurt they had better "piss off". The guards thinking that that was good advice had disappeared. Why when they were within hailing distance of the guard room they didn't call out I can't imagine!, though in all fairness they had only been in the Army a couple of weeks and hardly knew one end of a rifle from the other. There was a court of inquiry over the whole incident, accusations were cast in all directions. The Orderly Sergeant was to blame, the Orderly Officer was to blame, the Guard Commander was to blame, the two guards were to blame, everyone was to blame except of course the C.O., who apparently was pissed as a newt at the time, and was intent on playing silly buggers with his men. When all is said and done, if you are on guard in the middle of the night and you are confronted with a pissed commanding officer demanding access to his own castle it takes either a brave man, or an idiot, to tell him to bugger off and go and play elsewhere and yet that C.O. really thought that the guard who let him in failed in his duty. It was all just another case of the Army playing games with us. There was one small consolation to us however. We were led to believe that John broke two of the S.L.I. officer's ribs with his rifle butt, so I should think that he was well pleased with his part in the merry making raid on the Royal Citadel. Which is more than could be said about the S.L.I. officer who must have been been feeling pretty sore about the ribs!

CHAPTER 23

IN WHICH I AM INVITED TO PREPARE FOR CIVVY STREET

Approximately four weeks before I was due to be demobbed I received an urgent summons to attend the unit's Education Centre, for an interview with the Education Officer. The Education Officer in this instance being a sergeant in the Education Corps. I hadn't a clue what he might want me for, in the eight months that I had been stationed at the Royal Citadel the only other time I had previously been summoned to appear before the him was, much to my disgust, to receive a drubbing over the fact that I had off my own bat enrolled at the Plymouth Technical College for a course of evening classes without seeking his permission first. Surely he wasn't going to resurrect that old chestnut? I made my way over to the red brick building that served as the Education Centre, which was situated outside the confines of the Royal Citadel and close by the other ranks married quarters, found the Education Officer's room, and courteously for me, knocked on the door prior to entering swiftly, without waiting for a "come in". I always considered that it was prudent to conform to the system to a certain extent but at the same time show that you were not prepared to be completely subservient to the system. This was one of my ways showing that attitude. Childish I know, but then the Army was childish. I was only reciprocating.

The Sergeant was sitting at his desk looking expectantly at the door. From my limited experience of him I considered that for the Army he was almost a reasonable individual and in all probability a National Serviceman. I sometimes wondered if I had made an error of judgement in not taking up the offered opportunity of joining the Education Corps after I had failed W.O.S.B. With hindsight I'm sure that I would have had a much better time as a Sergeant in the Education Corps than I had had as a Craftsman in the R.E.M.E. for the last twenty two months or so! Too late to think about that now.

"Hello Sergeant. Skinner, I believe that you wanted a word with me", I said, wondering what that word could possibly be about, slightly intrigued but not really bothered.

"Ah yes, Skinner," said the Sergeant, "Please come in and sit down. Now I understand that you are to be demobbed next month", he continued.

"That is correct Sergeant, June the fourteenth", I replied.

"Now I've been checking on your education record and I see that you haven't got any of the Army's certificates of education, not even the third class one."

"No that's very true Sergeant I haven't". I was now becoming a trifle mystified.

"Now don't you think it would be to your advantage to leave the Army with some form of educational certificate? It will help you quite a lot to get a job in "civvy street", he explained in such a manner that it was clear to me that he felt sorry for this ignoramus of soldier that he had before him, who in the very near future was to be launched upon the civilian job market without any educational qualifications whatsoever, Army or otherwise, or so he thought. The penny dropped he'd cocked it up; he'd confused me with someone else. He was so used to dealing with the gunners in the Royal Artillery some of whom really did appear to be poorly educated that he probably hadn't even noticed that I was in the R.E.M.E. and not the RA. Rapidly summing up the situation I sensed that there was an opportunity for a little bit of sport here. So I decided to string the Sergeant along.

"The Army's third class certificate of education, that's the certificate that says you can read and write isn't it Sergeant, surely I need something more than that to get a job in *civvy street,* don't I?" I queried innocently.

"Ah, now then don't knock it Skinner", he countered, "Any qualification is better than none, even the third class certificate can be of use to you. Now I see that you have got slightly over four weeks before your discharge from the Army, if you work really hard in that time it might even be possible for you to obtain your second class certificate before you leave. Now that really would be something wouldn't it Skinner?" he beamed, in a not altogether optimistic manner.

Good heavens I thought this man really hasn't done his homework. He hasn't checked to see that I've been to W.O.S.B., admittedly failing it, that I'm an "X" class tradesman that took a seven month very intensive course to qualify. Or in my case twelve months, I wasn't a very enthusiastic student! That the course included higher mathematics, electronics, and a host of other subjects equally mystifying to me. The memories of the agony of the course came flooding back to me. How did I eventually pass it? Perhaps in the end the staff at Arborfield merely wanted to get rid of me! Anyhow that is beside the point, pass it I did and on paper at any rate in the eyes of the Army, if not mine, I was a highly qualified craftsman, and yet here was this idiot in front of me suggesting that I took the Army third class certificate of education so that I had some form of qualification when I left the Army.

"Er, the Army's second class certificate of education would that be better than my school certificate and my Higher National Certificate then Sergeant?" I asked, again in as innocent tone as I could muster, trying hard to hold back my innocent amusement. The arrow struck home.

"What school certificate and higher national certificate?" he demanded.

"I have a school certificate in seven subjects not that I am particularly proud of the fact, as unfortunately I didn't obtain matriculation exemption because I failed German, Then I have my higher national certificate in building studies, with distinction. If you recall", I continued, "Approximately six months ago you gave me a good telling off over the fact that I had enrolled at the local technical college without obtaining your permission first. The subjects that I had enrolled for were endorsements for my higher national certificate. I would have thought you that would have remembered that incident". I said a trifle sarcastically. "Incidentally I have just taken the exams and am quite confident that I have passed them, you will be pleased to hear", I said this with as much conviction as I could muster. He wasn't to know that inwardly I considered it a case of touch and go whether or not I had passed. If I had passed it would be due in no small part to Bill's tuition that he'd given me. Well let's face it the Army wasn't a very good atmosphere in which to study. "I'm surprised that you haven't got my service record in front of you Sergeant, because if you had you would find that I've been to the War Office Selection

Board, where the minimum education requirement is school certificate, and that my present Army trade is that of Electrician Control Equipment which as you are indubitably aware is an "X" class trade, which if my memory serves me correctly is one of only six in the whole of the British Army. Four being in R.E.M.E. and two I believe being in the Royal Signals. I'm sure that the fact that I have been an E.C.E. whilst in the Army will be far more impressive to a civilian employer than the Army's third class certificate of education. Thank you very much for your interest in my future but I have already had a successful interview for a job as an Architectural Assistant at British Oxygen Ltd, and that job is waiting for me when I leave the Army I am pleased to say. Or are you going to tell me that I should have sought your permission before I went for the interview?" I informed the Sergeant of these facts with a Put that in your pipe and smoke it, sort of attitude. The Sergeant sat there with a bemused look on his face without saying a word as if I'd pole axed him. I had nothing more to add on the subject so I was waiting for him to make the next move. We sat there staring at each other with neither of us saying a word. I wondered how long this pregnant pause was going to go on for. I didn't have long to wait!

"What are you doing here wasting my time", he exploded "Get out, get out before I put you on a charge". Feigning indignation I stood my ground. "But Sergeant you wanted to see me, I didn't ask for this interview.

"You know what I mean; you've been stringing me along. Now get out", he yelled, with I couldn't help noticing a broad grin on his face. Quick on the uptake was the Sergeant, he wasn't just a pretty face no wonder he was in the Education Corps! A National Serviceman without a doubt. Realizing that there was nothing more to be gained from the meeting, in my own time I made my way to the door, and turned as I reached it, and said in a sarcastic tone "I take it then Sergeant that you don't now want me to take the Army's third class certificate of education, or even the second?" I said this with as straight as face as I could muster.

"Get out," he yelled one last time.

A round to me I thought in my continuing guerrilla war against the Army. It went through my mind however that there was very little time left for me to fight many more battles before the war came to an end on June 14th. I returned to the workshop to finish off welding up my latest aquarium. I ruminated on the possibility of going into mass production and selling to the public. We had that loading platform at the side of the workshop that opened up directly onto the public footpath of the road that ran around the Citadel I could make a good display there and sell to the passing public. I dismissed the day dream from my mind; our CO would never wear it! or even if he did he would probably want the proceeds to go to the Army benevolent fund or some such organisation. In any case I only had a further four weeks of this boredom to endure before demobilization, and over a week of that time would be spent on leave. Although, in theory, we were only allowed 28 days privilege leave a year, I applied for leave at every opportunity as it arose, To date I had always been successful and in consequence obtained far more than 28 days leave a year. Even I however considered that I was being optimistic when I applied for 7 days Whitsun leave with only some four weeks service to complete, but no, once again I had been successful and was to go on leave the following day.

For once Doreen and I didn't try to crowd as much into the leave as humanly possible, as in three weeks time we would have all the time in the world to do as we pleased. One thing we did do however was to cycle down to Chelmsford for the day to see Bill, his wife and their new son.

My leave ended officially the following Saturday but naturally I wasn't going to go back to Plymouth until the Monday after. That was until Bill who was back off leave before me phoned up to inform that I was on fire piquet (again) Saturday night and all day Sunday. Reluctantly I had to return to Plymouth on the Saturday morning train. This time I found that my fire piquet duty consisted of me working in the Citadel N.A.A.F.I. acting as a skivvy clearing and washing down the tables as they were being used. An appropriate task for a highly trained Army specialist I must say, no wonder I couldn't wait to get out of the Army.

In the run down to my demobilization I still had one major obstacle to overcome, my final kit check. It was a fact, hard to believe as it may be, that you had to leave the Army with all of our equipment and clothing in perfect order, this in spite of the fact that your clothing had received two years unremitting wear, and your equipment a damned sight more than that as very little of it was new when it was issued to you. Remember the second hand boots for instance? Should any of your kit not come up to the quarter master's expectations you had to pay for new, or more correctly it was deducted from your credits, a system whereby whilst you were in the Army you were never paid all the money due to you, money was kept in your credits to be used for purposes as decided by the Army authorities. Any credit balances were paid to you when you left the Army. It was my observation that the Army did it's best to make sure there were none to be paid out. For instance I heard of people having to pay out £5.00 to £10.00 for worn clothing at the end of their service. The Army considered that this action was justified in view of the fact that the Army gave everyone a pittance of something like 3d a week clothing allowance for replacement of worn clothing. If therefore you hadn't replaced it previously they would make sure that you did so on termination of your service, in spite of the fact that the clothing you were handing in was presumably going to be thrown away. It appeared to me to be the last throw of the Army to show who had the upper hand. People were so pleased to be getting out of the Army that they just paid up without argument. I approached my own final kit inspection therefore with some trepidation, I was extremely relieved however to find that all my equipment was accepted by "Q" without demure. My last major hurdle had been overcome. I then handed in my own personal tool kit back into stores and collected all the 'chitties' I had to have before leaving the Army. I then took my tatty collection of paperwork to the battery clerk, himself a National Serviceman, to confirm the fact that everything was in order and that I was clear to leave in two days time.

"What the hell you still doing here?" he queried on seeing me approach.

"Oh, my demob date's not until Thursday," I explained

"Christ," he said, "Most of our people piss off at least one or two weeks before their official date nobody could care less around here."

"Do you mean to tell me I can go now if I want to?"

"I've signed you off, there's no one else for you to see, I'd piss off immediately if I was in your boots, you lucky bastard."

I couldn't believe it, here was I having been looking forward to leaving the Army for two years and it looks as if I could have left over a week ago. I was furious, if happily furious. I started to rush out of the Battery Office in excitement when a voice called out from behind me, "Here don't you want your travel warrant, or are you going to pay you own fare home?"

I turned round, grabbed the travel warrant from the clerk's hand, and disappeared out of the office at a great rate of knots to inform Bill and my R.E.M.E. compatriots the news that I was leaving there and then, sorry no time for the usual celebrations that we normally held when one of our number was being demobbed. As I appeared to have completed all the necessary formalities and was ready to leave the Royal Citadel, the R.E.M.E. and indeed the Army for the for the last time, it occurred to me that out of courtesy if nothing else I should go and say good-bye to Major Hounsell my C.O. There was also the possibility that I might have the opportunity of expressing my opinion of how I felt over having been deprived of two years of my life. Or at any rate of two years of how I would have liked to have spent it rather than how the Army wanted me to spend it! That is how I felt over National Service and I know that there were a lot of other young men who felt as I did. So with determined step I went out of the Royal Citadel down the steep embankment to the workshop area, and along to the Major's timber shed office. On entering the outer office with its collection of old trestle tables various assorted defective chairs and other accumulated rubbish, I found that there was surprisingly nobody in residence. A sense of bitter disappointment overcame me as it was unheard of to go "swanning" into the Major's office without being announced by the office Warrant Officer, or at least by one of the number of senior N.C.O.s that could usually be found hanging about in the outer office. Disappointed, I was about to effect a retreat from the office, when I thought hell, this is my last day in the Army what have I got to lose? I turned on my heel, made a beeline for the Major's office door, knocked on it with unnecessary force.

On receiving a shouted, "Come in," I did just that. The Major was sitting at his desk idly looking out of the window and absent mindedly playing with a government issue pencil, and no doubt at the same time trying to make a decision on what he was going to have to eat in the Officer's mess that lunchtime. Decisions, decisions, life was full of making decisions, if only life had been a little simpler for him! As I entered he glanced round.

"Hello Skinner, what can I do for you?", he enquired.

"I've just come to say cheerio Mr Hounsell". I replied, having long since given up calling anyone Sir in the Army.

"What, going on leave Skinner?" he questioned.

"Well, kind of", I responded.

"What do you mean kind of?" he queried?"

"Well", I sighed, "I am very pleased to say that I leave the Army today, so I suppose you could say that I am going on leave, one long leave as far as the Army and I are concerned that is.

The Major looked mystified, then glanced at the calendar on the wall of his office which had various hieroglyphics pencilled in on it.

"No, no," he said, "You've made a mistake, you don't leave the Army until next month".

"No", said I, "I haven't made a mistake, I do leave the Army today, I couldn't in fact make mistake like that. Not after looking forward to the day for two years.

"No", he replied, "You leave next month. Look I've got you pencilled in on my calendar for next month", as if pencilling in on his calendar was the ultimate confirmation on any particular matter.

"Wait a moment", I retorted, with a flash of inspiration. "We're both right".

"How come?" he said, looking at me in a manner as if I had just lost my marbles.

"I leave the Army today to go home, but the Army still pay me for a month's terminal leave. That is why I imagine you have me pencilled in on your calendar leaving the Army next month, the date on which the Army finally packs up paying me any money, Little as it is", I explained.

He looked extremely doubtful, and I began to feel very

agitated. Hell I thought. Is the Army going to be bloody-minded right to the end? The Major consulted the calendar again, very carefully this time.

"Ah yes I do believe you're right", he conceded in such a non-committal manner that I couldn't decide if he was relieved at getting rid of such an indifferent soldier, or disappointed at losing one of his flock. After all his command was getting smaller and smaller all the time and he must have wondered what the future held in store for him?

"Well", he beamed, "I hope you have enjoyed your stay with us Skinner?"

"No I haven't. I've hated every bloody minute of it," I replied with great conviction.

"What?" he exclaimed.

"I've hated every bloody minute of it", I repeated. "Oh with the exception of the leave that is, but then if I hadn't been in the Army I wouldn't have had to go on leave would I?"

"You surprise me Skinner, I think that it's a great life, especially for a young man like you!" he countered.

"Hm, I probably wouldn't mind it, if I lived in that very nice detached house that you live in, with my wife near at hand, instead of two hundred odd miles away like mine, came in to work at what, ten thirty, or eleven 'o'clock each morning, and left at three or three thirty each afternoon, having had a couple of hours for lunch at the officer' mess. Do you know I think that even I could force myself to enjoy that style of life". I thought what the hell I'm leaving the Army today there's nothing he can do about me expressing my feelings in this manner.

"Do many of the lads feel like you Skinner?" He queried.

"I can honestly say that I haven't come across a single National Serviceman who has said to me what, a wonderful life this is, I wish it would go on forever! I've come across quite a few who are completely indifferent to the life, shrug their shoulders and say, well it's not for ever, which it isn't thank goodness, but yes the majority of the lads as you call them, that I have met, hate the life and consider like I do that it has been a complete waste of two years of our lives".

"I just didn't realise that you chaps felt like this", he said in a tone that appeared to express genuine surprise.

Stick the knife in, I thought. "That's the trouble with you Officers you just don't realise how your men feel and frankly I don't think that you could care less". I was in full flight by now. I continued, "You are totally out of touch with your men, especially National Servicemen. For my own part I am absolutely fed up with having been treated like a schoolboy for two years. The fact that I am now twenty four years old, and that some National Servicemen are approaching thirty years old, has seemingly been totally ignored, and people like me are fed up with the life!"

"I see," he replied. He appeared to be completely lost for words, which was probably just as well for me. Little did I realise at the time, that he could, if he had been so minded, charged me, or had me charged, with conduct prejudicial to good order or some such, and had me detained for at least the duration of my month's terminal leave. Instead he just stood there with a look of astonishment on his face. He just didn't know what to do or to think, thank goodness. He had obviously had never had anyone speak so openly to him about what they thought over National Service.

"Right then I'll be off Mr Hounsell, I've got a train to catch, and two years of my life to catch up with. Good-bye," and with that parting remark, I turned on my heel with an un-military left about turn, just to show my newly found independence, and marched out of his office, out of his life and out of the Army. My very last act, before leaving the Royal Citadel was to collect that part of my equipment that I had to take home with me for my three and a half years service in the Army Emergency Reserve. Looking like the proverbial Christmas tree for the very last time I marched out through the archway of the Royal Citadel and made my way to the railway station and home. As a mild celebration I had tea on the train, and sat back and ruminated on my two years National Service, I came to the conclusion that I had never before (or since) hated two years of my life as much as I hated those two years of National Service and yet I see that recently an ex-cabinet minister has written a book on National Service entitled, "The Best Years of Their Lives". Not mine I assure both him and you.

Although in theory I was still in the Army, albeit only in the

Army Emergency Reserve, and although the Suez crisis flared up only three months after I was demobbed, I resolutely refused to answer any correspondence sent to me by the Army without any consequences whatsoever. Another person that I was working with at British Oxygen at the time, I know was threatened with dire consequences for not answering the directives sent to him. Mark you the person I am referring to had served his time in the R.A.F., maybe they were different in their approach to the subject! Perhaps I had got through to the Army after all, who knows? But then it did take me two years!

ND OF NATIONAL SERVICE

The end of National Service in 1960 was greeted by approval by both the Army and the civilian population. Whilst many National Servicemen had, at least in retrospect, enjoyed their time in the Army, since it enabled them to come in contact with other strata of society, others, like me, had resented both the interruption to their lives and the military discipline, or "bull" as it was referred to. While the Regulars had found the endless training of conscripts tedious and had often been hard pressed to keep them gainfully employed, the National Serviceman had fought alongside their Regular counterparts in Malaya, Korea, Cyprus, and Kenya and proved themselves just as good soldiers as the regulars, when they put their mind to it.

They also provided a large pool of reservists on which the Army could call in time of war, having to carry out a limited period of training with the T.A. each year for three years after they had left the Colours. An all-Regular Army, on the other hand, has only a small number to call upon, and many of them, with little or no training ability, are often very out of touch, as the Army found during exercises Crusader and Lionheart, two major reinforcement exercises carried out in Germany in 1980 and 1984.

ABOUT THE AUTHOR

I was educated at Latymers School North London, then gained my higher National in Building Construction at Tottenham Technical College studying three nights a week , hence I didn't do my National Service until I was 22. This book is my experiences during these two years.